A Day in the Life of a Happy Worker

This edited collection brings together some of the leading researchers in the study of the daily experience of work and well-being. The book covers both theoretical and methodological issues involved in studying workers' well-being as it evolves on an everyday basis.

Interest in the topic of daily fluctuations in worker well-being has grown rapidly over the past ten years. This is partly because of advances in research methods and statistical interests, but also because researchers have found that the psychological processes that influence well-being play out from moment to moment, and from day to day. Topics covered in this book include:

- the theoretical basis of studying work as a series of daily episodes;
- assessment of different components of daily well-being;
- factors involved in the regulation of well-being at work;
- qualitative and quantitative diary experience sampling and event reconstruction methods;
- latent growth curve modeling of diary data.

The final chapter of the book includes a preview of how daily methods may evolve in the future.

Intended as a guide for researchers with good knowledge of field research methods, the book will be particularly useful to researchers of work-related phenomena that seek to expand their knowledge of dynamic methods in field contexts, and those that want to start using these methods. It will also be of interest to students of work psychology and organizational behavior, and related disciplines.

Arnold B. Bakker is Full Professor at the Department of Work and Organizational Psychology at Erasmus University Rotterdam, the Netherlands. He is President of the European Association of Work and Organizational Psychology, and a fellow of the American Psychological Society. His research interests include positive organizational behavior (e.g. performance, flow and engagement at work), burnout, work–family balance, and crossover of work-related emotions. Further information can be found at: www.arnoldbakker.com.

Kevin Daniels is Professor of Organizational Behavior at the University of East Anglia, UK. He is a fellow of the British Psychological Society. His research concerns how cognitive and emotional processes are involved in the design of work influence well-being, safety and performance. As well as academic research, he is also involved in research on how to develop governmental policy and guidance to enhance health and well-being at work.

Current Issues in Work and Organizational Psychology
Series Editor: Arnold B. Bakker

Current Issues in Work and Organizational Psychology is a series of edited books that reflect the state-of-the-art areas of current and emerging interest in the psychological study of employees, workplaces and organizations.

Each volume is tightly focused on a particular topic and consists of seven to ten chapters contributed by international experts. The editors of individual volumes are leading figures in their areas and provide an introductory overview.

Example topics include: digital media at work, work and the family, workaholism, modern job design, positive occupational health and individualized deals.

A Day in the Life of a Happy Worker
Edited by Arnold B. Bakker and Kevin Daniels

The Psychology of Digital Media at Work
Edited by Daantje Derks and Arnold B. Bakker

New Frontiers in Work and Family Research
Edited by Joseph G. Grzywacz and Evangelia Demerouti

A Day in the Life of a Happy Worker

**Edited by Arnold B. Bakker
and Kevin Daniels**

Psychology Press
Taylor & Francis Group
LONDON AND NEW YORK

First published 2013
by Psychology Press
27 Church Road, Hove, East Sussex BN3 2FA

Simultaneously published in the USA and Canada
by Psychology Press
711 Third Avenue, New York NY 10017

Psychology Press is an imprint of the Taylor & Francis Group, an informa business

© 2013 Psychology Press

The right of the editors to be identified as the authors of the editorial material, and of the authors for their individual chapters, has been asserted in accordance with sections 77 and 78 of the Copyright, Designs and Patents Act 1988.

All rights reserved. No part of this book may be reprinted or reproduced or utilised in any form or by any electronic, mechanical, or other means, now known or hereafter invented, including photocopying and recording, or in any information storage or retrieval system, without permission in writing from the publishers.

Trademark notice: Product or corporate names may be trademarks or registered trademarks, and are used only for identification and explanation without intent to infringe.

British Library Cataloguing in Publication Data
A catalogue record for this book is available from the British Library

Library of Congress Cataloging-in-Publication Data
A day in the life of a happy worker / edited by Arnold B. Bakker and Kevin Daniels.
    p. cm.
    Includes bibliographical references and index.
  1. Work environment. 2. Well-being. I. Bakker, Arnold B. II. Daniels, Kevin.
  HD7261.D38 2013
  331.25'6–dc23   2012021728

ISBN13: 978–1–84872–085–5 (hbk)
ISBN13: 978–1–84872–086–2 (pbk)
ISBN13: 978–0–20307–899–0 (ebk)

Typeset in Times New Roman
by Swales & Willis Ltd, Exeter, Devon

Printed and bound in Great Britain by
TJ International Ltd, Padstow, Cornwall

Contents

List of Contributors vii
Acknowledgments viii

1 A Day in the Life of a Happy Worker: Introduction 1
  ARNOLD B. BAKKER AND KEVIN DANIELS

2 The Episodic Structure of Life at Work 8
  DANIEL J. BEAL AND HOWARD M. WEISS

3 State Work Engagement: The Significance of Within-Person Fluctuations 25
  DESPOINA XANTHOPOULOU AND ARNOLD B. BAKKER

4 Work-Related Flow 41
  CLIVE FULLAGAR AND E. KEVIN KELLOWAY

5 Job Characteristics and Problem-Solving 58
  KEVIN DANIELS

6 The Application of Diary Methods to Examine Workers' Daily Recovery During Off-Job Time 72
  CARMEN BINNEWIES AND SABINE SONNENTAG

7 Experience-Sampling and Event-Sampling Research 85
  NIKOLAOS DIMOTAKIS AND REMUS ILIES

8 Reconstruction Methods: Using Episodic Memory Traces to Capture Experiences at Work Efficiently 100
  GUIDO HERTEL AND CHRISTIAN STAMOV-ROßNAGEL

9 Latent Growth Modeling Applied to Diary Data: The   114
  Trajectory of Vigor Across a Working Week as an
  Illustrative Example
  SVEN GROSS, LAURENZ L. MEIER, AND NORBERT K. SEMMER

10 Using Qualitative Diary Research to Understand Emotion   132
   at Work
   KATHRYN WADDINGTON

11 Research Agenda   150
   PETER TOTTERDELL, DAVID HOLMAN, AND KAREN NIVEN

   Index   170

Contributors

Arnold B. Bakker, Erasmus University Rotterdam, the Netherlands
Daniel J. Beal, Rice University, USA
Carmen Binnewies, University of Mainz, Germany
Kevin Daniels, University of East Anglia, UK
Nikolaos Dimotakis, Michigan State University, USA
Clive Fullagar, Kansas State University, USA
Sven Gross, University of Bern, Switzerland
Guido Hertel, University of Münster, Germany
David Holman, University of Manchester, UK
Remus Ilies, National University of Singapore
E. Kevin Kelloway, Saint Mary's University, Halifax, Canada
Laurenz L. Meier, University of Bern, Switzerland
Karen Niven, University of Manchester, UK
Norbert K. Semmer, University of Bern, Switzerland
Sabine Sonnentag, University of Mannheim, Germany
Christian Stamov-Roßnagel, Jacobs University Bremen, Germany
Peter Totterdell, University of Sheffield, UK
Kathryn Waddington, City University, London, UK
Howard M. Weiss, Purdue University, USA
Despoina Xanthopoulou, University of Crete, Greece

Acknowledgments

Kevin Daniels' contributions to editing this collection have benefitted from the support of UK Engineering and Physical Sciences Research Council grants D04863X and EP/F02942X/1.

1 A Day in the Life of a Happy Worker

Introduction

Arnold B. Bakker and Kevin Daniels

Positive psychology emerged in the late 1990s with a renewed emphasis on what is right with people in contrast to the preoccupation psychology has had over the years with what is wrong with people (Seligman & Csikszentmihalyi, 2000; Snyder & Lopez, 2002). This approach rehabilitated the focus on positivity and people's strengths and virtues (Peterson & Seligman, 2004). Positive psychology is an attempt to adopt a more open and appreciative perspective regarding human potentials, motives, and capacities (Sheldon & King, 2001). Positive psychology and organizational theory merge in the new approach of positive organizational behavior (POB) defined as "the study and application of positively oriented human resource strengths and psychological capacities that can be measured, developed, and effectively managed for performance improvement in today's workplace" (Luthans, 2002, p. 59; see also Bakker & Schaufeli, 2008).

This book brings together authors who examine positive psychological states employees may experience during work. Such positive psychological states fall under the general rubric of well-being. Although the exact formation of well-being is subject to debate (cf. Busseri & Sadava, 2011) and some consider it is best considered an area of study – rather than a "thing" (Diener *et al.*, 1999) – there is general agreement that work-related well-being covers a range of experiences. These include positive affective states such as enthusiasm, the absence of negative affective states such as anxiety, good psychosomatic health, cognitive states such as aspiration, and judgments of job satisfaction (see e.g. Daniels, 2011). There is evidence that different aspects of work-related well-being are inter-related (e.g. van Horn *et al.*, 2004). Indicators of affective well-being are afforded a central place amongst the phenomena that make up well-being, as some consider affective reactions to be a leading indicator of environmentally induced changes in well-being (Daniels, 2011). Affective states can take many forms, but, in the workplace at least, happiness and its synonyms are seen as the principle indicators of a state of affective well-being (Daniels, 2000). So, the happy worker should experience a range of positive psychological states at work. In this book, the authors focus on positive emotions and mood, work-related flow, work engagement, and job satisfaction, among other positive psychological states.

Research conducted in the past two decades has clearly shown that workers scoring relatively high on positive psychological states demonstrate better job performance. For example, research has consistently shown that happy workers are productive workers (e.g. Cropanzano & Wright, 1999, 2001; Wright & Cropanzano, 2004). Typically, these studies found that individuals who are prone to experience positive affect (e.g. optimism) while also tending not to experience negative affect (i.e. feeling calm rather than anxious) received higher performance ratings from their supervisors. Similarly, research on employee work engagement (i.e. a fulfilling state of high energy and dedication to work) has shown that engaged workers are more creative, show higher in-role performance, and are more inclined to help their colleagues if needed – they show organizational citizenship behaviors (Bakker, 2009; Demerouti & Cropanzano, 2010). Moreover, engaged workers typically have more satisfied clients (Salanova *et al.*, 2005).

Taken together, the research evidence shows that happy workers are productive workers. However, it should be noticed that most researchers have not managed to explain a large amount of the variance in job performance. One of the reasons for this is that there are many other variables besides happiness that may play a role when it comes to differences between individuals in performance. For example, economic cycles may have an impact on performance as clients may not be willing to spend their budget on your products; or the quality of the overall service the company offers and its image may determine sales to a larger extent than employee work engagement. Perhaps a more worker focused approach is needed?

Daily Changes in Happiness

The central theme of the present book is that we need to look at short-term, within-person fluctuations in happiness and its consequences. Such an approach acknowledges that individuals who are generally happy with their job and engaged in their work may not be equally happy and engaged every day. Indeed, an increasing number of studies has shown that daily fluctuations in job satisfaction and work engagement are considerable, and that these fluctuations can be predicted and be used to predict important employee and organizational outcomes (Bakker & Xanthopoulou, 2009; Xanthopoulou *et al.*, 2009). Moreover, it is conceivable that short-term indicators (or within-person changes) of occupational well-being are better predictors of performance in organizations than long-term indicators (between-person differences).

The performance episodes model (Beal *et al.*, 2005) offers an explanatory theoretical framework for these findings. In contrast to traditional performance models that regard within-person differences as error variance, the performance episodes model focuses on an individual's variability in performance over short periods of time. Beal *et al.*'s main argument is that individuals perform better when fully concentrated on the task at hand. Specifically, Beal and his colleagues propose that resource allocation to the task is crucial for successful performance. If employees cannot allocate all of their resources to the task at hand – for example, because they are constantly interrupted by telephone calls – they cannot perform optimally. Thus, replenishing and conserving (self-regulatory) resources is critical for successful performance during performance episodes and during a day (see Beal *et al.*, 2005). For example, a financial investment manager will perform best when she is energetically engaged with information about the stock market. Similarly, a general practitioner may deliver the best care to patients to whom he listens empathically – a situation that is most likely when he dedicates all his energy to his work. If ongoing task performance is interrupted – for example by a colleague who wants to discuss his weekend experiences, or by the beep of an incoming e-mail message – the focus will shift from the task to the colleague or e-mail message, and the energy is no longer invested in the task.

This book is dedicated to short-term fluctuations in well-being. We titled the book *A Day in the Life of a Happy Worker* since we want to emphasize that a focus on short-term positive experiences in the workplace is meaningful and extremely useful. During the past two decades, scholars have developed sophisticated designs and methods to capture within-person fluctuations in happiness and work engagement, and statisticians have meanwhile developed software that can be used to take care of the dependency in the data when collecting data over the course of the days and weeks.

For example, simple paper-and-pencil diaries have been replaced with sophisticated electronic recording, with daily or hourly questionnaires administered by personal digital assistants or other electronic technologies (see e.g. Tennen *et al.*, 2006 for a discussion of electronic data collection methods). The development of multilevel modeling techniques has allowed researchers to tease out variability in how people usually are, how people are at a given point in time, and how different they are at a given point in time from how they usually are (see e.g. Kenny *et al.*, 2002). Such techniques also enable researchers to study whether stable between-person differences in workers' personality, attitudes, or work environments moderate relationships between variables with high-levels of daily variability (e.g. Semmer *et al.*, 2004).

Data captured on within-person changes in happiness, well-being, and other, related variables offer a number of strengths over the traditional survey methods. Collecting data in the field in real time gives researchers high ecological validity and minimizes recall bias, as data are captured about current or recently completed activity (Bolger *et al.*, 2003; Tennen *et al.*, 2006). Internal validity is also enhanced relative to cross-sectional methods, as prior levels of dependent variables and a range of other controls, such as personality and time of day, can be included in regression models (Bolger *et al.*, 2003). But more importantly, such methodological and statistical advances make theoretical models of short-term, within-person fluctuations in well-being, its consequences, and antecedents amenable to empirical investigation in real-world contexts.

The Present Book

How does a day in the life of a happy worker unfold? In this book, we have brought together some of the most influential researchers currently working on daily well-being in the workplace. We asked the authors to focus more on the happy worker because we believe that in the past there has been a bias toward negative phenomena.

This is not to say that the approaches described in this book cannot be applied to negative psychological phenomena: indeed, the methods described can and have been applied to tackling subjects like stress (Daniels, 2011). The authors of the chapters in this book have used different designs in their research, including experience sampling, day reconstruction, daily diaries, and combinations of these techniques. The commonality of these methods is that they are focused on collecting data about happiness, well-being, and other phenomena in relation to the working day or parts of the working day. The book comprises two parts: theory and methodology, which are integrated in a final chapter by Totterdell, Holman, and Niven.

The book starts with the theoretical part and focuses on substantive issues concerning well-being during the course of the working day. This part of the book addresses questions concerning why it is important to understand well-being as a within-person phenomenon and how theories can be developed to help us understand the ebbs and flows of daily well-being in and around the workplace. Chapters in this section of the book are concerned with the nature of daily work experience, capturing the experience of well-being, and how workers attempt to regulate and protect their well-being.

In the next chapter, Daniel Beal and Howard Weiss take up the notion of studying experience within the working day. Their chapter concerns the structure of the working day and how it is broken up into psychologically meaningful chunks. Beal and Weiss describe episodes through the day and the psychological principles that justify this level of analysis for understanding happiness and related phenomena. Without analyses such as that provided by Beal and Weiss, the study of daily work experience would be merely an exercise in technically sophisticated, dust bowl, empiricism. Beal and Weiss show that there is theoretical meaningfulness in studying the working day.

Having established the viability of the working day as a theoretically meaningful unit of analysis, the next two chapters are focused more firmly on well-being. These chapters are concerned with two closely related states associated with well-being and optimal psychological functioning: work engagement and flow. Despoina Xanthopoulou and Arnold Bakker examine within-person variations in work engagement – shifting the focus from *who* gets absorbed and engaged in their work to *when* engagement happens. The chapter illustrates some of the conceptual issues in shifting from one level of analysis (the worker) to another (the worker's experiences during the day). Clive Fullagar and Kevin Kelloway examine a concept that is usually conceived of as dynamic, momentary, and closely related to state work engagement – the concept of flow. Fullagar and Kelloway cover some of the methodological issues in researching this dynamic and elusive phenomenon, as well as examining its psychological and psychophysiological components.

Workers can be effective in regulating their well-being, and the next two chapters focus on factors that might serve to maintain well-being, or even enhance well-being at work in the face of threats to well-being, and examine some of the methodological issues in studying the psychological processes that can be seen as antecedents to well-being. Kevin Daniels considers how workers use job characteristics – specifically job control and social support – to solve problems. The chapter illustrates the importance of worker agency in shaping the daily experience of work, but also that job characteristics can be conceived of as highly dynamic, goal-directed, and behavioral phenomena, not stable characteristics of immutable organizational structures. Carmen Binnewies and Sabine Sonnentag examine recovery. Recovery is necessarily a dynamic concept that involves transitions from a state where personal resources are taxed to replenishment of those resources. Research in this area is often concerned with the frequent and daily transitions between work and non-work environments. This chapter anticipates the following chapters by describing quantitative diary methods and illustrating their application in recovery research.

Inevitably, any discussion of theoretical issues related to the daily experience of well-being strays into the territory of methods. Indeed, it is a tenable argument that the theoretical focus on daily work experience emerged as a consequence of developments in methods. Methodology is important in all areas of empirical research but has a special emphasis in the study of daily happiness and well-being at work. Most of the chapters in the methodological section are concerned with different methods for capturing the daily experience of work and well-being. Not only is there a choice of methods available, data on the daily dynamics of well-being at work also offer data analytic opportunities and challenges that other methods do not. Consequently, one of the chapters is concerned with data analytic methods suited to asking questions concerning how daily well-being progresses over time, and another chapter also devotes some space to the analysis of daily data.

Quantitatively oriented experience sampling, event sampling, and diary studies are the dominant methods in studies of daily well-being at work. In the first dedicated methodological chapter, Nikolaos Dimotakis and Remus Ilies discuss the general class of quantitative methods called experience- and event-sampling methods, and some of the major design decisions to be taken in using such methods. The methods described by Dimotakis and Ilies are the methods of choice for many researchers that look at daily and within-day processes. However, in the chapter that follows, Guido Hertel and Christian Stamov-Roßnagel note that experience and event-sampling methods require a lot of effort on the part of researchers and participants, and these methods can miss rare events. Hertel and Stamov-Roßnagel discuss alternatives to experience- and event-sampling methods – day and event reconstruction methods. Although not a substitute for experience- and event-sampling methods, day and event reconstruction methods get close to the key advantages of experience- and event-sampling methods and are useful when experience- and event-sampling methods are not possible. Hertel and Stamov-Roßnagel discuss not only the application of these methods in organizational research, but also how these methods can be used by practitioners (for example, in training evaluation).

For many quantitative researchers interested in daily variations in well-being, data are usually analyzed with variants of multilevel regression to ask research questions that are within-person variants of the kind of questions asked in more traditional survey designs. However, as patterns of change are integral to many theories in work psychology, examining workers over multiple days does allow the effects of time to be examined empirically. Sven Gross, Laurenz Meier, and Norbert Semmer describe one class of statistical methods – latent growth models – that can be used to investigate how well-being and other variables change over time and to examine inter-individual patterns in these changes.

Although most of the research in the area is quantitative, there are examples of qualitative diary studies in the literature. In her chapter, Kathryn Waddington discusses the issues in conducting qualitative diary studies that are able to capture participants' accounts of their experiences close to when they happen and to capture the richness and detail of those experiences. Waddington also discusses an approach to analyzing qualitative diary data. In citing Allport, Waddington reminds us that researching (working) life and its details as it unfolds should be the focus of (work and organizational) psychology. Waddington also argues that, at least in relation to researching emotion, examining working life as it unfolds can be a focus of integration for various academic disciplines.

Peter Totterdell, David Holman, and Karen Niven conclude the book with a retrospective look at the chapters in this volume and research in the area, and outline some of the underpinning assumptions of research on daily well-being. Totterdell and colleagues offer also a prospective view on how the field may develop and why researching the daily experience of happiness, well-being, and related phenomena will remain a lively, important, and theoretically fruitful research area. Of course, their considered but optimistic (could one say critical yet happy?) view is a view we share.

References

Bakker, A.B. (2009). Building engagement in the workplace. In R.J. Burke & C.L. Cooper (Eds), *The peak performing organization* (pp. 50–72). London: Routledge.

Bakker, A.B. & Schaufeli, W.B. (2008). Positive organizational behavior: Engaged employees in flourishing organizations. *Journal of Organizational Behavior, 29*, 147–154.

Bakker, A.B. & Xanthopoulou, D. (2009). The crossover of daily work engagement: Test of an actor-partner interdependence model. *Journal of Applied Psychology, 94*, 1562–1571.

Beal, D.J., Weiss, H.M., Barros, E., & MacDermid, S.M. (2005). An episodic process model of affective influences on performance. *Journal of Applied Psychology, 90*, 1054–1068.

Bolger, N., Davis, A., & Rafaeli, E. (2003). Diary methods: Capturing life as it is lived. *Annual Review of Psychology, 54*, 579–616.

Busseri, M.A. & Sadava, S.W. (2011). A review of the tripartite structure of subjective well-being: Implications for conceptualization, operationalization, analysis, and synthesis. *Personality and Social Psychology Review, 15*, 290–314.

Cropanzano, R. & Wright, T.A. (1999). A five-year study of change in the relationship between well-being and job performance. *Consulting Psychology Journal, 51*, 252–265.

Cropanzano, R. & Wright, T.A. (2001). When a "happy" worker is really a "productive" worker: A review and further refinements of the happy–productive worker thesis. *Consulting Psychology Journal, 53*, 182–199.

Daniels, K. (2000). Measures of five aspects of affective well-being at work. *Human Relations, 53*, 275–294.

Daniels, K. (2011). Stress and well-being are still issues and something still needs to be done: Or why agency and interpretation are important for policy and practice. In G.P. Hodgkinson & J.K. Ford (Eds), *International review of industrial and organizational psychology* (Vol. 26, pp. 1–46). New York: Wiley.

Demerouti, E. & Cropanzano, R. (2010). From thought to action: Employee work engagement and job performance. In A.B. Bakker & M.P. Leiter (Eds), *Work engagement: A handbook of essential theory and research* (pp. 147–163). New York: Psychology Press.

Diener, E., Suh, E.M., Lucas, R.E., & Smith, H.L. (1999). Subjective well-being: three decades of progress. *Psychological Bulletin, 125,* 276–302.

Horn, J.E. van, Taris, T.W., Schaufeli, W.B., & Schreurs, P.J.G. (2004). The structure of occupational well-being: A study among Dutch teachers. *Journal of Occupational and Organizational Psychology, 77,* 365–376.

Kenny, D.A., Bolger, N., & Kashy, D.A. (2002). Traditional methods for estimating multilevel models. In D.S. Moskowitz & S.L. Hershberger (Eds), *Modeling intraindividual variability with repeated measures data: Methods and applications* (pp. 1–24). Mahwah, NJ: Erlbaum.

Luthans, F. (2002). Positive organizational behaviour: Developing and managing psychological strengths. *Academy of Management Executive, 16,* 57–72.

Peterson, C. & Seligman, M.E.P. (2004). *Character strengths and virtues.* Oxford, UK: Oxford University Press.

Salanova, M., Agut, S., & Peiró, J.M. (2005). Linking organizational resources and work engagement to employee performance and customer loyalty: The mediation of service climate. *Journal of Applied Psychology, 90,* 1217–1227.

Seligman, M. & Csikszentmihalyi, M. (2000). Positive psychology: An introduction. *American Psychologist, 55,* 5–14.

Semmer, N.K., Grebner, S., & Elfering, A. (2004). Beyond self-report: Using observational, physiological, and situation-based measures in research on occupational stress. In P. Perrewé & D. Ganster (Eds), *Research in occupational stress and well being: Emotional and physiological processes and positive intervention strategies* (Vol. 3, pp. 205–263). Amsterdam: Elsevier.

Sheldon, K.M. & King, L. (2001). Why positive psychology is necessary. *American Psychologist, 56,* 216–217.

Snyder, C.R. & Lopez, S. (Eds) (2002). *Handbook of positive psychology.* New York: Oxford University Press.

Tennen, H., Affleck, G., Coyne, J.C., Larsen, R.J., & Delongis, A. (2006). Paper and plastic in daily diary research: Comment on Green, Rafaeli, Bolger, Shrout, and Reis (2006). *Psychological Methods, 11,* 112–118.

Wright, T.A. & Cropanzano, R. (2004). The role of psychological well-being in job performance: A fresh look at an age-old quest. *Organizational Dynamics, 33,* 338–351.

Xanthopoulou, D., Bakker, A.B., Demerouti, E., & Schaufeli, W.B. (2009). Work engagement and financial returns: A diary study on the role of job and personal resources. *Journal of Occupational and Organizational Psychology, 82,* 183–200.

2 The Episodic Structure of Life at Work

Daniel J. Beal and Howard M. Weiss

A day in the life of a happy worker? Yes, one volume about a single workday, a kind of scientific, work-related Joycean Ulysses. And Ulysses is an apt comparison in another way, as this volume is so self-consciously focused on the experiences of the day, the first-person stream of living at work. This is territory rarely explored in work psychology, and we are less for it.

But how should we approach this description of the happy worker's day? Most of the chapters in this volume take "happy" as the point of departure, focusing on issues of changes in emotional states or engagement. In our chapter, we will focus on the day itself, and more specifically the way the stream of daily work experience is given structure and how that structure influences the variations in personal and organizational outcomes of interest to work psychologists.

One of the more interesting aspects of lived-through personal experience is that it has, simultaneously, a sense of both continuous flow and discrete structure. Experience, as it is lived, has a fundamental feeling of flow and continuity. We may move from activity to activity, but we always have a sense of wholeness, of a seamless unity to it all. At the same time, we also experience a partitioning of that flow. Lived-through experience is continuous, to be sure, but it is given structure, organized and partitioned into discrete "experiences" by acts of the self. The "day in the life of the worker" is a continuous flow of conscious experience but it is naturally and inevitably partitioned into the episodes that are used to organize our memories, our narratives, our subjective lives. At the end of the day, a workers' partner might ask "what did you do today?" The answer is the product of that personal act of structuring which accompanies every lived-through workday.

Perhaps structure is the wrong term. Rather, we probably should think of "structures" as the stream of daily experience that can be subjectively partitioned in multiple ways simultaneously. To begin with, it is well known that autobiographical memory is structured hierarchically, with specific events nested within broader episodes (Conway & Pleydell-Pearce, 2000). It is also true that people create overlapping episodic structures that organize different aspects of their experiences.

Although some research has examined daily life structures (see Barker, 1963 and more recently Zacks *et al.*, 2001), very little has been done on the way daily work life is subjectively structured. In a previous paper, we (Beal *et al.*, 2005) described the "performance episode" as one aspect of work-life structure that we felt would be useful for better understanding the way transitory changes in affective states would influence within-person changes in work performance. In the next section of this chapter, we will summarize our thinking about performance episodes and how they are influenced by overlapping, transient episodes of affect. In doing so, we will elaborate on how we think of episodic structure generally. But our discussion in Beal *et al.* (2005) was primarily focused on better understanding affect–performance relationships, not on understanding episodic work structure generally, and our review here reflects that focus. Consequently, we will take the time in the second section to speculate on the nature of the subjective structure of work experience and why that is important.

Performance Episodes

There are numerous ways in which our immediate experiences might be translated or aggregated into more stable units. In Beal *et al.*, we argued for thinking of episodes as coherent segments of experience that are thematically organized around one's goals or objectives (Barker, 1963; Beal *et al.*, 2005) and performance episodes in particular as "behavioral segments that are thematically organized around organizationally relevant goals or objectives" (Beal *et al.*, 2005, p. 1055). Not everything that happens at work would be considered a performance episode; as such, in this section, we only consider episodes of behavior that relate to the goals of the organization and the implications this concept has for understanding within-person changes in performance and the relationship between those changes and changes in affective states.

Before we go further, it would be useful to provide a concrete sense of what we mean by episodes. Consider a recent day of your own; one that is still fresh in your memory. If you trace your experiences chronologically throughout the day, it is likely that you will naturally "chunk" the events, affective states, cognitions, and behaviors into discrete, meaningful units. For example, perhaps you woke up and had breakfast; then slogged through the morning commute to work; at work, you prepared for an upcoming class and then taught the class; afterward, you had lunch with some colleagues; then, you returned to your office and continued working on a chapter; after reaching the end of a section, you moved on to some analyses of recently collected data; noting the late hour, you decided to head home; there, you spent some time with your family and began preparations for dinner; after having dinner, you relaxed by reading a book before going to bed. The manner in which this day was described involves chunks or episodes of experience.

One of the more important aspects of this episodic structure is that it appears to be strongly guided by one's goals or objectives. For example, Zacks and colleagues (2001) found that individuals who were watching someone perform a series of behaviors made simultaneous descriptions of the behavior using goal-oriented language, referring to it largely in terms of the desired end-state. As a result, observers tended to agree on when the beginning and end of the episodes occurred. In addition, this effect was strengthened to the extent that people were familiar with the task (i.e. knew what the goal or desired end of the behavior stream should look like). These results suggest that our goals help dictate our perception of when episodes begin and end, and generally provide structure to our daily activities.

Emerging evidence concerning the segmentation of behavior streams suggests that boundaries between episodes are particularly important for the consolidation and encoding of our experiences into memory (Kurby & Zacks, 2008). That is, when people perceive the end to an episode, they update their memory for occurrences and objects that were present during the episode, allowing more of this information to be retrieved easily (Swallow *et al.*, 2009). Put differently, it appears that people automatically and efficiently chunk their experiences into episodes and that the beginnings and ends of episodes represent important moments when we evaluate and decide what to take away from our ongoing experiences.

To summarize, episodes are coherent segments of our life experience that are organized around goals. When our goals are organizationally relevant, we can characterize the associated segment of behavior as a performance episode. As we pass from episode to episode throughout the day, the most critical elements of these episodes are more deeply encoded in memory. The conclusion, therefore, is that by ascertaining what we take away from each episode, we will have a firmer grasp of the most crucial elements of our daily experience as it relates to performance at work.

Given that episodes provide a fairly natural way of structuring our day, a sensible next question is whether this fact can be useful for understanding our experiences at work. After all, there are many ways to structure a day; why would episodes carry any particular benefit? To this question, we offer two important reasons: first, if people naturally perceive their daily lives progressing in terms of episodes, then it seems likely that a commensurate episodic structure would be the appropriate level of analysis for the study of daily life (cf. Ajzen & Fishbein, 1977), particularly if this episodic structure helps us recall and understand the most crucial aspects of our experiences. Second, and more pragmatically, whereas experience-sampling or ecological momentary assessment techniques capture random and presumably representative moments of ongoing experience (Beal & Weiss, 2003), obtaining reports of episodes experienced throughout the day allows for a more efficient way of capturing all of, instead of a sample of, the critical elements of one's day.

We are not the first to recognize the usefulness of thinking about performance episodically. Motowidlo and colleagues (Motowidlo, 2003; Motowidlo *et al.*, 1997) also recognized that performance is best conceptualized as discrete behaviors and suggested that behavior at work is punctuated by occasions when people do something that either helps or hinders organizational goals. They also referred to such occasions as performance episodes and the episodic nature of work served as an underlying assumption in their distinction between task-related and contextual performance.

Similarly, we use the concept of performance episodes as a starting point for addressing two broad issues. First, as performance represents one of the largest and most important elements in this ongoing stream of experience, it is essential to our general aim of exploring the nature of experience at work. Second, performance episodes offer a means to better understand how people fluctuate in their effectiveness at work. Traditionally, performance is described in between-persons terms; that is, how effective people are relative to each other (i.e. "who is the best performer?"). Although people certainly differ from each other in time-aggregated effectiveness at work, there is a great deal of within-person variability that occurs throughout each workday. At times you may be at the "top of your game," while at other times it is a struggle to even think about accomplishing work-related goals. In trying to understand this variability, we believe that performance episodes represent the most viable unit of analysis from which we can understand the causes, corollaries, and consequences of effectiveness at work. Below, we explain a little more about the nature of episodes, as well as why we believe them to be a useful unit of experience.

As we stated earlier, one of our main aims in examining performance episodes is to understand how people fluctuate in their effectiveness at work. That is, what happens during any given performance episode that makes someone particularly effective? In prior work, we suggested that a maximally effective performance episode occurs when one's focus of attention is completely dedicated to the task at hand. Of course, some people have greater knowledge, skills, and abilities than others, so not all maximally effective performance episodes identified from a within-persons perspective are equally effective from a between-persons perspective. We are not concerned, however, with differences between individuals. If we examine a single individual's performance episodes over time, then our suggestion implies that a person's most effective episode is one where his or her attention is most completely devoted to the organizationally relevant task at hand. As with all models (Rodgers, 2010), there are caveats and exceptions that complicate our overarching definition of episodic performance effectiveness, and we will discuss some of these later. For the time being, however, this definition is useful for understanding the processes that govern our effectiveness during an episode.

Episodic Performance Processes

In our effort to determine what makes a performance episode effective or not, we will next consider the roles of two processes in particular. The first concerns the extent to which the content of our thoughts is related to the tasks undertaken during the performance episode. The second consideration is the effort involved in maintaining that focus of attention.

Allocation of Attention

As discussed by Beal and colleagues (2005), our model of episodic performance makes the assumption that one can be maximally effective during an episode to the extent that 100 percent of one's attention is allocated to the task or tasks at hand during the episode. Again, as we are discussing within-person aspects of performance variability, the maximal effectiveness to which we refer is relative to one's own possible effectiveness (i.e. it is limited by one's individual level of resources). This assumption is not meant to say that we should always strive to achieve 100 percent on-task thought or that it is even possible in any realistic setting. Instead, we merely point out that, if all of one's thoughts were directed toward performance, then there is essentially no other way for a person to be more effective. Of course, this perspective is true primarily for performances that involve controlled, deliberative thought. As we stated in our earlier work, if the performance activities do not require significant amounts of cognitive resources, then the degree to which thoughts are focused on the task are somewhat irrelevant to performance. We also recognize that some thoughts may be more effective than others, but for now, we will simplify our discussion by focusing only on the proportion of thought, not on the varieties of thought. The basis for this simplifying assumption is that intrusions into our on-task thought are likely to be primary factors that limit our ability to reach maximal performance during an episode.

Broadly, such intrusions occur as a result of the vagaries of our life at work. If we consider what we think about while at work, the task at hand often is only one of many potential topics. How we get along with co-workers, how we are treated by our supervisors, difficulties or triumphs at home, what the rest of the day holds for us, aspirations and regrets, and many other thoughts unrelated to the task at hand are constantly floating through our minds, vying for some portion of the allocation of our attention (Smallwood & Schooler, 2006). Part of the reason for such mind-wandering is that, even though we may have an organizationally relevant goal that is salient and driving our efforts to perform, it is quite unlikely that this is the only goal that we are pursuing. According to control theory (Carver & Scheier, 1982; Nelson, 1993), goals typically are thought to be arranged hierarchically; as a result, even while we are working on a particular task during a performance episode, it is often the case that other goals have yet to be attained. One consequence of having unattained or "open" goals is that we tend to experience recurring thought intrusions relevant to the open goal, commonly referred to as rumination (Martin & Tesser, 1996).

When such intrusions occur, attention shifts away from the task at hand. The off-task topic toward which one's attention shifts is immaterial; the result is that some attention is taken away from the focal task and effectiveness during the performance episode will necessarily be less than if attention had not shifted away. If the key to having effective performance episodes lies in the successful allocation of our cognitions to the focal task, then regulating our attention becomes a critical behavior within the stream of experience at work.

Regulation of Attention

There are two key factors involved in whether attention stays on-task during a performance episode or not: ability and motivation. The term ability often implies a stable individual difference, and it does seem likely that individuals vary in their ability to regulate their attention. Recall, however, that we are focused on within-person variability in behavior, and so our use of ability refers to the likelihood that someone will be able to regulate his or her attention to the task at any given moment during a performance episode. Recent research on self-control is supportive of this perspective. This research begins with the notion that regulating behavior (including attention) is a difficult and depleting action (Muraven & Baumeister, 2000). For example, anyone can attest to the palpable effort involved in focusing one's attention on one thing for an extended period of time. Research now has demonstrated that, even if we are successful in these efforts, it comes at a cost: subsequent regulation of our behavior and attention is less likely to meet with success. Baumeister and his colleagues have referred to this effect as ego-depletion (Baumeister *et al.*, 1998), and they suggest that the resources needed to control our thoughts and behavior are in limited supply at any given moment of the day. With rest, these resources return, but with continued efforts at regulation – regardless of whether that regulation involves attention, diet, interpersonal communication, or any other form of self-control – these resources diminish.

An important aspect of ego-depletion effects is that the cause and consequence are separated in time more so than is the case for other cognitive processes (e.g. perceptual effects, priming, appraisals, etc.). Most laboratory experiments find diminished capacity to regulate after a few minutes (e.g. Baumeister *et al.*, 1998; Muraven *et al.*, 2008), but some field research has demonstrated depletion effects at intervals as long as a few hours (e.g. Beal *et al.*, 2008; Trougakos *et al.*, 2008). As a result, diminished capacity to stay on-task could be observed both within the same performance episode as well as across two or more performance episodes.

Depletion effects also are cumulative in nature. That is, as one engages increasingly in effortful regulation without rest, the ability to continue regulating decreases more and more. For this reason, ego-depletion seems a likely mechanism linking emotionally laborious jobs and feelings of burnout or dissatisfaction (Beal *et al.*, 2006; Trougakos *et al.*, 2011). To a large extent, one's regulatory capacity at any given moment is determined by prior efforts at regulation that day. For example, Trougakos and colleagues (Trougakos *et al.*, 2008) found that – compared to occasions when breaks were used to relax – breaks used for engaging in relatively depleting chores resulted in less effective emotion regulation efforts later that same day.

Interacting with one's ability to regulate at any given moment of the day is one's motivation to stay on-task. Obviously, there are many considerations involved in dissecting the topic of work motivation and providing a comprehensive account of the topic would take us far outside of our purview (for reviews, see Kanfer *et al.*, 2008; Ambrose & Kulik, 1999). This is not to say, however, that motivation plays no role in the regulation of attention. In previous work (Beal *et al.*, 2005), we discussed several aspects of motivation within the performance episode framework in terms of *attentional pull*. Attentional pull refers generally to aspects of the task that make attending to the task easier. For example, one area of research that would affect attentional pull categorizes task motivation in terms of intrinsic versus extrinsic rewards (e.g. Porter & Lawler, 1968). Recent research in this area has emphasized the extent to which task-relevant behavior is autonomous or regulated. In particular, Self-Determination Theory (SDT: Deci & Ryan, 2002) discusses a continuum of motivation ranging from fully autonomous (i.e. freely chosen or self-determined) to completely controlled or contingent. In between these two poles are a variety of motivational states requiring different degrees of autonomy. For example, individuals could perform fairly undesirable tasks (i.e. they would not otherwise choose the task) either because their salary is contingent upon their performances or because they seek expertise. Neither scenario is completely autonomous, but the former is far less self-determined (see Gagné & Deci, 2005 for more details).

Our primary reason for discussing SDT in the context of episodic performance processes is that it has great implications for the effort involved in regulating one's attention during a performance episode. For example, the allocation of attention toward completely autonomous tasks (i.e. tasks which are perceived to be enjoyable) requires little to no effort, particularly compared to tasks that are less self-determined (Muraven et al., 2008; Ryan & Deci, 2008). As a result, the type of motivation one has for a given task will determine how much depletion occurs during a performance episode. In addition, motivational states for earlier performance episodes will have a bearing on one's ability to stay on-task during performance episodes later in the day.

Although self-determination tells us the amount of effort required to stay focused on one's tasks, it does not tell us much about what topics or goals are vying for our attention during a performance episode, nor does it tell us which of several potential goals will be attended to throughout the episode. Certainly there are numerous factors that converge to determine such complex and momentary attentional choices, but work motivation research does highlight several key factors. As discussed earlier, control theory suggests that goals are hierarchically arranged and that when discrepancies exist between current conditions and higher-level goals, these goals will often take priority over lower-level goals. For example, if someone has a high-level goal of flourishing socially, and progress toward this goal is perceived to be inadequate, it is possible that such a person would abandon lower-order goals (i.e. which might involve staying on-task) to instead pursue opportunities to engage in positive social interactions.

Taken to an extreme, this characterization implies that people will be in a near-constant state of flux, as goals and goal discrepancies come and go throughout the day. Clearly, this is not the case. Indeed, control theorists suggest that aspects of one's environment make associated goals more salient and more likely to be acted upon (Carver & Scheier, 1982). So, if someone is at work, then work-related goals have an associative advantage over non-work-related goals. This advantage suggests that staying on-task often is easier than it might seem if the contextual elements are consistent with the task in which one is engaged. Control theory also suggests that once a particular level in the hierarchy is active, it becomes prepotent or dominant over other potential goals or actions. So, once engaged in an activity, the goals that govern that activity tend to remain salient.

We discuss SDT and control theory here to demonstrate how motivation can play a role in the regulation of attention through attentional pull. We do not intend the discussion to be exhaustive; indeed, we view the interface of the work motivation literature and episodic performance to be one of the more fruitful areas of possible integration.

Performance Episodes and Emotion Episodes

Our initial discussion of performance episodes (Beal *et al.*, 2005) was confined to only the first section of the paper. Performance episodes, and the associated allocation and regulation of attention, served as the underlying structure and processes through which emotions influence within-person performance. Despite the emphasis of the current volume on happiness, we have not spent much time examining affective experiences, instead focusing on the episodic structure of our general and performance-related experiences. Indeed, our discussion of affect in this chapter is circumscribed to aspects of these states as they relate to episodic structure.

Historically, within the literature on emotions, there is a strong connection between emotions and episodes. Frijda (1993) elaborated extensively on the manner in which emotions occur in an episodic fashion, and most modern theories of emotions retain the episodic character of emotions as a central feature (e.g. Ekman, 2003; Izard, 2007; Russell & Feldman Barrett, 1999; Scherer, 2005). What then are the similarities and differences between these sorts of episodes and the episodes we have described so far?

In describing emotion episodes, theorists usually focus on the thematically related core of the experience, its punctuated beginning, and the often overwhelming nature of its intensity. From these characteristics, we can see some definite overlap: emotion episodes clearly are coherent segments of experience that are thematically organized; however, the organizing feature is not necessarily goals or objectives. Certainly our goals are often involved in the generation of emotions; when goals are either attained or blocked, emotions often result (Martin & Tesser, 1996; Scherer, 2005). The difference is that emotion episodes are specifically organized around the instigating event. These events often have direct relevance to our goals, but they need not. Events of all sorts intersect with our stream of experience and, when they do, there is the potential for an emotional reaction. The unfolding of thematically related processes (e.g. appraisals, action tendencies, physiological arousal, etc.) constitutes what scholars refer to as an emotion episode. Thus, emotion episodes reflect another way to structure our experiences. Performance episodes structure experiences around organizationally relevant goals; emotion episodes structure experiences around an instigating affective event.

The notion that performance and emotion episodes can have different bases to their structure suggests that these episodes hold the potential for partial or even complete overlap in our stream of experience. Although this may seem confusing at first, it provides us with an opportunity to discuss another aspect of episodes: episodes are not structures that are inherent to experience; they are structures that we impose on our continuous stream of experience in order to understand and remember the important occurrences and features of our lives. There are many elements to our experience (as we discuss further below), and so there are many potential ways for us to structure our lives in terms of episodes.

For example, let's say that Frank begins working on an important task. Soon after beginning, Frank experiences an "aha!" moment that provides the inspiration for how he then proceeds through the rest of the task. One way in which Frank might structure this stream of his experience is to consider the goals and objectives that initiated the task, organized the way in which he worked on the task, and signaled the conclusion of his work on the task. Yet another way in which Frank might structure this stream of experience is to consider his "aha!" moment and the thematically related feelings, thoughts, and behaviors that followed. Both structures are not only possible but, we would argue, are likely to occur. So, when Frank is asked to describe what he *did* during that time, he might base his response on aspects of his experience structured around the relevant performance episode; if Frank is instead asked about how he *felt* during that time, he might instead base his response on aspects of his experience structured around the relevant emotion episode. In this way, the same stream of experiences is quite likely to be structured around different episodes.

Elements of the Stream of Experience

At this point, we have referred occasionally to events, affective states, cognitions, and behaviors as elements in the stream of experience. They are elemental insofar as they characterize what is occurring within any particular episode. Whereas an episode describes a segment of experience, these elements provide substance and content to the episode in which they occur. Although these elements describe the processes that occur within an episode, they typically lack the temporal and hierarchical structure of the episodes they comprise. As such, we feel that they are most informative when they are examined within the context of a given episode or how their influence may transition from one episode to the next. Put differently, events, affective states, cognitions, and behaviors are best understood within the broader context in which they occurred. Episodes encapsulate this context and provide a basis for understanding how the elements within are interconnected. For example, if one wished to trace the path of one's affective states over the course of a day, knowing the sequence of states alone would be fairly uninformative and might appear quite chaotic. In contrast, if we examine all of the elements as they relate to the goals that structure the episode in which they occur, then we will be better able to understand and predict the shifts in any of the elements from episode to episode throughout the day.

As this notion is fairly abstract, consider the following example. Joan is at work on a typical day. We somehow are able to drop in and assess the events that are relevant to and perceived by Joan, as well as her affective states, cognitions, and behaviors. When we look at one sequence of these elements, we see that a friend of Joan's dropped by to see if she needed anything. Joan responds to her colleague in a curt and somewhat irritated manner and leaves no opening for further conversation. Alone, these elements of Joan's experience are somewhat ambiguous. We do not know why she reacted in this manner to her friend. If we were to know, however, that the episode in which this occurred was driven by a strong desire to complete a particular task, then it becomes clear that Joan is engaged in a performance episode and that interruptions, even from friends, represent a halting of goal progress. Understanding the goals that structure episodes is vitally important for the correct interpretation of the elements that occur within those episodes. From this example and our description of how episodes are comprised of events, affective states, cognitions, and behaviors, it should be clear that these elements are of great importance in understanding what happens during an episode. As such, we will briefly discuss how we conceptualize each of these elements.

Events

By "event," we refer to any aspect of or occurrence in one's environment that influences another element in the stream of experience. As such, events are the only elements that have the potential for being truly exogenous to one's experience. All the other elements of experience (i.e. affective states, cognitions, behaviors) are generated by the individual and so are endogenous elements in the stream of experience. This is not to say, however, that endogenous elements cannot influence each other. For example, an event may generate thoughts (e.g. event appraisals) that then trigger an emotional reaction. Both of these elements may then lead to some form of physical behavior.

Given this broad definition of "event," we can be certain that the nature of events varies widely. Furthermore, there are clearly many ways to classify events. For example, Beal and Ghandour (2011) made two classifications of events. First, consistent with Weiss and Cropanzano's (1996) discussion of affective events, these authors identified events that were likely to give rise to affective states. They then made a further distinction between mundane daily events and far more influential, shock-like events. This distinction was useful in determining the magnitude and duration of the event's influence on one's affective state. Of course, there are many other potential ways of classifying events: organizational relevance (perhaps as a comparison to family-related events in an analysis of work-family experiences), fairness relevance (or even type of fairness relevance, such as distributive, procedural, etc.), and source of responsibility for the event (e.g. supervisor, co-worker, customer, etc.) are some possibilities. Regardless of the classification of events, the importance of events for our purposes is that they can represent exogenous influences in the stream of experience and are potentially disruptive to the processes involved in making a performance episode effective.

Affective States

Affective experiences have received a great deal of attention in the work psychology literature. For example, Weiss and Cropanzano (1996) provided an excellent review of the various forms of affect and their relevance within the workplace. Beal *et al.* (2005) discussed the implications of emotions for the processes involved in making episodic performance effective. There are several aspects of affective states that are particularly relevant to understanding experiences at work. Emotions and moods represent a potentially constant aspect of experience that is initiated primarily by events occurring within one's environment. Such constancy implies that all of what we think and do is, to some extent, influenced by how we feel. This does not mean that we are always moving from one emotion to another throughout our days. Instead, emotions are triggered by some relevant event; the emotion has a strong influence on our immediate thoughts and behaviors, but then tends to taper off. Often, what are left behind are moods (cf. Russell and Feldman Barrett's [1999] concept of core affect). These states are more diffuse and have a subtle influence on other elements of experience. They can alter the valence of our perceptions (Bower & Forgas, 2001; Forgas, 1995); they can broaden or narrow the scope of what we make salient in our thoughts (Fredrickson, 2001); and they can influence the nature of how we appraise subsequent events (Lerner & Keltner, 2000, 2001).

Cognitions

Here we refer to the content of one's thoughts. Earlier, we discussed one way of categorizing cognitions in terms of on- versus off-task thought, and, much like events, there are likely innumerable ways to categorize or classify thought content. Cognitions play a central role in the stream of experience, as they tell us where we are placing our attention at any given moment in time. For example, during a class, a student might have the experience of attending to the lecture. While she is doing so, her thoughts will reflect the content of the lecture and her efforts to make sense of what the teacher is saying. It is possible, however, that she will occasionally become distracted by some other aspect of her environment. Perhaps something the teacher says reminds her of an assignment she has that is overdue; perhaps a fellow student is trying to get her attention. During these moments, despite her efforts to stay focused on the task of attending to the lecture, the content of her thoughts will reveal that she is not on-task. A fleeting thought concerning when she might complete the assignment or concerning the rudeness of the fellow student, however brief, implies that her attention has shifted focus. As could be seen with our discussion of off-task thought intrusions, knowing the content of our cognitions is centrally relevant in determining effectiveness during a performance episode.

Behaviors

During a performance episode, action is the translation of our thoughts into something that is either effective or ineffective at work. This simple fact is why behavior is the primary focus of the performance episode. It is easy to see, however, how the other elements in the stream of experience all play critical roles in determining the behaviors in which we engage. Consider the following depiction. Events often trigger a cascade of reactions. Some of these reactions are automatic, fast appraisals of the event which can lead directly to the experience of an emotion (LeDoux, 1995). Other cognitions may be more deliberative and mediate the relation between an event and an emotion (Smith & Lazarus, 1993). Still other cognitions may have no bearing on one's affective state whatsoever. Regardless of the particular course that is triggered by the event, all three of these elements (i.e. the event, affective states, and cognitions) can have direct or indirect effects on actual behavior.

An important aspect of behavior is that it can take the form of either overt physical action or unobservable mental processes. There is a strong precedent in the performance literature for treating mental processes as performance behaviors (Campbell, 1990; Campbell *et al.*, 1993). Here, however, the inclusion of mental efforts is complicated by our introduction of cognitions as elements of experience. Specifically, one might ask, "How are cognitions different from mental forms of behavior?" We describe mental behavior as cognitive processes such as attention, recall, reasoning, and other forms of information processing. Cognitions, as described earlier, refer instead to the contents of one's thought. For example, three sequential cognitions in the stream of mental experience might be 1) "I really did not get enough sleep last night"; 2) "What was I working on just now?"; and 3) "Oh, yes . . . Where will my company find the money to produce this design?" Irrespective of the content of these cognitions, each thought implies slightly different combinations of mental processes. The first thought might involve the recollection of last night's experience as well as a comparison (using working memory) made against one's prototype of a "restful night." These processes represent mental behavior, whereas the enumerated cognitions themselves reflect the contents of one's thought.

At this point, we have extensively described the nature of episodes as organizing structures to our continuous stream of experience. We have emphasized performance episodes in particular, as they are centrally relevant to understanding ongoing behavior at work and how one's effectiveness might fluctuate over time. We have also emphasized that, although performance episodes are important, they are but one way to structure our experience episodically. Finally, we have detailed other, more fundamental elements in the stream of experience that provide the grist for the episodic mill. In the final section of our chapter, we would like to return to some of the more philosophical questions of how our experiences are both perceived continuously and structured episodically.

The Structure of Work Life

Since our paper on performance episodes (Beal *et al.*, 2005) was published, we have encountered a variety of questions from other researchers concerning the temporal characteristics of an episode. How long is it? Who determines when it begins and ends? Can you have multiple episodes occurring simultaneously or are they only sequential? It would be pleasing to offer a definitive answer to all of these questions and leave it at that, but we suspect that, after all of the pondering over the response had faded, it would leave the distinctive aftertaste of disappointment. Episodes do not prescribe any particular duration. They are inherently subjective, but can be initiated by some external influence (e.g. boss says "get to work," the meeting commences at noon, etc.). The experiences that form episodes occur sequentially, yet the episodic structure that individuals then impose on those experiences may involve completely overlapping segments of experience.

Episodes simply refer to a general way that we structure our own experiences, and the title of this volume is a testament to this ubiquitous process of structuring life – of partitioning the continuous flow of experience into meaningful units. In our previous work and so far in this chapter, we have focused on a particular type of structure, the performance episode. Our focus on the performance episode is consistent with our interests in understanding the relationships between within-person fluctuations in affective states and within-person fluctuations in work performance. That interest is, in turn, consistent with the overall themes of this book. Yet the way people provide structure to their work experiences is an important experiential topic in its own right and we would like to use the last section of the chapter to make some general comments about this.

It has been understood at least since James (1890) that experience is both continuous and segmented. Certainly, in real time, we sense the continuous flow of experience. Yet, continuity is given meaning through structure; the continuous experience of life is turned into the "experiences" of life, the meaningful reportable units of an afternoon, a day, a career. Dewey (1934) suggested that people use the term "experience" in two ways. In one sense, they talk of the experience of doing this or that; the experience of stress or of being in love or of being frightened. "How did that feel?" is a question directed to that meaning of experience. The second way refers to the meaningful segments of one's life, the coherent units of one's personal history. Meeting in the morning with the boss, having lunch with colleagues: these are the "experiences" of the day.

Current research in work psychology is giving more and more attention to topics related to the first meaning. Research on emotional states or engagement (in the experiential sense of attentional focus) are examples of research on the experiential elements of work, the "what it is like" to be working. At the same time, there is very little research on the second meaning of experience, on the meaningful units created by the self, on the partitioning of experience, both in the moment and reflectively. Of course, as Weiss and Rupp (2011) point out, these two meanings are necessarily tied together. We want to know how you felt during that meeting or whether lunch was pleasant. Still, however related, the two meanings are conceptually separable and current research has clearly focused on the first meaning at the expense of the second.

This is unfortunate for a number of reasons. First, it is unfortunate because the process of creating structure from within continuity is a fundamental aspect of life experience, and therefore an important topic of work psychology. Second, because the structure that develops, the segments, the meaning given to segments, the recollected affect associated with segments, etc. are all critical to the personal meanings of and judgments about work. When your partner asks, at the end of the day (happy or otherwise), "what did you do today?", you will report the day in segments. When he or she asks "how was your day?", it is the meaning that you attached to particular critical segments that will determine your answer. How those segments are created, how they are evaluated, how they are labeled as important or discarded from memory are all critical questions for a psychology of work experience.

Historically, Barker (1963, 1968) was among the first to systematically study episodic organization to the stream of behavior, but Barker's ideas have rarely been discussed in the work psychology literature. More recently, Zacks has expanded on earlier work by Newtson and Engquist (1976) with the development of Event Segmentation Theory (Zacks *et al.*, 2007), a theory of how coherent units of behaviors are created. Although interesting, the research of Zacks, like the research of Newtson and Engquist, is entirely about how observers segment the behaviors of others. Consequently, it is only tangentially related to the issues of personal experience being discussed here. The processes by which meaningful units of experience are created, as well as their effects on judgments about work, remains a relatively unexplored topic.

The flip side of segmentation is continuity, and our discussion of the importance of understanding created structure should not lead to ignoring the continuity of it all. We may segment our experiences, but through it all there is a sense of continuity; there is always the sense that "this is my life." Episodes are the scenes and chapters of the autobiographies we write and edit. Whether each autobiography is the product of the "enduring self" or whether it is equivalent to the "enduring self" is something for philosophers to debate, but the self is the key to continuity in that each experience is uniquely perceived and interpreted by the self. As Weiss and Rupp (2011) state, "The self binds the experiences together." Consequently, as work psychologists examine the way structure is created, they must also examine how structure is integrated into the autobiographical narratives that describe work life.

Conclusion

The purpose of this chapter has been to describe not only performance episodes, but the more general episodic structure that we give to our continuous lives. Within the continuity and constancy of our experience are innumerable events, states, cognitions, and behaviors – so many, in fact, that we must create some sort of structure in order to understand and retain the elements that are of the most importance to us. Research demonstrates that compartmentalizing our experiences into thematically related, coherent chunks facilitates the general process of making sense of our lives. It allows us to extract what is most central to whatever it is that ties our continuous experiences together over time. As this volume is related to our work experiences, performance episodes represent an obvious and particularly useful means of structuring the elements that make up our daily work lives.

More pragmatically, understanding episodes may allow researchers to find some harmony between traditional, artificially aggregate perceptions of work and the more recent flurry of research associated with capturing immediate, online assessments of our lives (see Beal, 2012). Though an analysis of episodes is likely closer to online assessments, we have argued that the difference is an important one: episodes carry the information that we felt was important to take away from a stream of experience, whereas online assessments provide an accounting of the experiences themselves. Both perspectives allow for a more complete understanding of the experience of work.

References

Ajzen, I. & Fishbein, M. (1977). Attitude-behavior relations: A theoretical analysis and review of empirical research. *Psychological Bulletin, 84*, 888–918.

Ambrose, M.L. & Kulik, C.T. (1999). Old friends, new faces: Motivation research in the 1990s. *Journal of Management, 25*, 231–292.

Barker, R.G. (1963). The stream of behavior as an empirical problem. In R.G. Barker (Ed.), *The stream of behavior* (pp. 1–22). New York: Appleton-Century-Crofts.

Barker, R.G. (1968). *Ecological psychology: Concepts and methods for studying the environment of human behavior*. Stanford, CA: Stanford University Press.

Baumeister, R.F., Bratslavsky, E., Muraven, M., & Tice, D.M. (1998). Ego depletion: Is the active self a limited resource? *Journal of Personality and Social Psychology, 74*, 1252–1265.

Beal, D.J. (2012). I/O Psychology. In M.R. Mehl & T.S. Conner (Eds) *Handbook of research methods for studying daily life* (pp. 601–619). New York, NY: Guilford Press.

Beal, D.J. & Ghandour, L. (2011). Stability, change, and the stability of change in daily workplace affect. *Journal of Organizational Behavior, 32*, 526–546.

Beal, D.J. & Weiss, H.M. (2003). Methods of ecological momentary assessment in organizational research. *Organizational Research Methods, 6*, 440–464.

Beal, D.J., Weiss, H.M., Barros, E., & MacDermid, S.M. (2005). An episodic process model of affective influences on performance. *Journal of Applied Psychology, 90*, 1054–1068.

Beal, D.J., Trougakos, J.P., Weiss, H.M., & Green, S.G. (2006). Episodic processes in emotional labor: Perceptions of affective delivery and regulation strategies. *Journal of Applied Psychology, 91*, 1053–1065.

Beal, D.J., Trougakos, J.P., Dalal, R.S., Sundie, J.M., & Weiss, H.M. (2008, August). Dynamics of employee emotion regulation strategies and customer-related outcomes. In D. Wagner & R. Ilies (Co-Chairs), *What makes customers tick … and ticked off? Affect, justice, and emotions in customer service*. Symposium presented at the 68th annual meeting of the Academy of Management, Anaheim, California.

Bower, G.H. & Forgas, J.P. (2001). Mood and social memory. In J.P. Forgas (Ed.), *The handbook of affect and social cognition* (pp. 95–120). Mahwah, NJ: Erlbaum.

Campbell, J.P. (1990). Modeling the performance prediction problem in industrial and organizational psychology. In M.D. Dunnette & L.M. Hough (Eds), *Handbook of industrial and organizational psychology* (2nd ed., Vol. 1, pp. 687–732). Palo Alto, CA: Consulting Psychologists Press.

Campbell, J.P., McCloy, R.A., Oppler, S.H., & Sager, C.E. (1993). A theory of performance. In N. Schmitt &W.C. Borman (Eds), *Personnel selection in organizations* (pp. 35–70). San Francisco: Jossey-Bass.

Carver, C.S. & Scheier, M.F. (1982). Control theory: A useful conceptual framework for personality-social, clinical, and health psychology. *Psychological Bulletin, 92*, 111–135.

Conway, M.A. & Pleydell-Pearce, C.W. (2000). The construction of autobiographical memories in the self-memory system. *Psychological Review, 107*, 261–288.

Deci, E.L. & Ryan, R.M. (2002). *Handbook of self-determination research*. Rochester, NY: University of Rochester Press.

Dewey, J. (1934). *A common faith*. New Haven, CT: Yale University Press.

Ekman, P. (2003). *Emotions revealed.* New York, NY: Times Books.
Forgas, J.P. (1995). Mood and judgment: The affect infusion model (AIM). *Psychological Bulletin, 117*, 39–66.
Fredrickson, B.L. (2001). The role of positive emotions in positive psychology: The broaden-and-build theory of positive emotions. *American Psychologist, 56*, 218–226.
Frijda, N.H. (1993). Moods, emotion episodes, and emotions. In M. Lewis & J.M. Haviland (Eds), *Handbook of emotions* (pp. 381–403). New York, NY: Guilford Press.
Gagné, M. & Deci, E.L. (2005). Self-determination theory and work motivation. *Journal of Organizational Behavior, 26*, 331–362.
Izard, C.E. (2007). Basic emotions, natural kinds, emotion schemas, and a new paradigm. *Perspectives on Psychological Science, 2*, 260–280.
James, W. (1890). *The principles of psychology.* New York, NY: Holt.
Kanfer, R., Chen, G., & Pritchard, R.D. (2008). *Work motivation: Past, present, and future.* New York, NY, US: Routledge, Taylor & Francis Group.
Kurby, C.A. & Zacks, J.M. (2008). Segmentation in the perception and memory of events. *Trends in Cognitive Sciences, 12*, 72–79.
LeDoux, J.E. (1995). Emotion: Clues from the brain. *Annual Review of Psychology, 46*, 209–235.
Lerner, J.S. & Keltner, D. (2000). Beyond valence: Toward a model of emotion-specific influences on judgment and choice. *Cognition & Emotion, 14*, 473–493.
Lerner, J.S. & Keltner, D. (2001). Fear, anger, and risk. *Journal of Personality and Social Psychology, 81*, 146–159.
Martin, L.L. & Tesser, A. (1996). Some ruminative thoughts. In R.S. Wyer, Jr. (Ed.), *Advances in social cognition* (Vol. 9, pp. 1–47). Mahwah, NJ: Erlbaum.
Motowidlo, S.J. (2003). Job performance. In W.C. Borman, D.R. Ilgen, & R.J. Klimoski (Eds), *Comprehensive handbook of psychology, vol. 12: Industrial and organizational psychology.* New York, NY: Wiley.
Motowidlo, S.J., Borman, W.C., & Schmit, M.J. (1997). A theory of individual differences in task and contextual performance. *Human Performance, 10*, 71–83.
Muraven, M. & Baumeister, R.F. (2000). Self-regulation and depletion of limited resources: Does self-control resemble a muscle? *Psychological Bulletin, 126*, 247–259.
Muraven, M., Gagné, M., & Rosman, H. (2008). Helpful self-control: Autonomy support, vitality, and depletion. *Journal of Experimental Social Psychology, 44*, 573–585.
Nelson, T.D. (1993). The hierarchical organization of behavior: A useful feedback model of self-regulation. *Current Directions in Psychological Science, 2*, 121–126.
Newtson, D. & Engquist, G. (1976). The perceptual organization of ongoing behavior. *Journal of Experimental Social Psychology, 12*, 436–450.
Porter, L.W. & Lawler, E.E. III. (1968). *Managerial attitudes and performance.* Homewood, IL: Irwin-Dorsey.
Rodgers, J.L. (2010). The epistemology of mathematical and statistical modeling: A quiet methodological revolution. *American Psychologist, 65*, 1–12.
Russell, J.A. & Feldman Barrett, L. (1999). Core affect, prototypical emotional episodes, and other things called emotion: Dissecting the elephant. *Journal of Personality and Social Psychology, 76*, 805–819.
Ryan, R.M. & Deci, E.L. (2008). From ego depletion to vitality: Theory and findings concerning the facilitation of energy available to the self. *Social and Personality Psychology Compass, 2*, 702–717.
Scherer, K.R. (2005). What are emotions? And how can they be measured? *Social Science Information, 44*, 695–729.

Smallwood, J. & Schooler, J.W. (2006). The restless mind. *Psychological Bulletin, 132*, 946–958.

Smith, C.A. & Lazarus, R.S. (1993). Appraisal components, core relational themes, and the emotions. *Cognition & Emotion, 7*, 233–269.

Swallow, K.M., Zacks, J.M., & Abrams, R.A. (2009). Event boundaries in perception affect memory encoding and updating. *Journal of Experimental Psychology: General, 138*, 236–257.

Trougakos, J.P., Beal, D.J., Green, S.G., & Weiss, H.M. (2008). Making the break count: An episodic examination of recovery activities, emotional experiences, and positive affective displays. *Academy of Management Journal, 51*, 131–146.

Trougakos, J.P., Jackson, C.L., & Beal, D.J. (2011). Service without a smile: Comparing the consequences of neutral and positive display rules. *Journal of Applied Psychology, 96*, 350–362.

Weiss, H.M. & Cropanzano, R. (1996). Affective events theory: A theoretical discussion of the structure, causes, and consequences of affective experiences at work. *Research in Organizational Behavior, 18*, 1–74.

Weiss, H.M. & Rupp, D.E. (2011). Experiencing work: An essay on a person-centric work psychology. *Industrial and Organizational Psychology: Perspectives on Science and Practice, 4*, 83–97.

Zacks, J.M., Tversky, B., & Iyer, G. (2001). Perceiving, remembering, and communicating structure in events. *Journal of Experimental Psychology: General, 130*, 29–58.

Zacks, J.M., Speer, N.K., Swallow, K.M., Braver, T.S., & Reynolds, J.R. (2007). Event perception: A mind/brain perspective. *Psychological Bulletin, 133*, 273–293.

3 State Work Engagement
The Significance of Within-Person Fluctuations

Despoina Xanthopoulou and Arnold B. Bakker

The concept of work engagement was initially developed to capture an enduring, affective-motivational state of employees regarding their job. Schaufeli, Salanova, González-Romá, and Bakker (2002) indicated that "rather than a momentary and specific state, engagement refers to a more persistent and pervasive affective-cognitive state" (p. 74). Later, Sonnentag (2003) challenged this view by proposing that work engagement should not only be seen as an enduring experience. Rather, she argued and showed that levels of work engagement may vary within the same employee from one day to another, in response to specific situational and personal conditions (see also Sonnentag *et al.*, 2010). Thus, state work engagement (SWE) was introduced as complementary to enduring work engagement.

In this chapter, we explain the "how and why" of within-person variations in engagement. After defining enduring engagement, we discuss the added value of conceptualizing engagement as a dynamic state. Then, we review studies on the predictors of SWE, as well as its relationship to momentary performance in an attempt to address similarities and differences with findings concerning enduring work engagement. With regard to methodology, recent developments in the measurement of SWE are presented. Finally, we discuss a unique method to capture the crossover of SWE among dyads of colleagues, the actor–partner interdependence model (APIM; Kenny & Cook, 1999).

Defining Work Engagement

According to Schaufeli and Bakker (2004, 2010), work engagement is a positive, fulfilling, work-related state that comprises of three complementary dimensions: vigor, dedication, and absorption. Vigor concerns high levels of energy while working. Dedication refers to being involved in the job and experiencing a sense of significance, enthusiasm, and challenge. Absorption refers to being fully concentrated and happily engrossed in one's work. In other words, engaged employees are highly active, find their work to be significant and full of meaning, and are often fully concentrated and immersed in their work-related activities (Bakker *et al.*, 2011; Schaufeli *et al.*, 2002).

We argue against scholars who view engagement as a multidimensional construct that incorporates various psychological (e.g. commitment and satisfaction), behavioral (i.e. organizational citizenship behavior), as well as trait (i.e. proactive personality) facets (Macey & Schneider, 2008). Despite the fact that such a general definition of engagement seems popular among practitioners, it creates confusion when attempting to clarify the added (theoretical and methodological) value of SWE. The problem is that "all-inclusive" definitions incorporate various, different states that have been proven to be theoretically and empirically related but not identical (Bakker et al., 2011). Consequently, the use of such definitions makes it impossible to determine the motivational potential of engagement over and above different constructs, their predictors and outcomes.

In their recent theoretical analysis, Bakker and Oerlemans (2011) used Russell's (2003) circumplex model of affect to establish the conceptual distinction between work engagement and other indicators of work-related well-being. They positioned work engagement, together with happiness, in the quadrant of the model that is characterized by high levels of both pleasure and activation. Engaged employees are not only actively involved in their work, but they also like what they do because of the fulfillment they derive from it. Bakker and Oerlemans explain that happy employees experience high levels of pleasure, but in contrast to engaged employees, they only experience moderate and not high levels of activation. This theoretical analysis indicates that work engagement and happiness share similar qualities, and that engagement may be seen as a state that embodies pleasurable experiences that may be of limited duration, and may vary within the same person over short periods of time (Ekman, 1994). The strong link between engagement and happiness at work underlines the significance of the state character of employee engagement.

Measuring State Work Engagement

According to Allen and Potkay (1981), enduring and state facets of the same construct are measured with the same scale by changing the instructions and by adapting the items so as to refer to the specific time-frame one is interested in. When we measure states, participants are asked to respond to the items of the scale by taking into account their experience during the "past week," "today," or "right now." The most typical example is the Positive Affectivity Negative Affectivity Schedule, which consists of eight different temporal instructions depending on the experience that one is interested in measuring (Watson & Clark, 1994). These instructions vary from "right now" (i.e. momentary affect) to "in general" (i.e. general affect).

This tradition characterizes the research on SWE as well. The Utrecht Work Engagement Scale (UWES; Schaufeli et al., 2002; Schaufeli et al., 2006) is the most commonly used instrument to measure work engagement, both as an enduring trait and as a state (Sonnentag et al., 2010). The UWES incorporates items measuring each of the three sub-dimensions, such as "At my work, I feel bursting with energy" (i.e. vigor), "I am enthusiastic about my job" (i.e. dedication), and "I get carried away when I am working" (i.e. absorption; Schaufeli et al., 2006). Accordingly, when enduring work engagement is assessed, participants are asked to rate how vigorous, dedicated, and absorbed they generally feel at work. In contrast, when SWE is measured, these very same items of the UWES are adjusted so as to refer to the specific "week," "day" or "hour" that each study focuses upon.

Sonnentag and colleagues (2010) expressed doubts about the appropriateness of measuring SWE in this way. They argued that the modification of trait scales to measure states may be insufficient because these may not fully capture the specific state as experienced on a certain day or week. In more technical terms, due to the fact that some of the experiences captured with the general questionnaire may not be frequently encountered on a daily or weekly basis, it is likely to find low inter-item correlations, which consequently may result in more dimensions than the three dimensions of vigor, dedication, and absorption. SWE may embody additional, momentary experiences that are not incorporated in the definition of enduring work engagement. One may also argue that SWE concerns only those dimensions of enduring engagement that are encountered more frequently and that fluctuate more substantially on a day-to-day basis.

In an attempt to counteract these concerns, Breevaart, Bakker, Demerouti, and Hetland (in press) performed a multilevel factor analytic study on the state version of the UWES. The authors pooled data from three different studies among a total of 271 Dutch employees from various occupations. In all these studies, state (day-level) work engagement was assessed with an adaptation of the nine-item version of the UWES (Schaufeli *et al.*, 2006) across five workdays. A series of comparisons of competing models revealed that the multilevel model, which captured the interdependency between the levels of analysis (i.e. between-person and within-person level), was the model that fit best to the data. Importantly, the three-factor structure of the work engagement construct was confirmed on a day-to-day basis, and it showed a better fit than the one-factor solution. Furthermore, the factor loadings and factor correlations were substantial both at the between-person level and at the within-person level of analysis, indicating that the UWES operates very well at both levels of analysis. All in all, the study by Breevaart *et al.* (in press) provides evidence that supports the use of the adapted UWES as a valid and reliable instrument to capture within-person fluctuations in work engagement.

Enduring vis-à-vis State Work Engagement

It is clear from the above that work engagement is viewed both as an enduring trait and as a fluctuating state. But what is SWE exactly? What is the *meaning* of SWE that distinguishes it from enduring work engagement? Enduring (or trait) work engagement refers to how engaged employees feel in relation to their work in general, over long periods of time. For example, one academic is generally vigorous, dedicated and absorbed in his/her work, while another one is not. In contrast, SWE reflects a transient state of mind that exists on a given moment and fluctuates within the same individual over short periods of time (e.g. day to day or hour to hour; Sonnentag *et al.*, 2010). For instance, an academic may feel extremely vigorous, dedicated, and absorbed on the day she is writing a chapter on an interesting topic, whilst engagement evaporates on days she has to fill out administration forms.

It is clear that studies concerning enduring work engagement can only explain between-person differences (i.e. how employees differ from one another in terms of engagement). As such, these studies can be either cross-sectional or longitudinal with long time intervals. In contrast, SWE concerns within-person fluctuations of vigor, dedication, and absorption over short periods of time (e.g. days, weeks, or hours). Within-person variations are commonly measured with diary designs that allow the short-term dynamics of the experience to be captured (Ohly *et al.*, 2010).

Hitherto, there are several daily diary studies and one weekly diary study on SWE that have been published. All of these studies provide evidence for substantial within-person fluctuations. On the week level, the study by Bakker and Bal (2010) showed that 47 percent of the total variance in engagement was attributable to within-person fluctuations. Similarly, daily diary studies have shown that the amount of total variance in engagement that may be attributed to within-person fluctuations ranges from 28 percent to 72 percent ($M = 42$ percent; Bakker & Xanthopoulou, 2009; Petrou *et al.*, in press; Simbula, 2010; Sonnentag, 2003; Tims *et al.*, 2011; Xanthopoulou *et al.*, 2009; Xanthopoulou *et al.*, 2008) across different occupational settings.

Taken together, these studies suggest that at least one-third of the total variance in SWE is attributable to within-person fluctuations, supporting the significance of the state approach over and above enduring engagement. Also, these studies show that within-person fluctuations in engagement are more prevalent in settings where employees are in constant interaction with customers (e.g. consultants, Tims *et al.*, 2011; fast-food restaurant employees, Xanthopoulou *et al.*, 2009; service sector, Bakker & Xanthopoulou, 2009; Sonnentag, 2003; and flight attendants, Xanthopoulou *et al.*, 2008). This suggests that the ratio of between/within-person variance may be linked to the type of work environment under study.

The study of enduring work engagement is important for understanding employee well-being. However, it unfolds only part of the experience. Is it enough to think that even the most engaged employee is not equally engaged every day? A clear advantage of SWE is that it describes the specific experience when and as it occurs, thus providing insights into its dynamic character. Put differently, SWE captures inter-individual changes in vigor, dedication, and absorption. An additional advantage of this micro-approach is that the examination of work engagement at the time and in the situation that it occurs allows its proximal antecedents and outcomes to be investigated more accurately. What is it on a specific day that explains an employee's high levels of engagement? And what is the immediate outcome of this experience? Next to how individuals feel generally about their work and themselves, the characteristics of the specific situation and the feelings of the person in the specific situation play a significant role in determining SWE. Thus, it becomes clear that, by shifting the focus from enduring to state engagement, we gain new insights into the psychological mechanisms that explain the phenomenon of engaged employees that are impossible to obtain by focusing only on the enduring facet of the concept.

It should be emphasized that SWE does not discard the role of enduring work engagement. Rather, the two facets of engagement are complementary in better understanding this phenomenon. As proposed by George (1991), enduring dispositions may have an impact on the respective states, but states are the ones that initiate the psychological processes explaining day-to-day well-being. This premise is in line with Daniels' (2006) multilevel approach of dynamic processes that explain employee well-being. Accordingly, well-being concerns dynamic experiences that should be studied within short time-frames and that are determined by three inter-related, yet distinct, facets of job characteristics: latent, perceived, and enacted. Latent job characteristics are located at the organizational level and are independent of the perception and action of employees. Perceived job characteristics refer to employees' general perceptions of their job. Finally, the enacted facet is the most dynamic since it refers to the events at work that employees enact on a daily basis. By definition, enacted job characteristics are the most proximal determinants of employee well-being (i.e. these happen just before the occurrence of the actual experience). Thus, latent and perceived job characteristics may influence employee state experiences but mainly through their effect on enacted job characteristics.

Seeing work engagement within this multilevel framework, it may be argued that employees' general engagement levels are expected to influence their SWE. Indeed, previous studies showed that employees who feel generally engaged are more likely to be engaged on a specific day. Specifically, the between-person variance in SWE that can be attributed to trait engagement ranges from 13 percent to 68 percent (Sonnentag, 2003; Xanthopoulou *et al.*, 2008, 2009). However, it is SWE that denotes employee day-to-day coping. Consequently, the strongest influence is exerted by those conditions and feelings that happen right before the experience, suggesting that the examination of proximal antecedents provides richer information about the phenomenon (Sonnentag *et al.*, 2010). Furthermore, Salanova, Schaufeli, Xanthopoulou, and Bakker (2010) proposed that the engagement experience is cyclical. Accordingly, resources enhance SWE, which, in turn, leads to enhanced performance. Consequently, high performance may bring more resources, which, in turn, lead to higher levels of engagement and so on. In this context, frequent experiences of SWE may also determine trait work engagement over time.

Predictors of State Work Engagement

Do enduring work engagement and SWE share the same antecedents? Results of diary studies on SWE generally parallel the findings concerning enduring work engagement. However, certain antecedents seem to act differently when it comes to SWE, indicating a relative distinctiveness between the two types of engagement.

A significant antecedent of SWE is recovery or how well rested employees go to work on a specific day. Sonnentag (2003) studied 147 employees from six public service organizations over five consecutive workdays. Results of multilevel analyses showed that employees reported higher levels of vigor, dedication, and absorption on days that they went to work well rested. The beneficial effect of daily recovery was further supported in the study by Sonnentag and Niessen (2008). They showed that recovery accumulated during the preceding evening related positively to vigor at the end of the working day. Similarly, Bakker, van Emmerik, Geurts, and Demerouti (2010) found that daily recovery as reported in the morning predicted SWE during the day. To summarize these studies, employees who are able to rest during off-job hours regain the energy and resources they lost while at work, which makes subsequent work engagement more likely.

Moving to more proximal antecedents of SWE, it is essential to take the work environment into consideration (Bakker & Leiter, 2010). In this context, there is a growing number of diary studies examining how within-person variations in job resources (i.e. social, psychological, or organizational aspects of the job that act as means to achieve goals and promote employee growth and development; Demerouti et al., 2001) determine SWE. Xanthopoulou et al. (2008) conducted a study among 44 flight attendants, who filled out diaries over consecutive flights to three intercontinental destinations. Results revealed that, on trips that flight attendants worked with supportive colleagues, they experienced higher levels of SWE. The role of co-worker support in determining SWE was also emphasized in the study by Simbula (2010) among 61 Italian teachers. She found that, on days that teachers received more support from their colleagues, they were more engaged. Further, in a diary study among 42 Greek fast-food restaurant employees, Xanthopoulou et al. (2009) showed that daily fluctuations in autonomy, supervisory coaching, and team atmosphere related positively to SWE. Similarly, Tims et al. (2011) found that employees were more engaged on days that their supervisors behaved in a transformational manner (i.e. showed individual consideration and support to the employees, and motivated them toward excellent performance). Finally, variations in job resources relate positively to SWE not only on a daily but also on a weekly basis. In the study by Bakker and Bal (2010), 54 Dutch teachers filled out a diary every Friday for five consecutive weeks. Multilevel analyses revealed that week levels of autonomy, exchange with the supervisor, and opportunities for development related positively to teachers' weekly work engagement.

Next to job resources, fluctuations in employee personal resources seem equally important for SWE. Personal resources are positive self-evaluations that are linked to resiliency and refer to individuals' sense of their ability to control and impact upon their environment successfully (Hobfoll et al., 2003). Xanthopoulou et al. (2008) found flight attendants' feelings of self-efficacy before the inbound flight to have a positive impact on their work engagement during the flight. Similarly, daily fluctuations in self-esteem, self-efficacy, and optimism related positively to fast-food restaurant employees' daily engagement (Xanthopoulou et al., 2009). Interestingly, the latter study showed that day-level personal resources mediated the relationship between day-level job resources and engagement. In other words, the exposure to job resources enhances employees' beliefs that they can adequately deal with their tasks on a daily basis. Such beliefs encourage employees to invest effort and energy in the task, which results in engagement. Support for the mediating role of personal resources is of particular theoretical significance because it suggests that personal resources are the most proximal determinants of SWE that transform the beneficial effects of job resources into increased motivation (Sonnentag et al.,

2010). This also practically means that job redesign toward work engagement is more important than selection of employees with specific personality traits.

To conclude, previous diary studies clearly show that it is fluctuations particularly in social types of job resources and autonomy, as well as in personal resources, that determine employees' SWE. The underlying theoretical assumption is that job and personal resources provide employees with the necessary means and psychological strength to face their work goals and, as a result, employees become more motivated and engaged in their work. It may be concluded that results concerning the relationship between state resources and SWE parallel results of studies at the between-person level, which clearly suggest that job and personal resources are the most crucial determinants of engagement (for reviews, see Bakker & Demerouti, 2008; Halbesleben, 2010). Empirical support for parallel processes at different (between and within) levels is of particular theoretical importance. Namely, it favors the homology of the proposed assumptions across levels of analysis (Kozlowski & Klein, 2000), which adds to the parsimony and breadth of the theoretical framework. In contrast, rejection of homology sets boundaries and indicates the need for theory refinement.

Such a need for theory refinement seems to be necessary with regard to the relationship between job demands and SWE. Despite the fact that in between-person analyses job demands relate negatively to engagement in a consistent manner (for a meta-analysis, see Halbesleben, 2010), not all studies at the within-person level have yielded similar findings. Sonnentag and Niessen (2008) in their diary study among 75 employees from service and public administration organizations found that day-specific workload (i.e. number of work hours and time pressure) related negatively to daily vigor (i.e. the energy dimension of work engagement). Using Hobfoll's (1989) conservation of resources theory, the authors suggested that a high workload requires energy expenditure from the side of the employee, which may result in low levels of vigor. However, it is important to note that this study conceptualized vigor as levels of energy at the end of work, and not how employees felt during work.

In contrast to these results, the two-week diary study by Bakker, van Emmerik, Geurts, and Demerouti (2010) among 53 assembly line workers showed that daily workload (i.e. quantitative, physically and mentally demanding aspects of the job) related *positively* to daily engagement – suggesting that workload acted as a challenge. In a similar vein, Petrou *et al.* (in press) performed a five-day diary study among 95 employees from different organizations to study the effect of job crafting on SWE. Results suggested that seeking more resources and challenges during the workday enhanced employee SWE. Based on these results, there are reasons to believe that, at the within-person level of analysis, job demands function largely as challenges that consequently have a positive impact on SWE. This is in line with Sonnentag and colleagues (2010), who argued that, on days that there are enough challenging things to do, employees are more likely to mobilize their energy and to concentrate on the task, and as a result engagement is more likely to occur.

According to LePine, Podsakoff, and LePine (2005), when individuals appraise demands as challenges, they increase their effort, which may lead to positive emotions (e.g. enjoyment, enthusiasm). The proposition that job demands are likely to function as challenges at the day level is further supported by the study of Ohly and Fritz (2010), who showed that daily time pressure was positively related to challenge appraisal. To conclude, contrary to studies on enduring engagement, daily job demands relate positively to SWE. The instrumentality aspect of meeting the demands in relation to the profit gained when demands are met (Le Pine *et al.*, 2005) seems to be more prominent on a day-to-day basis (see also Daniels, this volume).

State Work Engagement and Performance

The increased interest of scholars and managers in the concept of work engagement may be explained by the strong empirical evidence supporting the link between engagement and employee performance both at the between- and at the within-person level (for a review, see Demerouti & Cropanzano, 2010). The added, theoretical value of examining within-person fluctuations in job performance is outlined in Beal, Weiss, Barros, and MacDermid's (2005) episodic process model. In contrast to traditional, static approaches, they define a time structure for performance, the performance episode (i.e. naturally parted, short-lived behavioral episodes that are organized around immediate work goals), that focuses on within-person variability. Indeed, systematic within-person variability has been recorded with regard to task performance (Trougakos *et al.*, 2008), in-role performance (Xanthopoulou *et al.*, 2008), and proactive behaviors (Binnewies *et al.*, 2009; Sonnentag, 2003).

According to Beal *et al.* (2005), fluctuations in performance do not happen at random. Rather, they are caused by systematic fluctuations in affect, affect regulation, as well as in the characteristics of the specific context within which the episodes develop (see also Fay & Sonnentag, 2010). Thus, the study of dynamic performance episodes is analogous to and complements the study of SWE, and indicates that it is worth looking at whether SWE and successful performance episodes are linked.

In line with the findings of between-person studies, diary studies have supported a positive link between SWE and performance episodes. Sonnentag (2003) supported the positive relationship between daily engagement and day levels of personal initiative and pursuit of learning (i.e. proactive behavior). In addition, Xanthopoulou and colleagues (2008) showed that flight attendants' work engagement during the flight related to more favorable self-assessments of momentary in-role and extra-role performance. Similarly, Bakker and Bal (2010) revealed that teachers' weekly engagement related positively to weekly (in-role and extra-role) self-rated performance. Importantly, in the latter study, teachers' self-ratings of performance were strongly related to supervisors' ratings of teachers' performance that were collected during the first week of the study. Also, Bakker and his co-workers (2010) found evidence for a positive link between daily engagement and task performance among assembly line workers. Finally, work engagement has also been found to relate positively to "bottom-line" financial indicators of performance: On days that fast-food restaurant employees were more engaged, restaurants reported higher financial returns (Xanthopoulou et al., 2009). In these studies, the unique within-person variance in job performance explained by SWE ranged from 2 percent to 32 percent.

Crossover of State Work Engagement: The Actor–Partner Interdependence Model

According to Bakker and Demerouti (2008), one reason why engaged employees perform better is that engagement is contagious. Engagement may cross over from one employee to another within the same work environment, even on a day-to-day basis. Considering that, in the majority of jobs, productivity indicators depend on the collaborative effort of a team of individuals, it is conceivable that the crossover of engagement from one colleague to another may be particularly beneficial for performance outcomes. The results of the study by Xanthopoulou et al. (2009) provided indirect support for this argument. This study showed that, on days that fast-food restaurant employees were more engaged, the financial returns of the restaurant during the specific shift were higher. It is clear that financial returns do not depend on the work of one employee only. However, the fact that SWE of an individual may impact the financial returns of a whole team implies that crossover may be the underlying psychological mechanism explaining this effect.

Crossover is the process that occurs when the psychological well-being experienced by one person affects the level of well-being of another person (Westman, 2001). How exactly does work engagement cross over from one colleague to another on a day-to-day level? Bakker and Xanthopoulou (2009) argue that each sub-dimension of engagement crosses over via a slightly different mechanism. The crossover of vigor and absorption may be attributed to an unconscious modeling process, where colleagues imitate each other's behavior. Indeed, studies have shown that people tend to automatically mimic the facial expressions, postures, and behaviors of others (Bavelas et al., 1987; Bernieri et al., 1988). Therefore, an employee may become unconsciously more vigorous on days that his/her colleague is very energetic. Similarly, an employee who notices that her colleague is so concentrated in her work that she neglects other stimuli is likely to model such behavior. In the case of dedication, the crossover mechanism is more conscious in the sense that employees actively "put themselves in the shoes" of their colleagues. Thus, the dedication and enthusiasm expressed by one employee may fuel his/her colleagues' dedication because their thoughts are focused on the positive aspects of work that make them enthusiastic.

Although the crossover of SWE may be applied to extended networks of employees, the current analysis is restricted to dyads of colleagues. According to Kenny and Cook (1999), such a crossover effect constitutes a typical case of a *partner effect* since the work engagement of the one person reflects the work engagement of the other person within the dyad. It is known that dyadic data is non-independent because the responses of the two people, as members of the same dyad, are highly correlated (Kenny, 1996). One of the most promising models to analyze such data is the Actor–Partner Interdependence Model (APIM; Campbell & Kashy,

2002; Kenny & Cook, 1999). The APIM enables estimation of how a person's independent variable has an effect on his/her *own* dependent variable (i.e. an actor effect), as well as on his/her partner's dependent variable (i.e. a partner effect; Campbell & Kashy, 2002). The advantage of this model is that it includes the dyad as the highest unit of analysis, with individuals nested within the dyad (i.e. two-level model).

An additional challenge when studying the crossover of SWE is that within-person fluctuations in engagement for each member of the dyad need to be taken into account as well. This leads to a three-level model that takes into consideration the interdependence between the members of the dyad, as well as the fact that day-level measurements are nested within each person. An additional advantage is that the APIM directly models the *mutual* influence that may occur between the members of the dyad. This means that the crossover of SWE from "colleague A" to "colleague B" is tested simultaneously with the crossover from "colleague B" to "colleague A."

Bakker and Xanthopoulou (2009) made use of the advantages of the APIM to study the daily crossover of engagement among 62 dyads of colleagues from various occupations that worked closely together. Multilevel analyses revealed that daily work engagement crossed over from one colleague to the other and vice versa on days they had more business and informal (phone, e-mail, face-to-face) contacts than usual; on these days, particularly vigorous co-workers facilitated each other's performance. Building on this study, Bakker and Xanthopoulou (2010) performed a similar diary study among 78 dyads of co-workers. Analyses of the data collected in this latter study provided strong evidence for the bi-directional crossover of daily work engagement from one colleague to the other, after controlling for the degree of liking between colleagues. These findings substantiate the theoretical assumption that work engagement contributes to enhanced performance because it is contagious. Nevertheless, future studies that use the APIM to examine the crossover of SWE may provide further insights particularly with regard to personal (e.g. colleagues' extraversion), situational (e.g. daily resources), or dyadic (e.g. degree of collaboration) factors that may determine the strength of the crossover effect.

Avenues for Future Research

Since the very first studies on enduring work engagement, a lot of effort has been invested in the development of the construct, as well as in exploring the psychological processes that explain this phenomenon. The published studies on SWE are fewer, yet significant. Almost ten years after the first publication on SWE (Sonnentag, 2003), we know a lot more about its proximal predictors and outcomes, as well as the underlying psychological mechanisms. Nevertheless, there are some unresolved issues with regard to the concept of SWE that require further attention.

One point of interest concerns the theoretical and methodological distinction between SWE and the concept of work-related flow. Flow refers to peak affective experiences during any activity of everyday life, including work (Csikszentmihalyi, 1975). Work-related flow is characterized by enjoyment (i.e. feelings of happiness), total absorption in the activity (i.e. the feeling that "time flies"), and intrinsic work motivation (i.e. activities are partaken regardless of external rewards or costs; Bakker, 2008). Clearly, there is some overlap between the dimensions of work-related flow and SWE. Fullagar and Kelloway (2009) argued and showed that flow is best conceptualized as a dynamic and not as an enduring state. This proposition has been further supported by Rodriguez-Sánchez, Schaufeli, Salanova, Cifre, and Sonnenschein (2011), who showed that flow varies within the same employee even from one hour to another. In this context, the question is whether SWE could best be conceptualized as the frequency of peak flow experiences at work. The main theoretical point here is that the core dimension of flow is absorption, while absorption has been considered by some scholars to be a constituent dimension of work engagement (Gonzàlez-Romà et al., 2006). Furthermore, SWE does not concern peaks of the experience. In other words, engagement is more about being energetic and dedicated to the job, while flow concerns peaks of total immersion in the activity. In any case, these are theoretical assumptions implying a distinction between SWE and work-related momentary flow that require further empirical support from future studies.

In an attempt to further disentangle methodological as well as theoretical issues, future studies should make more extensive use of Beal et al.'s (2005) episodic approach in examining SWE. Instead of capturing SWE experiences across the course of the workday or week, this approach would allow examination of the engagement experience for each work episode across a workday, separately. Such an approach would enable fluctuations over shorter periods of time to be captured and closer examination of the experience of SWE and its specific components. As Fay and Sonnentag (2010) suggested, the use of the episodic approach in practice may reveal alternative psychological mechanisms underlying the relationship between SWE and performance. For instance, one may argue that an employee who is extremely engaged in a task on a given moment may choose not to interrupt his work in order to help a colleague, which would suggest low extra-role performance. Further insights into the mechanisms that explain SWE are needed in order to either establish the current theoretical framework or proceed to specific refinements.

Another theoretical and methodological issue that requires further attention concerns the incorporation of time in the empirical examination of the processes that explain SWE. Time and SWE are inter-related in two important ways. First, time constitutes a core element in the definition of SWE (i.e. an experience that varies within the same person over the course *of time*). Second, the study of SWE involves determining its proximal antecedents and outcomes, those that take place more or less at the same *time*. The majority of studies on SWE imply that changes in the antecedents go hand-in-hand with changes in SWE, which, in turn, go hand-in-hand with changes in performance. In other words, dynamic effects or growth models are hypothesized. However, most of these studies (for an exception, see Bakker et al., 2010) do not test these dynamic relationships in a manner consistent with theory because the role of time is excluded from the empirical testing. Pitariu and Ployhart (2010) suggest that it is not enough to include time-varying predictors in models that examine dynamic relationships. Rather, it is important to incorporate time as an independent variable (fixed or random) in the analyses in order to describe change. Failing to model temporal factors implies that we neglect the dynamic character of our data (for a detailed discussion, see Gross, Meier, & Semmer, this volume), which may lead to inferences about theory that are unwarranted. Thus, future studies should take into account this methodological suggestion in order to be able to arrive at more robust theoretical conclusions with regard to the psychological processes that explain SWE.

Practical Implications

What are the practical implications of knowledge about SWE? Since SWE seems more closely related to daily performance than enduring engagement, organizations could monitor SWE on an individual basis and find out on which days individual employees are most engaged. It is on these days that the employees should be given the more challenging tasks. Additionally, since daily job and personal resources influence daily engagement, managers should try to inspire and stimulate their employees on a daily basis, perhaps particularly on days that are extremely challenging – for example, on the days before Christmas for salespersons and at the end of the tax year for accountants. The main message for organizations is that the creation of resourceful work environments may keep employees engaged on a daily basis via the enhancement of their personal resources (see Xanthopoulou *et al.*, 2008, 2009). This implies that, for cultivating SWE, more emphasis should be placed on (re)designing the work environment, rather than on optimizing recruitment and selection processes.

Additionally, employees may themselves use their experience of SWE on a daily basis to mobilize their resources and to set high goals. On days employees feel highly engaged, they may engage in complex tasks that would be stressful on other days. Petrou *et al.* (in press) examined the situational conditions influencing job crafting on a daily basis, as well as the relationship between job crafting and SWE. Job crafting has been defined as the changes employees may make regarding their job demands and job resources (Tims & Bakker, 2010; see also Wrzesniewski & Dutton, 2001). Petrou and his colleagues conducted their research among 95 employees from several organizations, who filled in a diary for five consecutive days. The results showed that on days that work pressure and autonomy were both high (i.e. active jobs) employees showed more job-crafting behaviors (increased their job resources), which in turn was related to more state work engagement. These findings suggest that job crafting may occur on a daily basis, but only when employees have a high work pressure and perceive the autonomy to engage in job crafting.

Conclusion

In this chapter, we discussed the how and why of within-person variations in engagement. Conceptualizing engagement as a dynamic state has certain advantages, since it yields insights into processes that cannot easily be captured with survey studies. Recent studies clearly suggest that SWE can be reliably measured with the state version of the UWES. Whereas job and personal resources seem important predictors of state and enduring work engagement, job demands seem to act as challenges on a daily basis and as hindrances in the long run. SWE is positively related to momentary performance and may cross over from one employee to the other. These findings indicate that SWE is highly relevant for organizations – managers may use information about SWE for performance improvement in the workplace. We hope that this chapter inspires future research on the dynamics of work engagement.

References

Allen, B.P. & Potkay, C.R. (1981). On the arbitrary distinction between states and traits. *Journal of Personality and Social Psychology, 41*, 916–928.

Bakker, A.B. (2008). The work-related flow inventory: Construction and initial validation of the WOLF. *Journal of Vocational Behavior, 72*, 400–414.

Bakker, A.B. & Bal, P.M. (2010). Weekly work engagement and performance: A study among starting teachers. *Journal of Occupational and Organizational Psychology, 83*, 189–206.

Bakker, A.B. & Demerouti, E. (2008). Towards a model of work engagement. *Career Development International, 13*, 209–223.

Bakker, A.B. & Leiter, M.P. (2010). Where do we go from here: Integration and future research on work engagement. In A.B. Bakker & M.P. Leiter (Eds), *Work engagement: A handbook of essential theory and research* (pp. 181–196). New York: Psychology Press.

Bakker, A.B. & Oerlemans, W.G.M. (2011). Subjective well-being in organizations. In K.S. Cameron & G.M. Spreitzer (Eds), *The Oxford handbook of positive organizational scholarship* (pp. 178–189). New York: Oxford University Press.

Bakker, A.B. & Xanthopoulou, D. (2009). The crossover of daily work engagement: Test of an actor-partner interdependence model. *Journal of Applied Psychology, 94*, 1562–1571.

Bakker, A.B. & Xanthopoulou, D. (2010). The convergence of job performance during interactions with engaged colleagues: An actor-partner interdependence analysis. *Erasmus University Rotterdam, The Netherlands.*

Bakker, A.B., Van Emmerik, H., Geurts, S., & Demerouti, E. (2010). Recovery turns job demands into challenges: A diary study on work engagement and performance. *Manuscript submitted for publication.*

Bakker, A.B., Albrecht, S.L., & Leiter, M.P. (2011). Key questions regarding work engagement. *European Journal of Work and Organizational Psychology, 20*, 4–28.

Bavelas, J.B., Black, A., Lemery, C.R., & Mullett, J. (1987). Motor mimicry as primitive empathy. In N. Eisenberg & J. Strayer (Eds), *Empathy and its development* (pp. 317–338). New York: Cambridge University Press.

Beal, D.J., Weiss, H.M., Barros, E., & MacDermid, S.M. (2005). An episodic process model of affective influences on performance. *Journal of Applied Psychology, 90*, 1054–1068.

Bernieri, F.J., Reznick, J.S., & Rosenthal, R. (1988). Synchrony, pseudosynchrony, and dissynchrony: Measuring the entrainment process in mother–infant interactions. *Journal of Personality and Social Psychology, 54*, 1242–1253.

Binnewies, C., Sonnentag, S., & Mojza, E.J. (2009). Daily performance at work: Feeling recovered in the morning as a predictor of day-level job performance. *Journal of Organizational Behavior, 30*, 67–93.

Breevaart, K., Bakker, A.B., Demerouti, E., & Hetland, J. (in press). The measurement of state work engagement: A multilevel factor analytic study. *European Journal of Psychological Assessment.*

Campbell, L. & Kashy, D.A. (2002). Estimating actor, partner, and interaction effects for dyadic data using PROC MIXED and HLM: A user-friendly guide. *Personal Relationships, 9*, 327–342.

Csikszentmihalyi, M. (1975). *Beyond boredom and anxiety: Experiencing flow in work and play.* San Francisco, CA: Jossey-Bass.

Daniels, K. (2006). Rethinking job characteristics in work stress research. *Human Relations, 59*, 267–290.

Demerouti, E. & Cropanzano, R. (2010). From thought to action: Employee work engagement and job performance. In A.B. Bakker & M.P. Leiter (Eds), *Work engagement: A handbook of essential theory and research* (pp. 147–163). Hove: Psychology Press.

Demerouti, E., Bakker, A.B., Nachreiner, F., & Schaufeli, W.B. (2001). The job demands-resources model of burnout. *Journal of Applied Psychology, 86*, 499–512.

Ekman, P. (1994). Moods, emotions, and traits. In P. Ekman & R.J. Davidson (Eds), *The nature of emotion: Fundamental questions* (pp.56–58). New York: Oxford University Press.

Fay, D. & Sonnentag, S. (2010). A look back to move ahead: New directions for research on proactive performance and other discretionary work behaviors. *Applied Psychology: An International Review, 59*, 1–20.

Fullagar, C.J. & Kelloway, K.E. (2009). 'Flow' at work: An experience sampling approach. *Journal of Occupational and Organizational Psychology, 82*, 595–615.

George, J.M. (1991). State or trait: Effects of positive mood on prosocial behaviors at work. *Journal of Applied Psychology, 76*, 299–307.

Gonzàlez-Romà, V., Schaufeli, W.B., Bakker, A.B., & Lloret, S. (2006). Burnout and work engagement: Independent factors or opposite poles? *Journal of Vocational Behavior, 68*, 165–174.

Halbesleben, J.R.B. (2010). A meta-analysis of work engagement: Relationships with burnout, demands, resources, and consequences. In A.B. Bakker & M.P. Leiter (Eds), *Work engagement: A handbook of essential theory and research* (pp. 102–117). New York: Psychology Press.

Hobfoll, S.E. (1989). Conservation of resources: A new attempt at conceptualizing stress. *American Psychologist, 44*, 513–524.

Hobfoll, S.E., Johnson, R.J., Ennis, N., & Jackson, A.P. (2003). Resource loss, resource gain, and emotional outcomes among inner city women. *Journal of Personality and Social Psychology, 84*, 632–643.

Kenny, D.A. (1996). Models of nonindependence in dyadic research. *Journal of Social and Personal Relationships, 13*, 279–294.

Kenny, D.A. & Cook, W. (1999). Partner effects in relationship research: Conceptual issues, analytic difficulties, and illustrations. *Personal Relationships, 6*, 433–448.

Kozlowski, S.W.J. & Klein, K.J. (2000). A multilevel approach to theory and research in organizations: Contextual, temporal, and emergent processes. In K.J. Klein & S.W.J. Kozlowski (Eds), *Multilevel theory, research, and methods in organizations: Foundations, extensions, and new directions* (pp. 3–90). San Francisco: Jossey-Bass.

LePine, J.A., Podsakoff, N.P., & LePine, M.A. (2005). A meta-analytic test of the challenge stress-hindrance stress framework: An explanation for inconsistent relationships between stressors and performance. *Academy of Management Journal, 48*, 764–775.

Macey, W.H. & Schneider, B. (2008). The meaning of employee engagement. *Industrial and Organizational Psychology: Perspectives on Science and Practice, 1*, 3–30.

Ohly, S. & Fritz, C. (2010). Work characteristics, challenge appraisal, creativity, and proactive behavior: A multi-level study. *Journal of Organizational Behavior, 31*, 543–565.

Ohly, S., Sonnentag, S., Niessen, C., & Zapf, D. (2010). Diary studies in organizational research: An introduction and some practical recommendations. *Journal of Personnel Psychology, 9*, 79–93.

Petrou, P., Demerouti, E., Peeters, M., & Schaufeli, W. (in press). Crafting a job on a daily basis: Contextual antecedents and the effect on work engagement. *Journal of Organizational Behavior*.

Pitariu, A.H. & Ployhart, R.E. (2010). Explaining change: Theorizing and testing dynamic mediated longitudinal relationships. *Journal of Management, 36*, 405–429.

Rodriguez-Sánchez, A.M., Schaufeli, W.B., Salanova, M., Cifre, E., & Sonnenschein, M. (2011). An electronic diary study on flow experiences involving working and non-working tasks. *Work & Stress, 25*, 75–92.

Russell, J.A. (2003). Core affect and the psychological construction of emotion. *Psychological Review, 110*, 145–172.

Salanova, M., Schaufeli, W.B., Xanthopoulou, D., & Bakker, A.B. (2010). The gain spiral of resources and work engagement: Sustaining a positive worklife. In A.B. Bakker & M.P. Leiter (Eds), *Work engagement: A handbook of essential theory and research* (pp. 118–131). New York: Psychology Press.

Schaufeli, W.B. & Bakker, A.B. (2004). Job demands, job resources and their relationship with burnout and engagement: A multi-sample study. *Journal of Organizational Behavior, 25*, 293–315.

Schaufeli, W.B. & Bakker, A.B. (2010). Defining and measuring work engagement: Bringing clarity to the concept. In A.B. Bakker & M.P. Leiter (Eds), *Work engagement: A handbook of essential theory and research* (pp.10–24). New York: Psychology Press.

Schaufeli, W.B., Salanova, M., González-Romá, V., & Bakker, A.B. (2002). The measurement of engagement and burnout: A two sample confirmatory factor analytic approach. *Journal of Happiness Studies, 3*, 71–92.

Schaufeli, W.B., Bakker, A.B., & Salanova, M. (2006). The measurement of work engagement with a short questionnaire: A cross-national study. *Educational and Psychological Measurement, 66*, 701–716.

Simbula, S. (2010). Daily fluctuations in teachers' well-being: A diary study using the job demands-resources model. *Anxiety, Stress, & Coping, 23*, 1–22.

Sonnentag, S. (2003). Recovery, work engagement, and proactive behaviour: A new look at the interface between nonwork and work. *Journal of Applied Psychology, 88*, 518–528.

Sonnentag, S. & Niessen, C. (2008). Staying vigorous until work is over: The role of trait vigour, day-specific work experienced and recovery. *Journal of Occupational and Organizational Psychology, 81*, 435–458.

Sonnentag, S., Dormann, C., & Demerouti, E. (2010). Not all days are created equal: The concept of state work engagement. In A.B. Bakker & M.P. Leiter (Eds), *Work engagement: A handbook of essential theory and research* (pp. 25–38). New York: Psychology Press.

Tims, M. & Bakker, A.B. (2010). Job crafting: Towards a new model of individual job redesign. *South African Journal of Industrial Psychology, 36*, Art. #841.

Tims, M., Bakker, A.B., & Xanthopoulou, D. (2011). Do transformational leaders enhance their followers' daily work engagement? *The Leadership Quarterly, 22*, 121–123.

Trougakos, J.P., Beal, D.J., Green, S.G., & Weiss, H.M. (2008). Making the break count: An episodic examination of recovery activities, emotional experiences, and positive affective displays. *Academy of Management Journal, 51*, 131–146.

Watson, D. & Clark, L.A. (1994). The PANAS-X: Manual for the positive and negative affect schedule-expanded form. *Unpublished Manuscript, University of Iowa*. Retrieved from: http://ir.uiowa.edu/cgi/viewcontent.cgi?article=1011&context=psychology_pubs&sei-redir=1#search=%22PANAS+questionnaire%22.

Westman, M. (2001). Stress and strain crossover. *Human Relations, 54*, 557–591.

Wrzesniewski, A. & Dutton, J.E. (2001). Crafting a job: Revisioning employees as active crafters of their work. *Academy of Management Review, 26*, 179–201.

Xanthopoulou, D., Bakker, A.B., Heuven, E., Demerouti, E., & Schaufeli, W.B. (2008). Working in the sky: A diary study on work engagement among flight attendants. *Journal of Occupational Health Psychology, 13*, 345–356.

Xanthopoulou, D., Bakker, A.B., Demerouti, E., & Schaufeli, W.B. (2009). Work engagement and financial returns: A diary study on the role of job and personal resources. *Journal of Occupational and Organizational Psychology, 82*, 183–200.

4 Work-Related Flow

Clive Fullagar and E. Kevin Kelloway

In the last two weeks of July in 1950, the photographer Hans Namuth was given the opportunity to observe and record Jackson Pollock, the abstract expressionist painter, as he worked on one of his large paintings in his East Hampton studio in New York. It was the first time that anyone had seen Pollock at work. Namuth noted that Pollock became completely absorbed in the act of painting, dancing around the canvas on the floor, totally oblivious that his actions were being observed and photographed. This intense physical activity and involvement lasted perhaps an hour, after which the artist looked up and said, "This is it." It was this same state of immersion that prompted Mihaly Csikszentmihalyi, a decade later, to study creative painters in order to understand why individuals become absorbed in an activity in the absence of any extrinsic rewards (Csikszentmihalyi, 1975, 2000). Although psychologists had studied intrinsic motivation (e.g. Deci, 1972; White, 1959), Csikszentmihalyi was the first to systematically research the subjective phenomenology of intrinsic motivation when individuals were engaged in a skillful activity. He interviewed chess players, dancers, rock climbers, surgeons, and many others, and found that the psychological state associated with engaged activity was remarkably similar across all domains. He termed this optimal experience of absorption "flow," as many interviewees described the experience as flowing from moment to moment. Csikszentmihalyi defined this dynamic state as "the holistic sensation that people feel when they act with total involvement" (1975, p. 36).

Most of the research on flow has focused on voluntary and pleasurable leisure and sporting activities. However, the experience of flow has been reported while engaging in work-related tasks as well (Csikszentmihalyi, 1975; Csikszentmihalyi & LeFevre, 1989; Fave & Massimini, 1988). The purpose of this chapter is to focus on work-related flow. This book is about applying the theories and constructs of positive psychology to understand what makes us flourish and be happy at work. Luthans (2002) has stipulated that any such application should focus on constructs that "can be measured, developed, and effectively managed for performance improvement" (p. 58). This chapter is an exposition of whether work-related flow fulfills these criteria and its potential to make a contribution to both positive organizational research and the promotion of occupational health. We start off by outlining the dimensionality of flow and its enabling preconditions. Next, we describe the methodologies that have been used to study the experience of flow.

We then proceed to discuss the psychophysiology of flow and elaborate on whether it is a state or a trait. Finally, we discuss research that has identified the individual and organizational consequences of flow as well as studies that have investigated how to restructure work to make it more intrinsically rewarding and conducive to flow.

The Preconditions and Dimensionality of Flow

Many theories of intrinsic motivation are based on the notion of *regulatory compatibility* (Keller & Bless, 2008). This refers to the experience of compatibility between individual characteristics (e.g. skill level, need for achievement, dispositional factors) and situational characteristics (e.g. task demands, goal clarity, resources). There are three situational or task-related preconditions that have been found to be conducive to flow (Nakamura & Csikszentmihalyi, 2002).

Challenge/Skill Balance

Csikszentmihalyi (1990, 1997) has stipulated that, in order to experience flow, the challenges of the activity must be in balance with the skills necessary to perform the activity. Furthermore, both challenges and skills must be at a moderate to high level for optimal experience to occur (Massimini & Carli, 1988; Massimini *et al.*, 1987). This balance between challenge and skill has been a core tenet of flow theory (Csikszentmihalyi, 1975).

When challenges far exceed skills, individuals will experience anxiety. Conversely, when individuals are over-skilled for the performance of an activity, they will experience boredom. Flow occurs when both challenges and skills are balanced and at above-average levels (Haworth & Evans, 1995; Massimini & Carli, 1988; Massimini *et al.*, 1987; Massimini & Delle Fave, 2000). Flow theory suggests that the relationship between the perceived challenge of a task and flow is a curvilinear one. If the task is perceived as being too challenging or too easy, then optimal experience is less likely to occur. An optimal level of challenge is necessary for flow to be experienced and this optimal level is determined by the skills of the individual performing the task.

The theoretical centrality of challenge/skill balance in flow theory has been partially supported by empirical studies (Eisenberger *et al.*, 2005; Engeser & Rheinberg, 2008; Fullagar *et al.*, 2009; Haworth & Evans, 1995; Hektner & Asakawa, 2000). Specifically, these studies confirm that degree of challenge in a task is significantly associated with enjoyment and interest. However, several of these studies (e.g. Engeser & Rheinberg, 2008; Fullagar *et al.*, 2009; Haworth & Evans, 1995; Hektner & Asakawa, 2000) also found that tasks where skill exceeds challenge were also conducive to flow. This is contrary to flow theory, which predicts that tasks low in challenge and exceeded by skill should generate a state of "boredom" (Csikszentmihalyi, 1975; Massimini & Carli, 1988). Such inconsistencies suggest that the relationship between challenge/skill balance and flow may be moderated by task-related factors.

Two task characteristics that have been found to be important moderators are the volitional nature and importance of the activity. Several studies have found that performance of low-challenge/high-skill volitional leisure activities (e.g. playing a musical instrument, knitting, cooking) produces relatively high levels of flow (e.g. Fullagar *et al.*, 2009; Hektner & Asakawa, 2000). The perceived importance of the task has also been found to moderate the relationship between challenge/skill balance and flow (Engeser & Rheinberg, 2008). In highly important activities (such as learning statistics), flow was found to be high even in low-challenge situations. For less important activities (such as playing the computer game Pac-Man), flow was highest when there was a balance between challenge and skill, but low when the challenge of the task was too high or too low.

Clear and Specific Goals

A second precondition of flow is that the task should have clear and proximal goals (Csikszentmihalyi, 1990, 1997). This is consistent with goal-setting theory, which stipulates that human behavior is driven by goals (Locke *et al.*, 1981). Such goals are the basis of human motivation and engagement in a task in that they determine effort, persistence, and direction (Pinder, 2008). Both goal-setting theory and flow theory emphasize that goals should be both proximal and specific if they are to direct attention and action (Csikszentmihalyi *et al.*, 2005; Locke *et al.*, 1981). For Csikszentmihalyi, goals focus attention on the task at hand, thereby filtering out extraneous stimuli from the individual's consciousness and promoting the experience of flow. Flow theory supports goal theory in suggesting that challenging goals that are compatible with individual skill levels would be associated with both optimal experience and performance. Despite being an important precondition of flow, no research has been undertaken that has applied goal-setting theory to understanding flow.

Feedback

The final precursor to flow is that the task should provide the individual with clear feedback as to how much progress is being made toward goal achievement (Csikszentmihalyi, 1990, 1997). Both goals and feedback are necessary for both the experience of flow (Csikszentmihalyi, 1975) and for peak performance (Locke *et al.*, 1981). Feedback provides information to the individual regarding whether moment-to-moment goals are being met (Latham & Locke, 1991). For feedback to have its maximum impact on generating a state of intrinsic motivation, such as flow, it is important that the individual believes that it is his/her own skills, efforts, and abilities that are the cause of successful performance of the task (Thomas & Mathieu, 1994). However, no research has been done that has investigated the importance of feedback as a necessary precondition for flow to occur.

It is these conditions that are conducive to the subjective state of flow. Qualitative and quantitative research has indicated that the constitution of flow is remarkably consistent across diverse work and leisure activities (Csikszentmihalyi, 1990, 1993; Jackson, 1996; Jackson & Marsh, 1996; Nakamura & Csikszentmihalyi, 2009) and consists of the following characteristics:

Intense absorption. Perhaps the most frequently reported state associated with the flow experience is a deep involvement in the task at hand. Attention and energies are completely focused on the task and there is an absence of extraneous thoughts and distractions. The individual becomes so absorbed in what he/she is doing that the distinction between the self and the activity disappears. It is this core dimension of flow that drives the other components.

Intrinsic motivation. Csikszentmihalyi (1975) described flow as an autotelic state, from the Greek words "auto" meaning self and "telos" meaning goal. The experience of flow is intrinsically motivating and independent of extrinsic rewards or punishments. The process of the activity is so enjoyable that it is rewarding in and of itself.

A sense of control. When individuals describe their experience of flow, they report a sense of exercising control over both the outcomes and the process of the task, while not having to exercise effort to try and be in control. As soon as attention shifts to try to maintain control, flow dissipates.

A merging of action and awareness. Involvement in the task is such that behavior becomes automatic and spontaneous. Athletes in flow report a sense of effortlessness, where practiced routines become subconscious and attention is fully focused on the task. There is little awareness of the self, other than what one is doing.

A loss of self-consciousness. People in flow report such an absorption in the task that they lose all concern for self and their surroundings as they become immersed in the activity. This un-self-conscious form of action is accompanied by a lack of concern for what others may be thinking or how well one is performing.

A transformation of time. In the very intense stages of the flow state, the notion of time disappears to the extent that later individuals report that time becomes distorted. Similar to other states of focused cognitive attention, time is reported as speeding up. The more attention dedicated to performing the task, the shorter the perceived duration of the task.

Despite the fact that these core dimensions of flow have been consistently reported in the literature, very few studies have empirically tried to confirm the dimensionality of flow. There has been some work that has attempted to establish the construct validity of a multidimensional measure of state and trait flow that assesses optimal experience among athletes (Jackson & Eklund, 2004; Jackson & Marsh, 1996; Marsh & Jackson, 1999). One of the problems with this research is that it confounds the preconditions of flow with the cognitive and affective components of optimal experience. Nonetheless, using confirmatory factor analysis, this research has established clear support for a multi-factor construct, although there is some ambiguity as to whether it is significantly better than a higher-order global measure of flow. The global approach has received satisfactory psychometric support and is almost predominantly used in research on flow (Jackson & Eklund, 2004), perhaps as a result of the experience-sampling method that has been the predominant methodology used to study flow (see below).

A work-related flow measure (WOLF; Bakker, 2008) has been developed that focuses on three of the above dimensions; absorption, enjoyment, and intrinsic motivation. Using both exploratory and confirmatory factor analysis, Bakker found that a three-factor model of flow provided a better fit than a one-factor or global model in a variety of occupational and organizational samples. Although it is encouraging to have a reliable measure of flow that is specific to work, the development of such applied psychological constructs necessitates establishing their conceptual distinctiveness from previously established constructs. As long ago as 1927, Kelley was warning against the "Jangle Fallacy" (p. 63) – the tendency to use a different term to describe a construct that is essentially no different from one already coined (Kelley, 1927). There is a considerable amount of conceptual overlap between Bakker's operationalization of work-related flow and the concept of work engagement defined as "a positive, fulfilling, work-related state of mind that is characterized by vigor, dedication, and absorption" (Schaufeli et al., 2002). Both work engagement and the WOLF assess chronic involvement in a broad range of work activities, whereas flow is typically described as a more acute and intense absorption with a specific work task (Csikszentmihalyi, 1975; Mills & Fullagar, 2008; Schaufeli & Salanova, 2007).

In sum, establishing the dimensionality of flow is an important part of both its theoretical development and its measurement. Further research is needed that (a) confirms the factorial structure of flow through factor analysis, (b) establishes the conceptual distinctiveness of the different factors of the flow experience, and (c) determines the construct and predictive validity of the various unidimensional and multidimensional operationalizations of flow. As Luthans and colleagues have pointed out, the scientific credibility of such constructs as flow and their potential to contribute to the development of a positive psychology of work is dependent on their valid measurement, which in turn facilitates the systematic analysis, control, and prediction that is necessary to establish their utility (Luthans et al., 2007).

Capturing Flow

Early research on flow used qualitative methodologies, such as interviews, to produce subjective, albeit retrospective, descriptions of optimal experiences (e.g. Csikszentmihalyi, 1975; Fave & Massimini, 1988; Jackson, 1992; Privette & Bundrick, 1991). These interviews provided an in-depth view of flow by allowing respondents to describe their associated thoughts, feelings, and experiences. Such qualitative research was well suited for the purpose of describing, interpreting, and explaining the experience of flow and appropriate for generating and elaborating upon a theory of optimal experience.

More typically, researchers have used the experience sampling method (ESM) to measure flow in daily life. ESM is a methodology that was specifically developed by Larson and Csikszentmihalyi (1983) to longitudinally examine the thoughts, feelings, and behaviors associated with flow across a range of situations and activities as they occur in the participants' natural environment (see also Dimotakis & Ilies, this volume). Typically, ESM consists of providing subjects with an electronic pager and a questionnaire booklet. Researchers activate the pagers several times a day, contingent upon a fixed interval of time, a specific event, or a random signal (Reis & Gable, 2000). Upon being signaled, the participant completes a short survey that assesses thoughts and feelings at that moment. These studies usually last from one to several weeks. ESM has been used to assess flow experiences in a variety of samples and domains, including students (Carli *et al.*, 1988; Csikszentmihalyi & Larson, 1984), family members (Larson & Richards, 1994), psychiatric patients (Massimini *et al.*, 1987), nursing home residents (Voelkl, 1990), and architecture students (Fullagar & Kelloway, 2009).

ESM is a methodological approach that has four strengths (Scollon *et al.*, 2003). First, ESM provides data concerning the relationship between dynamic situational characteristics and a variety of response outcomes. Second, because ESM studies individuals operating in real settings, it enhances the ecological validity of the findings. Third, it enables examination of both within- and between-person variation and allows researchers to disentangle the state-like and trait-like components of flow. Finally, because cognitive, affective, and behavioral constructs are assessed immediately following an event, recall biases are minimized. However, ESM can be extremely intrusive, frequently impractical, and disruptive of the flow experience.

Despite the difficulty of applying empirical methods to phenomenological experiences, quantitative approaches to the study of flow have recently begun to emerge. Jackson and Marsh (1996) have developed the Flow State Scale, a psychometrically valid scale that assesses the flow experience in sport and physical activity settings. Also more quantitative methodologies have been used to specifically study work flow (Demerouti, 2006; Eisenberger *et al.*, 2005; see discussion below).

Even more recently, innovative, controlled, laboratory methods have been used to move beyond correlational studies to experimentally induce flow and to test the core tenets of flow theory (Engeser & Rheinberg, 2008; Keller & Bless, 2008; Keller & Blomann, 2008; Moller *et al.*, 2010). Most of this research manipulates the skill/challenge balance of video game tasks to create different levels of flow and enable the documentation of the causal impact of the compatibility of skills and demands on the emergence of flow. Advances in computer game technology have enabled researchers to create laboratory simulations that are capable of recreating complex cognitive and affective states, such as flow. Precise levels of experimental control and improved accuracy and efficiency of data-collection procedures are characteristic of such microworlds. These benefits are achieved with concomitant gains in both internal validity and external validity, as a result of high levels of cognitive realism and the replication of complex, dynamic, task environments (DiFonzo *et al.*, 1998). Such computer simulations attempt to reconcile the complexity of field research with the rigor of laboratory study.

Several concerns have been raised regarding attempts to quantify subjective experiences. Csikszentmihalyi (1992) is skeptical about empirical measures of flow and is concerned that the process of measurement detracts from the experience of flow: "The moment we say ... 'flow is a score of "x" on the flow questionnaire,' we have lost it. We have mistaken the reflection for the reality" (p. 183). Nonetheless, such empirical attempts present an additional perspective on the understanding of the flow construct and facilitate research that identifies the antecedents and consequences of flow (Jackson & Marsh, 1996). It is not our intention to resuscitate the quantitative versus qualitative debate here, but to emphasize that a variety of methodological approaches are available, appropriate, and necessary to fully understand the complexity and prevalence of the flow experience.

The Physiology of Flow

Establishing the physiological and cognitive anatomy of flow is important in order to confirm its construct validity and to differentiate it from other cognitive and mental states of mind. Empirical research on the physiology of flow is sparse. The main reason for this is that it is very difficult to obtain non-invasive physiological measures of flow that do not disrupt the state.

Recently, however, research has begun to map out the physiology of flow. This research is predicated by the notion that flow is a state of "effortless attention" (Bruya, 2010). Building on neuropsychological research on athletes and recent theoretical and empirical research in cognitive neuroscience, Dietrich (2004, 2006; Dietrich & Stoll, 2010) has developed a framework for understanding the neurocognitive mechanisms underlying flow. He proposes that flow is a state of "transient hypofrontality" in that there is a temporary suspension of the higher cognitive functions (the analytic and meta-conscious capacities of the explicit system) so that highly practiced, overlearned skills (the more efficient, skill-based knowledge of the implicit system) can be engaged without interference. The most sophisticated cognitive processes of consciousness, such as sustained and directed attention, working memory, and temporal integration are located in the prefrontal cortex and it is these functions that are affected first when flow is experienced. As flow deepens or intensifies, there is a progressive down-regulation of these prefrontal regions. The various lower levels of consciousness are pared away leaving only the highest levels of consciousness fully operational (Dietrich & Stoll, 2010). So certain explicit, metacognitive processes are deregulated in the flow state and are thus prevented from interfering with the automaticity of implicit systems, thereby enabling more skilled movement to proceed effortlessly. This automation of sequences of action is necessary to enable more attention to be focused on the important elements of the activity (Csikszentmihalyi & Nakamura, 2010). Consequently, experts or skilled performers will automate many of the routine aspects of their performance in order to shift attention to the more dynamic and critical elements of the task.

Other research (e.g. De Manzano *et al.*, 2010) has attempted to distinguish the psychophysiology of flow as a state of effortless attention from the physiology of states of *effortful* attention. Attention is a core component of human cognition and a necessary element of goal-oriented behavior (Raz & Buhle, 2006). De Manzano *et al.* (2010), in an attempt to identify the physiological correlates of flow, studied 21 professional classical pianists as they performed five trials of a short piece of self-selected music that generated variable levels of flow. Repeated measures were taken of muscle tone, thoracic respiration, heart period, heart rate variability, and blood pressure, as well as self-reported flow. States of high flow exhibited the same physiological characteristics as high arousal emotions, such as joy (e.g. higher activity in muscles associated with smiling, decreased heart period, and larger respiratory depth). Such a psychophysiology has important implications for health. For example, a consistent prevalence of joyful emotions has been associated with low blood pressure (Theorell et al., 1993). Another positive emotion, optimism, has been correlated with a reduced incidence of coronary heart disease (Bygren et al., 1996). Furthermore, the ability of flow to regulate both sympathetic and parasympathetic nervous systems has implications for stress. Parasympathetic activity levels have been argued to counteract stress arousal. There is some support that flow and anxiety are incompatible states in that the experience of one precludes the other (Fullagar et al., 2009). So there is emerging evidence that frequent exposure to flow experiences may have beneficial health consequences.

Both of these research streams suggest that flow is associated with automaticity and that optimal experience is a state where those higher-order cognitive functions that could be distracting are inhibited from interfering with attention to the task (Beilock et al., 2004). This enables more efficient and automated motor output. Automaticity is an important characteristic of expertise (Ericsson et al., 2006). There is evidence that practice is a better predictor of expert performance than general cognitive ability (Ericsson et al., 2006). Nonautomatic work routines can become automated through extensive practice, training, and repetition until skills become overlearned (Ullén et al., 2010). The above research is recent and emergent. More work needs to be done to establish a clearer understanding of the relationship between work flow, cognitive ability, expertise, and practice and to study these variables in different work domains and on larger samples of workers.

Flow: State or Trait

Part of the process of clarifying constructs is distinguishing whether a construct is trait-like or state-like (Allen & Potkay, 1981). A trait is a durable and chronic predisposition to behave in certain way. On the other hand, a state is something that is variable, a reaction to certain situational characteristics. Trait-like and state-like constructs are distinguishable along several criteria (Chaplin et al., 1988). Specifically, they differ in terms of their temporal stability, cross-situational consistency, and source of causation (internal versus external).

There is some debate as to whether flow is a state or a trait. Flow as a state is defined as a psychological state of mind that is transitory, existing at a given moment in time and at a particular level of intensity, and experienced while performing a specific activity. However, Csikszentmihalyi (1990) has also referred to the "autotelic personality," in that certain individuals may have psychological characteristics that make them more prone to the experience of flow, regardless of the situation. However, the distinction between trait and state flow is frequently and arbitrarily made by varying the instructions on scales that contain the same items. Dispositional assessments of the flow experience (e.g. the Dispositional Flow Scale, Jackson & Eklund, 2004) measure the general tendency to experience flow during an activity usually selected by the participant. Respondents are required to recall and rate the frequency with which they experience the various characteristics of flow (Jackson & Eklund, 2004). The premise behind this approach is that individuals who report higher frequencies of flow characteristics have a greater predisposition to experience flow. State measures of flow (e.g. the Flow State Scale, Jackson & Eklund, 2004) are usually administered immediately following an activity and assess the level of flow characteristics during the activity. By surveying participants close to the conclusion of an activity, it is assumed that a more accurate assessment of the flow experience is assessed, one that is less susceptible to recall bias. Changing the instructions presumes that there is a change in the respondent's orientation from state to trait. Using such minor alterations in the framing of survey instructions to differentiate between state and trait constructs is an arbitrary and tenuous distinction.

More recently, Fullagar and Kelloway (2009) tracked the flow experiences of architecture students longitudinally as they performed studio work. These researchers used hierarchical linear modeling to differentiate within- and between-individual variation in flow. This study found that flow exhibited more state-like than trait-like characteristics. Within-individual variance in flow accounted for 74 percent of the overall variability in the construct. In other words, flow varied considerably as the situational contingencies and characteristics of architectural work changed (Fullagar & Kelloway, 2009). This is not to say that flow does not exhibit trait-like properties. For example, flow has been found to correlate with other trait variable characteristics, such as achievement motivation, aestheticism, and inquisitiveness (Csikszentmihalyi *et al.*, 1993; Jackson, 1984). Nonetheless there seems to be some confusion in the literature as to whether flow constitutes a state or a trait. Recent operationalizations of flow (e.g. Jackson & Eklund, 2002, 2004) have defined it as both a state and a trait construct. Flow is described as a psychological state influenced by state-based factors, with individuals varying in their propensity to regularly experience flow (Jackson *et al.*, 1998).

Most research that has investigated both the trait and the state aspects of flow has proposed that the relationship between situational characteristics and state-based flow is moderated by dispositional elements. Csikszentmihalyi (Csikszentmihalyi & Rathunde, 1993) and Adlai-Gail (1994) have suggested that individuals with an "autotelic personality" are more predisposed to seek out challenging tasks and experience flow. However, very little empirical research has been undertaken to identify what the characteristics of the autotelic personality are. One study (Eisenberger *et al.*, 2005) found that the relationship between challenge/skill balance and flow was moderated by achievement orientation. High achievement-oriented employees were more likely to experience positive mood and task interest on work tasks that required high skill and were challenging. Keller and Bless (2008) found that individuals who had a high "habitual action orientation," or ability to persevere with a task and stay focused, were more sensitive to challenge/skill compatibility.

Work-Related Flow

With the interest in applying positive psychology to an understanding of behavior in the workplace (Cameron et al., 2003; Luthans, 2001, 2002; Turner et al., 2002), it is important to distinguish between the trait-like and state-like properties of work flow. There is some evidence that work flow behaves like a state and so consequently is capable of being developed. This means that we can begin to understand what characteristics of the work environment facilitate optimal experience.

Although flow research has often concentrated on leisure activities (e.g. sports or artistic activities), researchers have suggested that adults are most likely to experience flow in the work setting (e.g. Csikszentmihalyi, 1990; Csikszentmihalyi & LeFevre, 1989; Haworth and Hill, 1992). In particular, Csikszentmihalyi and his colleagues have reported that the enabling conditions for flow (i.e. high challenges and high skills) (a) occur three times as often in the work environment as in other domains; (b) are present for approximately 50 percent of the work day (as opposed to only 18 percent of the non-working day); and (c) are more likely to occur in the work environment than in the non-work environment, even for assembly-line workers (Hektner et al., 2007).

Paradoxically, experiencing flow conditions (i.e. high challenge and high skill use) in the work setting is not always associated with experiencing flow. Although these conditions are reliably associated with the experience of flow in non-work activities, experiencing high demands and high skill use at work can actually be associated with negative, rather than positive, outcomes (Hektner et al., 2007). Although the reasons for this paradoxical finding are poorly understood, there are several likely explanations.

First, researchers (Hektner et al., 2007) have pointed to the fact that the flow conditions might increase the individuals' experience of workplace stress and this perspective is consistent with models of stress that identify job demands as a central component (for a review, see Kelloway & Day, 2005). Second, it is possible that individual motivations moderate the relationship between flow conditions and negative or positive outcomes. There may, for example, be different outcomes associated with experiencing the flow conditions in tasks for which one is intrinsically motivated (e.g. that one chooses to do for enjoyment) versus tasks for which one is more extrinsically motivated (e.g. that one does for money). Third, although the conditions necessary to experience flow may occur more often at work, it is possible that one simply cannot sustain the level of experience characteristic of flow. In this case, an unrelenting state of increased job challenges may be seen as stressful rather than an optimal experience. Finally, it is plausible that the state of intense involvement characteristic of flow may actually impede performance of some aspects of the job. For example, performing surgery is technically demanding and likely to create the flow conditions mentioned earlier. However, surgeons are also expected to demonstrate a number of non-technical skills, including teamwork, leadership, communication, and decision-making (Yule et al., 2006). Being in a state of flow might enhance technical performance at the expense of these non-technical components of the job.

Antecedents of Work-Related Flow

As noted earlier, considerable effort has been expended to identify the task characteristics that lead to flow. These "flow conditions" are commonly viewed as comprising (a) a high level of task challenge, and (b) a high degree of skill use (see, for example, Hektner *et al.*, 2007). Flow is thought to occur when these two conditions are in balance. When skills exceed demands, the resulting state is boredom, and when demands exceed skills, the result may be overwhelming and stressful.

Demerouti (2006) initially expanded this view and reported that the motivating job characteristics identified in the job characteristics model (e.g. autonomy, skill variety, task significance, task identity, and feedback; Hackman & Oldham, 1975, 1980) were predictive of flow. However, that study used an overall measure of job characteristics and could not identify which characteristics of tasks were more likely to result in flow. Fullagar and Kelloway (2009) further elaborated on this finding by measuring individual job characteristics. They reported that flow was more likely in situations characterized by skill variety and autonomy. This is consistent with the finding that flow is associated with performance of voluntary activities (Csikszentmihalyi, 1975; Csikszentmihalyi & LeFevre, 1989; Fave & Massimini, 1988).

Salanova, Bakker and Llorens (2006) focused on the contribution of work-related resources to the experience of flow. In a two-wave longitudinal study, they found that personal (i.e. self-efficacy) and organizational (i.e. social support, innovation orientation, rules orientation, goals orientation) resources contributed to the experience of flow. In turn, flow contributed to participants' personal and organizational resources. The authors interpreted this pattern of findings as evidence for an upward spiral in which flow is both a predictor and an outcome of organizational resources.

In their three-wave longitudinal study, Mäkikangas *et al.*, (2010) focused on job resources as a contributor to work-related flow as measured using the WOLF. They found an overall association between the level of, and changes in, job resources (i.e. autonomy, social support, professional development, supervisory coaching, and performance feedback) and flow. They also noted that there appeared to be different groups within their sample, indicating that the relationship between job resources and flow varies across individuals.

Consequences of Work-Related Flow

Flow is, by definition, an optimal state and it will come as no surprise that flow is linked to the experience of positive moods and emotions, such as excitement, joy, ecstasy, happiness, and pride (Bloch, 2002; Eisenberger *et al.*, 2005; Fullagar & Kelloway, 2009), and subjective well-being (Clarke & Haworth, 1994; Delle Fave & Massimini, 2003; Seongyeul, 1988). There is also some longitudinal evidence that flow predicts subsequent positive mood and not vice versa (Fullagar & Kelloway, 2009).

Although these associations are important in and of themselves in terms of individual mental health (Fredrickson & Losada, 2005), researchers have also suggested that positive mood is an important link or mediator between flow and outcomes such as performance or creativity. Indeed, Eisenberger et al. (2005) have shown that the relationship between flow and employee performance is *partially* mediated by positive mood and this is consistent with a large body of empirical literature showing that positive moods have a favorable impact on performance (Bolte *et al.*, 2003; Fredrickson & Branigan, 2005; Isen *et al.*, 1987), particularly performance on tasks that require spontaneity and creativity (Eisenberger & Rhoades, 2001; George & Brief, 1992).

This view is consistent with Fredrickson's (1998, 2001, 2010) broaden and build theory of positive emotions. She pointed to the fact that negative emotions tend to narrow the focus of individuals (e.g. individuals experiencing fear often focus solely on the cause of their fear), whereas experiencing positive emotions both broadens and builds our focus. That is, individuals who are experiencing positive emotions are more open to new experiences, more aware of their surroundings, and more attuned to a wide variety of opportunities – this is the "broaden" function of positive emotions. Individuals who are experiencing positive emotions are also more likely to build resources by learning new skills, making new friendships or contacts, and acquiring new experiences.

Webster, Klebe Trevino, and Ryan (1993) provide an interesting set of findings that demonstrate the connection between flow and the broaden and build hypotheses. These authors found that experiencing flow in human–computer interactions led to a variety of positive outcomes, including "more positive attitudes, more system use, and more positive work outcomes such as perceived communication effectiveness" (p. 420). The authors suggest that systems that are designed to enhance flow will also enhance user playfulness and use of computer systems.

Conclusion

Throughout this chapter, we have pointed to the growing body of research that has indicated that flow is a state-like construct. The finding that flow is manageable, in that it is affected by situational and task-related contingencies, has considerable implications for the workplace. Organizations can construct work to consist of tasks that optimize the "flow conditions" and facilitate the state. There is an increasing amount of evidence that suggests that providing individuals with the opportunity to experience flow at work has outcomes that are important to both individuals (e.g. positive mood, well-being) and organizations (e.g. innovation, performance). Although there is more work to do in defining and measuring the construct of flow, as well as establishing the links between flow and hypothesized outcomes, the existing data suggest that flow is a construct that has the potential to contribute to the field of positive organizational behavior.

References

Adlai-Gail, W.S. (1994). *Exploring the autotelic personality.* Unpublished doctoral dissertation, University of Chicago: Chicago, IL.

Allen, B.P. & Potkay, C.R. (1981). On the arbitrary distinction between states and traits. *Journal of Personality and Social Psychology, 41*, 916–928.

Bakker, A.B. (2008). The work-related flow inventory: Construction and initial validation of the WOLF. *Journal of Vocational Behavior, 72*, 400–414.

Beilock, S.L., Bertenthal, B.I., McCoy, A.M., & Carr, T.H. (2004). Haste does not always make waste: Expertise, direction of attention and speed versus accuracy in performing sensorimotor skills. *Journal of Experimental Psychology: Applied, 8*, 6–16.

Bloch, C. (2002). Moods and the quality of life. *Journal of Happiness Studies, 3*, 101–128.

Bolte, A., Goschkey, T., & Kuhl, J. (2003). Emotion and intuition: Effects of positive and negative mood on implicit judgments of semantic coherence. *Psychological Science, 14*, 416–421.

Bruya, B. (2010). Introduction: Toward a theory of attention that includes effortless attention and action. In B. Bruya (Ed.), *Effortless attention: A new perspective in the cognitive science of attention and action* (pp. 1–28). Cambridge, MA: MIT Press.

Bygren, L.O., Konlaan, B.B., & Johansson, S.E. (1996). Attendance at cultural events, reading books or periodicals, and making music or singing in a choir as determinants of survival: Swedish fourteen-year cohort follow-up. *British Medical Journal, 313*, 1577–1580.

Cameron, K.S., Dutton, J.E., & Quinn, R.E. (Eds) (2003). *Positive organizational scholarship: Foundations of a new discipline.* San Francisco, CA: Berrett-Koehler Publishers, Inc.

Carli, M., Delle Fave, A., & Massimini, F. (1988). The quality of experience in the flow channels: Comparison of Italian and U.S. students. In M. Csikszentmihalyi & I.S. Csikszentmihalyi (Eds), *Optimal experience: Psychological studies of flow in consciousness* (pp. 266–306). New York: Cambridge University Press.

Chaplin, W.T., John, O.P., & Goldberg, L.R. (1988). Conceptions of states and traits. *Journal of Personality and Social Psychology, 54*, 541–557.

Clarke, S.G. & Haworth, J.T. (1994). "Flow" experience in the daily lives of sixth-form college students. *British Journal of Psychology, 85*, 511–523.

Csikszentmihalyi, M. (1975). *Beyond freedom and anxiety.* San Francisco, CA: Jossey-Bass.

Csikszentmihalyi, M. (1990). *Flow: The psychology of optimal experience.* New York: Harper & Row.

Csikszentmihalyi, M. (1992). A response to Kimiecik & Stein and Jackson papers. *Journal of Applied Sport Psychology, 4*, 181–183.

Csikszentmihalyi, M. (1993). *The evolving self.* New York: Harper & Row.

Csikszentmihalyi, M. (1997). *Finding flow: The psychology of engagement with everyday life.* New York: Basic Books.

Csikszentmihalyi, M. (2000). The contribution of flow to positive psychology: Scientific essays in honor of Martin E.P. Seligman. In J.E. Gillham, (Ed.), *The science of optimism and hope* (pp. 387–395). Philadelphia: Templeton Foundation Press.

Csikszentmihalyi, M. & Larson, R. (1984). *Being adolescent: Conflict and growth in the teenage years.* New York, NY: Basic Books.

Csikszentmihalyi, M. & LeFevre, J. (1989). Optimal experience in work and leisure. *Journal of Personality and Social Psychology, 56*, 815–822.

Csikszentmihalyi, M. & Nakamura, J. (2010). Effortless attention in everyday life: A systematic phenomenology. In B. Bruya (Ed.), *Effortless attention: A new perspective*

in the cognitive science of attention and action, (pp. 179–190). Cambridge, MA: MIT Press.
Csikszentmihalyi, M. & Rathunde, K. (1993). The measurement of flow in everyday life: Toward a theory of emergent motivation. In J. E. Jacobs (Ed.), *Developmental perspectives on motivation: Volume 40 of the Nebraska symposium on motivation* (pp. 57–97). Lincoln, Nebraska: University of Nebraska Press.
Csikszentmihalyi, M., Rathunde, K. & Whalen, S. (1993). *Talented teenagers: A longitudinal study of their development.* New York: Cambridge University Press.
Csikszentmihalyi, M., Abuhamdeh, S., & Nakamura, J. (2005). Flow. In A.J. Elliott & C.S. Dweck (Eds), *Handbook of competence and motivation* (pp. 598–608). New York: Guilford.
De Manzano, O., Theorell, T., Harmat, L., & Ullén, F. (2010). The psychophysiology of flow during piano playing. *Emotion, 10*, 301–311.
Deci, E. (1972). Intrinsic motivation, extrinsic reinforcement, and inequity. *Journal of Personality and Social Psychology, 22*, 113–120.
Delle Fave, A. & Massimini, F. (2003). Optimal experience in work and leisure among teachers and physicians: Individual and bio-cultural implications. *Leisure Studies, 22*, 323–342.
Demerouti, E. (2006). Job characteristics, flow, and performance: The moderating role of conscientiousness. *Journal of Occupational Health Psychology, 11*, 266–280.
Dietrich, A (2004). Neurocognitive mechanisms underlying the experience of flow. *Consciousness and Cognition, 13*, 746–761.
Dietrich, A. (2006). Transient hypofrontality as a mechanism for the psychological effects of exercise. *Psychiatry Research, 145*, 79–83.
Dietrich, A. & Stoll, O. (2010). Effortless attention, hyperfrontality, and perfectionism. In B. Bruya (Ed.), *Effortless attention: A new perspective in the cognitive science of attention and action,* (pp. 159–178). Cambridge, MA: MIT Press.
DiFonzo, N., Hantula, D. A., & Bordia, P. (1998). Microworlds for experimental research: Having your (control and collections) cake, and realism too. *Behavior Research Methods, Instruments, and Computers, 30*, 278–286.
Eisenberger, R. & Rhoades, L. (2001). Incremental effects of reward on creativity. *Journal of Personality and Social Psychology, 81*, 728–741.
Eisenberger, R., Jones, J.R., Stinglhamber, F., Shanock, L., & Randall, A.T. (2005). Flow experiences at work: For high need achievers alone? *Journal of Organizational Behavior, 26*, 755–775.
Engeser, S. & Rheinberg, F. (2008). Flow performance and moderators of challenge-skill balance. *Motivation & Emotion, 32*, 158–172.
Ericsson, K.A., Charness, N., Feltovich, P.J., & Hoffman, R.R. (Eds) (2006). *The Cambridge handbook of expertise and expert performance.* New York: Cambridge University Press.
Fave, A.D. & Massimini, F. (1988). Modernization and the changing contexts of flow in work and leisure. In M. Csikszentmihalyi & I.S. Csikszentmihalyi (Eds), *Optimal experience: Psychological studies of flow in consciousness* (pp. 193–213). New York: Cambridge University Press.
Fredrickson, B.L. (1998). What good are positive emotions? *Review of General Psychology, 2,* 300–319.
Fredrickson, B.L. (2001). The role of positive emotions in positive psychology: The broaden and build theory. *American Psychologist, 56*, 218–226.
Fredrickson, B.L. (2010). *Positivity: Top notch research reveals the 3 to 1 ratio that will change your life.* New York: Crown Publishing.

Fredrickson, B.L. & Branigan, C.A. (2005). Positive emotions broaden the scope of attention and thought–action repertoires. *Cognition and Emotion, 19*, 313–332.

Fredrickson, B.L. & Losada, M.F. (2005). Positive affect and the complex dynamics of human flourishing. *American Psychologist, 60*, 678–686.

Fullagar, C. & Kelloway. E.K. (2009). "Flow" at work: An experience sampling approach. *Journal of Occupational and Organizational Psychology, 81*, 595–615.

Fullagar, C., Knight, P.K., & Sovern, H. (2009). *Flow and performance anxiety.* Paper presented at the 24th Annual Conference of the Society for Industrial and Organizational Psychology. New Orleans, LA, April 2–4, 2009.

George, J.M. & Brief, A.P. (1992). Feeling good-doing good: A conceptual analysis of the mood at work-organizational spontaneity relationship. *Psychological Bulletin, 112*, 310–329.

Hackman. J.R. & Oldham, G.R. (1975). Development of the job diagnostic survey. *Journal of Applied Psychology, 60*, 159–170.

Hackman, J.R. & Oldham, G.R. (1980). *Work redesign.* Reading, MA: Addison-Wesley Publishing Company.

Haworth, J. & Evans, S. (1995). Challenge, skill and positive states in the daily life of a sample of YTS students. *Journal of Occupational and Organizational Psychology, 68*, 109–121.

Haworth, J.T. & Hill, S. (1992). Work, leisure and psychological well-being in a sample of young adults. *Journal of Community and Applied Psychology, 2*, 147–160.

Hektner, J. & Asakawa, K. (2000). Learning to like challenges. In M. Csikszentmihalyi & B. Schneider (Eds), *Becoming adult: How teenagers prepare for the world of work* (pp. 95–112). New York: Basic Books.

Hektner, J.M., Schmidt, J.A., & Csikszentmyhali, M. (2007). *Experience sampling method: Measuring the quality of everyday life.* Thousand Oaks, CA: SAGE Publications.

Isen, A.M., Daubman, K.A., & Nowicki, G.P. (1987). Positive affect facilitates creative problem solving. *Journal of Personality and Social Psychology, 52*, 1122–1131.

Jackson, D. (1984). *Personality research form manual.* Port Huron, MI: Research Psychologists Press.

Jackson, S.A. (1992). Athletes in flow: A qualitative investigation of flow states in elite figure skaters. *Journal of Applied Sport Psychology, 4*, 161–180.

Jackson, S.A. (1996). Toward a conceptual understanding of the flow experience in elite athletes. *Research Quarterly for Exercise and Sport, 67*, 76–90.

Jackson, S.A. & Eklund, R.C. (2002). Assessing flow in physical activity: The Flow State Scale-2 and Dispositional Flow Scale-2. *Journal of Sport and Exercise Psychology, 24*, 133–150.

Jackson, S.A. & Eklund, R.C. (2004). *The Flow Scales manual.* Morgantown, WV: Fitness Information Technology, Inc.

Jackson, S.A. & Marsh, H.W. (1996). Development and validation of a scale to measure optimal experience: The Flow State Scale. *Journal of Sport & Exercise Psychology, 18*, 17–35.

Jackson, S.A., Kimiecik, J.C., Ford, S., & Marsh, H.W. (1998). Psychological correlates of flow in sport. *Journal of Sport and Exercise Psychology, 20*, 358–378.

Keller, J. & Bless, H. (2008). Flow and regulatory compatibility: An experimental approach to the flow model of intrinsic motivation. *Personality and Social Psychology Bulletin, 34*, 196–209.

Keller, J. & Blomann, F. (2008). Locus of control and the flow experience: An experimental analysis. *European Journal of Personality, 22*, 589–607.

Kelley, E.L. (1927). *Interpretation of educational measurements.* Yonkers, NY: World Book Company.

Kelloway, E.K. & Day, A.L. (2005). Building healthy organizations: What we know so far. *Canadian Journal of Behavioural Science, 37,* 223–236.

Larson, R. & Csikszentmihalyi, M. (1983). The experience sampling method. *New Directions for Methodology of Social and Behavioral Science, 15,* 41–56.

Larson, R. & Richards, M.H. (1994). *Divergent realities: The emotional lives of mothers, fathers, and adolescents.* New York: Basic Books.

Latham, G.P. & Locke, E.A. (1991). Self-regulation through goal-setting. *Organizational Behavior and Human Decision Processes, 50,* 212–247.

Locke, E.A., Shaw, K.M., Saari, L.M., & Latham, G.P. (1981). Goal setting and task performance: 1969–1980. *Psychological Bulletin, 90,* 125–152.

Luthans, F. (2001). The case for positive organizational behavior (POB). *Current Issues in Management, 1,* 10–21.

Luthans, F. (2002). Positive organizational behavior: Developing and managing psychological strengths. *Academy of Management Executive, 16(1),* 57–72.

Luthans, F., Youssef, C.M., & Avolio, B.J. (2007). *Psychological capital: Developing the human competitive edge.* New York, NY: Oxford University Press.

Mäkikangas, A., Bakker, A.B., Aunola, K., & Demerouti, E. (2010). Job resources and flow at work: Modelling the relationship via latent growth curve and mixture model methodology. *Journal of Occupational and Organizational Psychology, 83,* 795–814.

Marsh, H.W. & Jackson, S.A. (1999). Flow experiences in sport: Construct validation of multidimensional, hierarchical state and trait responses. *Structural Equation Modelling, 6,* 343–371.

Massimini, F. & Carli, M. (1988). The systematic assessment of flow in daily life. In M. Csikszentmihalyi & I. Csikszentmihalyi (Eds), *Optimal experience: Psychological studies of flow in consciousness* (pp. 266–287). New York: Cambridge University Press.

Massimini, F. & Delle Fave, A. (2000). Individual development in a bio-cultural perspective. *American Psychologist, 55,* 24–33.

Massimini, F., Csikszentmihalyi, M., & Carli, M. (1987). The monitoring of optimal experience: A tool for psychiatric rehabilitation. *Journal of Nervous and Mental Disease, 175,* 545–549.

Mills, M.J. & Fullagar, C.J. (2008). Motivation and flow: Toward an understanding of the dynamics of the relation in architecture students. *Journal of Psychology, 142,* 533–553.

Moller, A.C., Meier, B.P., & Wall, R.D. (2010). Developing an experimental indication of flow: Effortless action in the lab. In B. Bruya (Ed.), *Effortless attention: A new perspective in the cognitive science of attention and action* (pp. 191–204). Cambridge, MA: MIT Press.

Nakamura, J. & Csikszentmihalyi, M. (2002). The concept of flow. In C.R. Snyder & J.S. Lopez (Eds), *Handbook of positive psychology* (pp. 89–105). New York: Oxford University Press.

Nakamura, J. & Csikszentmihalyi, M. (2009). Flow theory and research. In C.R. Snyder & S.J. Lopez (Eds), The Oxford handbook of positive psychology, 2nd edition (pp. 195–206). New York, NY: Oxford University Press.

Pinder, C.C. (2008). *Work motivation in organizational behavior* (2nd edition). New York: Taylor & Francis.

Privette, G. & Bundrick C.M. (1991). Peak experience, peak performance, and flow: Correspondents of personal descriptions and theoretical constructs. *Journal of Social Behavior and Personality, 6,* 169–188.

Raz, A. & Buhle, J. (2006). Typologies of attentional networks. *National Review of Neuroscience, 7*, 367–379.
Reis, H.T. & Gable, S.L. (2000). Event sampling and other methods for assessing everyday experience. In H.T. Reis & C. Judd (Eds), *Handbook of research methods in social psychology* (pp. 190–222). New York: Cambridge University Press.
Salanova, M., Bakker, A.B., & Llorens, S. (2006). Flow at work: Evidence for an upward spiral of personal and organizational resources. *Journal of Happiness Studies, 7*, 1–22.
Schaufeli, W.B. & Salanova, M. (2007). Work engagement: An emerging psychological concept and its implications in organizations. In S.W. Gilliland, D.D. Steiner, & D.P. Skarlicki (Eds), *Research in social issues management* (pp. 135–177). Greenwich, CT: Information Age Publishers.
Schaufeli, W.B., Salanova, M., Gonzales-Romá, V., & Bakker, A.B. (2002). The measurement of engagement and burnout: A confirmative analytic approach. *Journal of Happiness Studies, 3*, 71–92.
Scollon, C.N., Kim-Prieto, C., & Diener, E. (2003). Experience sampling: Promises and pitfalls, strengths and weaknesses. *Journal of Happiness Studies, 4*, 5–34.
Seongyeul, H. (1988). The relationship between life satisfaction and flow in elderly Korean immigrants. In M. Csikszentmihalyi & I.S. Csikszentmihalyi, *Optimal experience: Psychological studies of flow in consciousness* (pp. 138–149). New York: Cambridge University Press.
Theorell, T., Ahlberg-Hulten, G., Jodko, M., Sigala, F., & de la Torre, B. (1993). Influence of job strain and emotion on blood pressure in female hospital personnel during workhours. *Scandinavian Journal of Work and Environmental Health, 19*, 313–318.
Thomas, K.M. & Mathieu, J.E. (1994). Role of attributions in dynamic self-regulation and goal processes. *Journal of Applied Psychology, 79*, 812–818.
Turner, N., Barling, J., & Zacharatos, A. (2002). Positive psychology at work. In C.R. Snyder & S.J. Lopex (Eds), *Handbook of positive psychology* (pp. 715–728). New York: Oxford University Press.
Ullén, F., de Manzano, O., Theorell, T., & Harmat, L. (2010). The physiology of effortless attention: Correlates of state flow and flow proneness. In B. Bruya (Ed.), *Effortless attention: A new perspective in the cognitive science of attention and action* (pp. 205–217). Cambridge, MA: MIT Press.
Voelkl, J.E. (1990). The challenge skill ratio of daily experiences among older adults residing in institutional environments. *Therapeutic Recreation Journal, 24*, 7–17.
Webster, J., Klebe Trevino, L., & Ryan, L. (1993). The dimensionality and correlates of flow in human-computer interactions. *Computers in Human Behavior, 9*, 411–426.
White, R. (1959). Motivation reconsidered: The concept of competence. *Psychological Review, 66*, 297–333.
Yule, S., Flin, R., Patterson-Brown, S., Maran, N., & Rowley, D. (2006). Development of a rating system for surgeons' non-technical skills. *Medical Education, 40*, 1098–1104.

5 Job Characteristics and Problem-Solving

Kevin Daniels

Many theories of job design treat job characteristics as stable, independent of the person performing the job, and as an "objective" determinant of workplace health, well-being, and performance. Drawing on the job crafting and coping literatures, in this chapter, I portray job characteristics as dynamic phenomena which are enacted by people for specific purposes. I show how this approach to job design can be used to help understand how some job characteristics can protect and enhance daily levels of well-being, learning, creativity, innovation, and cognitive performance through facilitating the generation and implementation of solutions to workplace problem-solving demands.

Next, I will review how traditional approaches to job design have furthered our understanding of what makes for good and productive work. I will also review some of the unstated assumptions of this approach that are inherent to the methodologies used in this stream of literature. Following from this, I will examine some of the major principles from the emerging literature on job crafting. Together with some of the literature on coping, I will show how the literature on job design can be extended to examine how workers shape their work over the short-term for specific purposes. These purposes include solving problems at work. I will then outline how experience-sampling and diary methods can add to our understanding of job design and its consequences because they allow researchers to look at job design in a new way. Before concluding the chapter with implications for job design theories, I will review research that indicates the importance of examining how workers shape their work over the short-term for specific purposes. This research indicates implications for well-being and different facets of work performance, such as learning, creativity, innovation, and cognitive performance.

Traditional Job Design Research: Some Triumphs and Assumptions

I do not intend to review the whole of job design research in this section, rather to give some of the highlights of these approaches. More comprehensive and recent reviews have been provided elsewhere (e.g. Grant & Parker, 2009; Parker & Ohly, 2008). While there are many approaches to job design that have appeared over the years, many share features with two of the most influential models, which are

Hackman and Oldham's job characteristics theory (JCT, 1980) and Karasek and Theorell's job demands, control, support model (DCSM, 1990).

These models provide complementary explanations as to why good job design is related to better health, well-being, and performance. In the JCT, well-designed jobs are characterized by, for example, high levels of job control, variety, and skill use. Such jobs are thought to be intrinsically motivating and satisfying. In the DCSM, well-designed jobs, specifically those with high levels of control over work and good relationships with co-workers, give workers the latitude, information, and support they need to solve problems caused by high work demands and otherwise cope with these demands: that is, rather than being intrinsically motivating, good job design serves workers' instrumental purposes of adapting to high work demands. The ability to cope with work demands prevents the deterioration of well-being. Solving problems also leads to workers learning how to deal with demands more efficiently or more quickly, which in turn leads to enhanced performance and well-being.

This traditional approach to job design has been successful in generating a large body of empirical evidence and in elaborating our understanding of good and productive work (see e.g. Grant & Parker, 2009; Parker & Ohly, 2008). Even a cursory examination of the major work and organizational or occupational health psychology journals indicates how influential this approach continues to be. Of relevance to this book and this chapter are two areas in which the traditional approach has been particularly useful: first, in relation to furthering our understanding of healthy and safe work; and second, in furthering our understanding of creativity and innovation.

There are many reviews and studies that underscore the importance of job design for health, well-being, and safety. In relation to health and well-being, a large body of evidence indicates that aspects of psychological and physical health can be predicted from assessments of well-designed jobs (see e.g. Marmot *et al.*, 2010). The literature on job design and safety is less well developed, but there is evidence that safer work might be associated with good job design (Barling *et al.*, 2003; Elfering *et al.*, 2006; Parker *et al.*, 2001) or wider human resource management practices that include aspects of good job design (Tregaskis *et al.*, in press; Zacharatos *et al.*, 2005).

The relationship between job design and creativity, or the generation of new and useful ideas (e.g. George, 2007), seems well established. For example, research has demonstrated that creativity is associated with different kinds of work demands, job control, social support, and team working (e.g. Amabile, 1988; Binneweis *et al.*, 2008; Oldham & Cummings, 1996; Taggar, 2002; Scott & Bruce, 1994). Creativity is the precursor to innovation, which is the implementation of new and useful ideas (George, 2007). Support from co-workers might be particularly useful for the implementation of ideas because support has informational value that may help in the collective acceptance, selection, modification, and implementation of ideas in the social environments that characterize most work organizations. Where teams have good social processes, teams may be able to select, modify, and implement the ideas suggested by team members (e.g. De Dreu, 2006; De Dreu & West, 2001; West, 2002).

The demonstrable associations between job design and various outcomes are based mainly on the assumption that job characteristics, once set through job design, are both stable and objective. That is, traditional approaches to job design assume job characteristics do not change much unless there are intentional change efforts (stability) and two people doing exactly the same job will be subject to the same job characteristics. These assumptions are being questioned, both from the perspective of job design research (Grant & Parker, 2009) and from the perspective of research concerned more specifically with job design and worker health and well-being (Daniels, 2006, 2011).

For Grant and Parker (2009), relaxing these assumptions enables job design research to capture a wider array of phenomena and allows researchers to develop theories and research that capture more readily the realities of contemporary working environments. For Daniels, relaxing these assumptions provides researchers with additional conceptual bases for using event-sampling and diary designs (Daniels, 2006) and enables policy makers to develop policy and guidance that works with workers' subjective experiences of the work environment and natural inclinations to self-regulate their well-being, rather than against it through managerially imposed job redesign (Daniels, 2011).

In relation to objectivity, the dominant approach to assessing job characteristics is based on self-report questionnaires in which participants rate their jobs as they usually are (see Daniels, 2006). Strictly, such data provide subjective rather than objective data. Self-reports of how jobs usually are can be subject to numerous biases, including those linked to trait affect (Spector, 1992) and social interaction (Salancik & Pfeffer, 1978). In response, there have been calls for researchers to use other methods to assess job characteristics objectively and/or to triangulate findings from multiple methods.

Other methods either reflect perceptions (e.g. line manager reports), cannot detect local but important variations in working practices (e.g. using nationally representative databases to impute job characteristics for a focal individual), or reflect institutionalized portrayals of how managers would like jobs to appear rather than how they really are (e.g. job descriptions) (Daniels, 2006). There are also examples where triangulation has failed, indicating it is not a failsafe strategy (Daniels, 2006). Therefore, it might be better to develop theory further on the basis of the phenomena which we can measure, rather than assuming job characteristics such as job control are unitary constructs independent of the person doing a job and that can be measured, albeit imperfectly, from multiple perspectives. Rather, convergence across measures may indicate how different phenomena, such as individual perceptions of job characteristics and institutional factors, are related (Daniels, 2006).

In relation to stability, Grant and Parker (2009) point out that work is no longer stable because work is now more complex and interdependent than when traditional job design theories were first developed. Indeed, there is evidence that job characteristics are not stable. For example, there is evidence that the experience of job characteristics changes from week to week, from day to day, and within the same day (Daniels, 2011). Because organizational life is dynamic, it has been argued that it might be productive to include short-term changes in the experience of work in our thinking on job design and worker well-being (e.g. Beal & Weiss, this volume).

New Developments in Job Design and Implications for Theory and Methods

The emerging literature on job crafting has moved researchers away from viewing job characteristics as stable entities. Instead, job crafting emphasizes the workers' own agency in shaping their work (Wrzesniewski & Dutton, 2001) and also emphasizes the dynamic nature of job design, as job characteristics become open to change (Clegg & Spencer, 2007). Job crafting has been defined as changes that alter the nature of job tasks, work relationships, or perceptions of work in ways that are beneficial to individuals (Berg, Wrzesniewski, & Dutton, 2010; Wrzesniewski & Dutton, 2001; Wrzesniewski et al., 2010). Job crafting can be seen as a proactive and goal-driven behavior that is done for a purpose (Bindl & Parker, 2010; Parker et al., 2010). Job crafting can alter the meaning of work or how people view themselves at work (Wrzesniewski & Dutton, 2001). Those that engage in job crafting are called job crafters (Wrzesniewski & Dutton, 2001).

Because job crafters exercise control over the nature of their jobs and often alter their jobs to make work a more positive experience, it would be expected that job crafting would be associated with positive outcomes, such as greater work motivation and better well-being at work (Berg et al., 2010; Wrzesniewski et al., 2010). However, the evidence on job crafting is less clear cut. For example, Wrzesniewski et al. (2010) caution that job crafting might be harmful if it is done to take on too much at work and that it might lead to conflict with others unless others are informed or involved. In support of this, Leana, Appelbaum, and Sevchuk (2009) reported that individual job crafting was associated with lower job satisfaction, but collective job crafting was associated with better job satisfaction. As well as conflict with others through unilateral changes to job design, job crafting might lead to intra-personal conflict, as job crafting to attend to some motivations might lead to frustration that other aspects of the job role are not being fulfilled (Berg et al., 2010). Similarly, job crafting might be easier in some circumstances than others, for example, because workers have higher autonomy or more ambiguity in their job roles or because workers feel less restricted by the expectations of others (Berg et al., 2010).

However, the literature on job crafting tends to portray crafting as an activity that leads to permanent or semi-permanent changes in job design so that workers can achieve quite abstract goals (e.g. to make work more interesting, Berg et al., 2010). However, it is not necessary to view job crafting, or activities related to the shaping of the content of work, as involving long-run changes or as one-off or infrequent activities. It may be that job crafting can be a more ongoing, day-to-day activity. In this respect, Daniels (2006) referred to enacted job characteristics as those aspects of work that are emergent, dynamic, and shaped by the activities of people at work. It may also be the case that job crafting is not always done to achieve abstract, higher-order goals, but the content of work might be shaped for more short-term, concrete, and instrumental purposes, such as to solve specific problems or regulate specific emotions (Daniels et al., 2011). The active and motivated aspects of job crafting and the potential for job crafting to be short-term and instrumental are points of connection with the coping literature.

The experience of stressors motivates activity to regulate the impact of stressors: this activity is more commonly known as coping (Lazarus, 1999). Coping is not a unitary concept and various aspects can be identified. Of relevance here is the distinction between coping function, coping behavior, and coping resources (Latack & Havlovic, 1992; Lazarus, 1999; Skinner et al., 2003).

Coping function is the target of coping. Common typologies of coping function in the literature refer to problem-focused coping, avoidance coping, regulation of affective experience, and regulation of perceptions (Skinner et al., 2003). How coping function comes to be is through coping behavior, or those actions that enable coping function to have its desired effect. For example, a worker may reschedule work activities to spend time to reach a solution to a problem. In this case, the coping behavior is the act of rescheduling activities, which fulfills the purpose or function of problem-solving. Coping resources refer to those things that enable coping behavior and, in the context of job design, represent a sub-set of job resources that are specifically concerned with mitigating the impact of job stressors (Demerouti et al., 2001). For the worker who rescheduled work activities to spend time on solving a problem, the coping resource refers to the control or discretion over work schedules that allow the worker to reschedule activities. As well as job control, another commonly researched coping resource tied to increasing interest in relational aspects of job design (e.g. Humphrey et al., 2007) is support from work colleagues (Daniels et al., 2004).

It is important to differentiate coping behavior from coping function, since it is possible for the same behavior to fulfill more than one function, perhaps simultaneously (Skinner et al., 2003). For the worker rescheduling activities, rather than spending time on solving a problem, the worker may reschedule activities in order to spend time doing routine e-mails and so facilitating detachment from the stressor. Here detachment is the coping function. Therefore, by just assessing coping behavior, it is not possible to get a full picture of the coping process, since the target of coping is unknown. So, in the example here, asking whether a worker has rescheduled activities cannot give any information on whether rescheduling activities is beneficial because it facilitates detachment or whether it is beneficial because it facilitates problem-solving. Similarly, simply assessing coping function cannot indicate whether problem-solving is more effective if facilitated by rescheduling activities or if some other coping behavior is better or worse for problem-solving.

Like the job crafting literature, the coping literature indicates specific behaviors can be executed for specific purposes (Daniels & de Jonge, 2010). However, in the coping literature, the motivations for executing specific coping behaviors are more often concerned with the short-term regulation of the impact of work stressors rather than longer-term changes to work often considered in the existing job crafting literature, and coping functions are more specific and concrete than the more abstract motivations listed by some participants in much of the existing job crafting literature.

Juxtaposing the existing job crafting literature with the coping literature can lead us to differentiate job crafting along two dimensions. The first dimension relates to the time course over which job crafting takes place (Daniels *et al.*, 2011). This can be longer term as in much of the job crafting literature and lead to permanent or semi-permanent changes in work. Or job crafting can take place over a much shorter period and refer to temporary changes or the short-term enactment of specific job characteristics. For example, a worker may build into his or her job the ability to reschedule activities (longer term) or simply reschedule activities at a given point in time (short term). It is perhaps logical to assume that crafting more permanent changes to work may build up resources that allow short-term job crafting around specific activities. A second dimension refers to the purposes for which jobs are crafted (cf. Daniels *et al.*, 2011): is the purpose of job crafting concerned with more abstract goals, such as creating meaningful or interesting work, or is the purpose of job crafting more instrumental and concrete, such as making a change to work in order to solve a specific problem?

This differentiation of purpose may also point to different theoretical processes through which job crafting promotes well-being and work performance. Crafting for more abstract goals may reflect a purely motivational process as higher-order needs are met, in a way described in the JCT (Hackman & Oldham, 1980). Crafting for more specific purposes, such as problem-solving, may protect workers from the deleterious effects of work demands and promote learning, which might have an effect on work performance, as in the DCSM (Karasek & Theorell, 1990). Of course, because jobs might be crafted over the longer or shorter term, such motivational and instrumental explanations may have longer-term and shorter-term variants.

This differentiation of purpose also indicates that elements of jobs crafted for general purposes may not have a direct relationship with elements of jobs crafted for specific purposes. For example, individuals who craft their work to be able to reschedule activities so they can be flexible about their leisure activities (more general purpose) may not be willing, able, or knowledgeable of how to reschedule activities in order to help them solve work-related problems. That is, if jobs are crafted over the longer term to provide resources for short-term job crafting, there may need to be a match between the purpose for which a job is crafted over the longer term and the purpose for which a job is crafted over the shorter term (van den Tooren & de Jonge, 2010).

Of the specific purposes for which jobs can be crafted, problem-solving is important not just for well-being, but also for learning, creativity, and innovation (Griffin *et al.*, 2007; Parker *et al.*, 2006; Scott & Bruce, 1994). Problem-solving is also embedded in Karasek and Theorell's DCSM in the "active learning hypothesis," in which job control and social support facilitate solving problems caused by high job demands; in turn, problem-solving enhances learning and protects well-being. As argued above, the beneficial effects of job control and social support for problem-solving might be specific to job control and social support crafted over the short term and for the specific instrumental purposes of problem-solving. This view of linking the purpose or function of job crafting (problem-solving) to a specific job-crafting behavior (executing job control or eliciting social support), within the context of responding to problem-solving demands, has a number of implications for methods.

Implications for Methods

The most obvious implication for differentiating between the time course of different job-crafting strategies is that methods must be capable of detecting the dynamic processes of job crafting. For problem-solving facilitated by job control or social support, this entails using methods that are capable of detecting short-term changes because problem-solving, problem-solving demands, job control, and social support can fluctuate between working days and also within-working days, as can many of the presumed consequences of problem-solving, such as indicators of well-being and learning (e.g. Ilies *et al.*, 2010; Daniels *et al.*, 2009). As such, experience-sampling methods, daily diary studies, and event reconstruction interviews are suitable methods (see e.g. Daniels & Harris, 2005; Daniels *et al.*, 2009; Hertel & Stamov-Roßnagel, this volume; Waddington, this volume). Experience-sampling and daily diary methods in particular have the added advantages of greater accuracy compared with other methods reliant on recall and, for quantitative research, easily enable statistical controls for prior levels of dependent variables and stable factors (Bolger *et al.*, 2003).

For quantitative researchers, there remain other challenges. Most research on the DCSM and other models of job characteristics is reliant on methods that simply assess levels of job characteristics. For problem-solving, this then requires that the beneficial effects of problem-solving are inferred from a pattern of relationships between job demands, job control, and social support, rather than being examined directly. As follows from the argument that job crafting might reflect crafting for more abstract or more instrumental goals, simply assessing levels of job characteristics cannot give any information on how job characteristics might influence well-being or other outcomes. Such ambiguity also has practical implications because clear evidence for specific underpinning theoretical processes indicates ancillary interventions that might aid job redesign. For example, if there is direct evidence that control enables workers to solve problems, problem-solving skills training might be introduced alongside increases in job control.

An alternative strategy, therefore, is to link crafting of specific job characteristics to specific motivations. For problem-solving research, this means developing items that link the execution of job control or elicitation of support to problem-solving, and also necessarily involves linking the items to the incidence of problem-solving demands. In some recent studies, my colleagues and I have done this using personal digital assistants to administer questionnaires several times per day (Daniels *et al.*, 2008, 2009, 2011). Our questionnaire begins with a filter question on whether participants have experienced any problems in the previous hour and, if so, the frequency of problems. If participants have experienced problems, they are then asked a series of questions that taps the extent to which they have executed job control to solve problems (operationalized as "changing work practices to solve problems") or elicited social support to solve problems (operationalized as "discussing problems with others to solve problems"). Example items include "In the past hour, did you change the order in which you normally do work tasks to solve the issues?" as part of the "changing work practices to solve problems" scale and "In the past hour, did you discuss the issues to help you solve them?" as part of the "discussing problems with others to solve problems" scale. If participants report experiencing no problems, they are automatically given the lowest score on all problem-solving items, to reflect that they have not engaged in any problem-solving because there have been no problems to solve.

Such items link the specific purpose (problem-solving) to a specific job-crafting behavior (e.g. executing job control), and therefore unambiguously provide a test of whether the beneficial effects of certain job-crafting activities are due to problem-solving, rather than due to some other theoretical process (Daniels *et al.*, 2009). There is also evidence from confirmatory factor analyses reported in a number of studies that the items that make up the "changing work practices to solve problems" and "discussing problems with others to solve problems" scales tap separate constructs rather than a general problem-solving construct or general job control and social support constructs (Daniels *et al.*, 2008, 2009, 2011).

However, using such complex items does raise some issues. First, there is the interpretability of such complex items. Extensive piloting and interpretability checks with participants have helped to overcome this issue. For example, we provide contact numbers and presentations to participants, so participants can contact us if they have difficulties with data collection and we can check whether the constructs and items make sense to participants. Second, there is the issue of validation of the scales through correlations with similar constructs. In two studies, measures of stable levels of job control and social support that have not been linked to specific motivations, goals, or purposes did not correlate significantly with the hourly measures of "changing work practices to solve problems" and "discussing problems with others to solve problems" scales (Daniels *et al.*, 2009, 2011). However, this should not be surprising, since one set of measures has no specific time-frame or purpose and the other set of measures has a specific time-frame and purpose. A stronger test of the validation of the scales might come from correlating the hourly measures of "changing work practices to solve problems" and "discussing problems with others to solve problems" with measures that assess levels of "changing work practices to solve problems" and "discussing problems with others to solve problems" over the longer term.

Third, there is the issue of assigning the lowest possible score on the problem-solving scales to participants that have not experienced problems. The question is whether such data should be included or excluded from analyses because the experience of no problems might be qualitatively different from experience of problems but not engaging in problem-solving. In general terms, we tend to include incidences of no problems in the data analysis for three main reasons: first, we control for level of problems experienced in our analyses, and so we take into account incidences when people do not encounter problems (and so cannot engage in problem-solving), incidences when they do encounter problems but choose not to engage in problem-solving, and incidences when they encounter problems and engage in problem-solving; second, from a substantive point of view, an absence of problems in any given hour reflects ordinary work experiences as much as encountering problems, so including data from hours when there are no problems forms a legitimate comparison; and third, from a statistical point of view, restricting the range of problems by excluding zero incidences can reduce statistical power by restricting the size of correlations and reducing the number of observations that can be used in analyses.

Nevertheless, findings from research using quantitative measures and statistical analyses might be greatly enhanced if findings were triangulated using different methods. Qualitative event reconstruction interviews and qualitative diaries might be especially useful in this regard. This is because qualitative methods can be less restrictive in how questions are asked and can probe for specific motivations, goals, or purposes used to craft specific job characteristics. Such qualitative methods are also more likely to illustrate *how* jobs are crafted over the short term rather than *whether* specific features are crafted or not.

A Brief Overview of Some Recent Findings

The first study to couple the short-term crafting of job characteristics to problem-solving was a daily diary study of 29 hospital workers conducted over two weeks, where workers reported problem-solving in response to job demands at the end of each working day (Daniels & Harris, 2005). As well as assessing daily job demands and the use of job control and social support for problem-solving, participants provided data on a range of control variables completed before the start of the diary study (e.g. trait affect) and assessed at the start of each working day (e.g. affective well-being in the morning). We examined within-person variation in problem-solving by subtracting each participant's values for the variables from the participant's mean value over the period of the study (Kenny *et al.*, 2002). We found that within-person variation in using support to solve problems was associated with better affective well-being at the end of work on both the same day and the following day. Within-person variation in using job control to solve problems was associated with higher levels of goal attainment at the end of work on the following day. The study also found some between-person covariation between using job control to solve problems and goal attainment.

The differentiation of between-person variation and within-person variation was examined in more detail in another study (Daniels *et al.*, 2008). In this study, a sample of 32 nuclear design engineers provided data on hourly problem-solving four times per day during one working week. This was the first study to use the hourly measures of "changing work practices to solve problems" and "discussing problems with others to solve problems" that have also been used in subsequent studies. After controlling for a range of variables, including between-person differences in frequency of encountering problems, between-person variation in "changing work practices to solve problems," indexed by taking participants' average levels across the week, was related to less frequent experience of negative affect and lower levels of risk-taking in decision-making. However, within-person variation in "changing work practices to solve problems" was related to more frequent experience of negative affect and more frequent experience of cognitive lapses, such as distractability. Between-person variability in "discussing problems with others to solve problems" was associated with more frequent experience of positive affect, while within-person variability in "discussing problems with others to solve problems" was associated with more frequent risk-taking in decision-making.

It is unclear from these two studies (Daniels & Harris, 2005; Daniels *et al.*, 2008) whether within-person or between-person variation in problem-solving is more or less beneficial or harmful for well-being and performance. While these two studies do indicate the potential for meaningful between-person and within-person variation, Karasek and Theorell's (1990) DCSM implies it is the absolute level of problem-solving that leads to benefits. Therefore, in a direct test of Karasek and Theorell's active learning hypothesis, absolute levels of "changing work practices to solve problems" and "discussing problems with others to solve problems" were related to hourly learning and affective well-being (Daniels *et al.*, 2009). The study was conducted on two samples of workers ($N = 78$ and $N = 106$), in which workers provided data four times per day for one working week. Between-person and within-person variation was taken into account by controlling for each participant's average levels of problems, "changing work practices to solve problems," and "discussing problems with others to solve problems" (see Kenny *et al.*, 2002). After controlling for hourly levels of problems and a range of other variables, we found, as predicted by the active learning hypothesis, that hourly levels of both "changing work practices to solve problems" and "discussing problems with others to solve problems" were related to higher levels of hourly learning, and that hourly learning mediated the effect of both "changing work practices to solve problems" and "discussing problems with others to solve problems" on the experience of positive affect.

In extending this line of reasoning to creativity and innovation, a sample of 89 workers provided data on hourly problems, "changing work practices to solve problems," "discussing problems with others to solve problems," hourly generation of ideas, and hourly implementation of those ideas four times per day for one working week (Daniels *et al.*, 2011). The results indicated that relationships between problem-solving on the one hand and generating and implementing ideas on the other were moderated by personal initiative: people high in personal initiative can be characterized as self-starting, persistent in implementing goals, and having a long-term orientation (Frese & Fay, 2001). The analyses controlled for a range of variables, including the incidence of problems in any given hour and between-person variation in problems. Absolute levels of "changing work practices to solve problems" were associated with more frequent generation of ideas only for people with high personal initiative. Absolute levels of "discussing problems with others to solve problems" were associated with more frequent implementation of ideas only for people with high personal initiative.

These last two studies (Daniels et al., 2009, 2011) indicate that absolute levels of "changing work practices to solve problems" and "discussing problems with others to solve problems" might be more important than a person's average levels or deviations from a person's average levels. This would accord with most of the literature on job crafting, job characteristics, and coping in the workplace. However, because this research has focused on between-person differences, it has confounded between-person variation with absolute variation. In general, it also appears that, when confronted by problem-solving requirements or demands in the workplace, temporarily crafting work so that job control or social support are used to solve problems is beneficial for well-being and aspects of performance such as learning, and for people high in personal initiative, creativity, and innovation.

However, because we have found the potential for detrimental effects of problem-solving (Daniels et al., 2008), the contingencies or contexts remain to be discovered that may modify the effects of "changing work practices to solve problems" or "discussing problems with others to solve problems." One such contingency may be methodological. "Changing work practices" and "discussing problems" are behaviors that are not simply tied to problem-solving, but can be enacted for other reasons, such as to avoid problems or regulate affective experience (Daniels & Harris, 2005). It may be that "changing work practices" and "discussing problems" can be enacted for multiple and simultaneous purposes (Skinner et al., 2003). Although some of our studies have controlled for "changing work practices" and "discussing problems" to regulate affect (Daniels et al., 2009, 2011), mapping out the effects of the different functions of "changing work practices" and "discussing problems" relative to each other may give a more precise picture.

Conclusion

The concept of job crafting has highlighted the active role of workers in job design as well as the dynamic nature of job characteristics. As workers craft jobs for a purpose, the job-crafting literature has also highlighted that the purposes for which jobs are crafted may be just as important as the features of work that are crafted. For more traditional, management-led, and top-down approaches to job redesign (Grant & Parker, 2009), the purposes for which jobs are redesigned (for example, to facilitate safety or innovation) may also deserve more focus than has been the case hitherto. Understanding the intended purposes underpinning job design, whether management or worker initiated, may enable more precise examination of how job design affects the experience of work. Drawing attention to the potential for jobs to be crafted over the short term as well as the long term also draws attention to the importance of day-to-day variation in how work is shaped and experienced.

Acknowledgement

Parts of this work have been supported by grants from the UK Engineering and Physical Sciences Research Council (grants nos D04863X and EP/F02942X/1).

References

Amabile, T.M. (1988). A model of creativity and innovation in organizations. *Research in Organizational Behavior, 10*, 123–167.

Barling, J., Kelloway, E.K., & Iverson, R.D. (2003). High-quality work, job satisfaction, and occupational injuries. *Journal of Applied Psychology, 88*, 276–283.

Berg, J.M., Grant, A.M., & Johnson, V. (2010). When callings are calling: Crafting work and leisure in pursuit of unanswered occupational callings. *Organization Science, 21*, 973–994.

Berg, J.M., Wrzesniewski, A., & Dutton. J.E. (2010). Perceiving and responding to challenges in job crafting: When proactivity requires adaptivity. *Journal of Organizational Behavior, 31*, 158–186.

Bindl, U.K. & Parker, S.K. (2010). Proactive work behavior: Forward-thinking and change-oriented action in organizations. In S. Zedeck (Ed.), *APA handbook of industrial and organizational psychology* (Vol. 2, pp. 567–598). Washington, DC: American Psychological Association.

Binnewies, C., Ohly, S., & Niessen, C. (2008). Age and creativity at work: The interplay between job resources, age and idea creativity. *Journal of Managerial Psychology, 23*, 438–457.

Bolger, N., Davis, A., & Rafaeli, E. (2003). Diary methods: Capturing life as it is lived. *Annual Review of Psychology, 54*, 579–616.

Clegg, C.W. & Spencer, C. (2007). A circular and dynamic model of the process of job design. *Journal of Occupational and Organizational Psychology, 80*, 321–339.

Daniels, K. (2006). Rethinking job characteristics in work stress research. *Human Relations, 59*, 267–290.

Daniels, K. (2011). Stress and well-being are still issues and something still needs to be done: Or why agency and interpretation are important for policy and practice. In G.P. Hodgkinson & J.K. Ford (Eds), *International review of industrial and organizational psychology* (Vol. 25, pp. 1–46). Chichester: Wiley.

Daniels, K. & Harris, C. (2005). A daily diary study of coping in the context of the job demands-control-support model. *Journal of Vocational Behavior, 66*, 219–237.

Daniels, K. & de Jonge, J. (2010). Matching-making and match-breaking: The nature of match within and around job design. *Journal of Occupational and Organizational Psychology, 83*, 1–16.

Daniels, K., Harris, C., & Briner, R.B. (2004). Linking work conditions to unpleasant affect: Cognition, categorisation and goals. *Journal of Occupational and Organizational Psychology, 77*, 343–364.

Daniels, K., Beesley, N.J., Cheyne, A.J.T., & Wilmarisiri, V.P. (2008). Coping processes linking the Demands-Control-Support model, affect, and risky decisions at work. *Human Relations, 61*, 845–874.

Daniels, K., Boocock, G., Glover, J., Hartley, R., & Holland, J. (2009). An experience sampling study of learning, affect, and the Demands Control Support model. *Journal of Applied Psychology, 94*, 1003–1017.

Daniels, K., Wimalasiri, V.P., Cheyne, A.J.T., & Story, V. (2011). Linking the Demands-Control-Support Model to innovation: The moderating role of personal initiative on the generation and implementation of ideas. *Journal of Occupational and Organizational Psychology, 84*, 581–598.

De Dreu, C. (2006). When too little or too much hurts: Evidence for a curvilinear relationship between task conflict and innovation in teams. *Journal of Management, 32*, 83–107.

De Dreu, C.K.W. & West, M.A. (2001). Minority dissent and team innovation: The importance of participation in decision making. *Journal of Applied Psychology, 86*, 1191–1201.

Demerouti, E., Bakker, A.B., Nachreiner, F., & Schaufeli, W.B. (2001). The job demands-resources model of burnout. *Journal of Applied Psychology, 86*, 499–512.

Elfering, A., Semmer, N.K., & Grebner, S. (2006). Work stress and patient safety: Observer-rated work stressors as predictors of characteristics of safety-related events reported by young nurses. *Ergonomics, 49*, 457–469.

Frese, M. & Fay, D. (2001). Personal initiative: An active performance concept for work in the 21st century. *Research in Organizational Behavior, 23*, 133–187.

George, J.M. (2007). Creativity in organizations. *Academy of Management Annals, 1*, 439–477.

Grant, A.M. & Parker, S.K. (2009). Redesigning work design theories: The rise of relational and proactive perspectives. *Academy of Management Annals, 3*, 317–375.

Griffin, M.A., Neal, A., & Parker, S.K. (2007). A new model of work role performance: Positive behavior in uncertain and interdependent contexts. *Academy of Management Journal, 50*, 327–347.

Hackman, J.R. & Oldham, G.R. (1980). *Work redesign.* Reading, MA: Addison Wesley.

Humphrey, S.E., Nahrgang, J.D., & Morgeson, F.P. (2007). Integrating motivational, social and contextual work design features: A meta-analytic summary and theoretical extension of the work design literature. *Journal of Applied Psychology, 92*, 1332–1356.

Ilies, R., Dimotakis, N., & De Pater, I.E. (2010). Psychological and physiological reactions to high workloads: Implications for well-being. *Personnel Psychology, 63*, 407–436.

Karasek, R.A. & Theorell, T. (1990). *Healthy work.* New York: Basic Books.

Kenny, D.A., Bolger, N., & Kashy, D.A. (2002). Traditional methods for estimating multilevel models. In D.S. Moskowitz & S.L. Hershberger (Eds), *Modeling intraindividual variability with repeated measures data: Methods and applications* (pp. 1–24). Mahwah, NJ: Erlbaum.

Latack, J.C. & Havlovic, S.J. (1992). Coping with job stress: a conceptual evaluation framework for coping measures. *Journal of Organizational Behavior, 13*, 479–508.

Lazarus, R.S. (1999). *Stress and emotion: A new synthesis.* New York: Springer.

Leana, C., Appelbaum, E., & Sevchuk, I. (2009). Work process and quality of care in early childhood education: The role of job crafting. *Academy of Management Journal, 52*, 1169–1192.

Marmot, M., Allen, J., Goldblatt, P., Boyce, T., McNeish, D., Grady, M., & Geddes, I. (2010). *Fair society, healthy lives: Strategic review of health inequalities in England post-2010.* London: The Marmot Review.

Oldham, G.R. & Cummings, A. (1996). Employee creativity: Personal and contextual factors at work. *Academy of Management Journal, 39*, 607–634.

Parker, S.K. & Ohly, S. (2008). Designing motivating jobs: An expanded framework for linking work characteristics and motivation. In R. Kanfer, G. Chen, & R. Pritchard (Eds), *Work motivation: Past, present, and future* (pp. 233–284). New York: Routledge.

Parker, S.K., Axtell, C., & Turner, N. (2001). Designing a safer work place: Importance of job autonomy, communication quality, and supportive supervisors. *Journal of Occupational Health Psychology, 6*, 211–228.

Parker, S.K., Williams, H.M., & Turner, N. (2006). Modeling the antecedents of proactive work behavior. *Journal of Applied Psychology, 91*, 636–652.

Parker, S.K., Bindl, U., & Strauss, K. (2010). Making things happen: A model of proactive motivation. *Journal of Management, 36*, 827–856.

Salancik, G.R. & Pfeffer, J. (1978). A social information processing approach to job attitudes and task design. *Administrative Science Quarterly, 23*, 224–253.

Scott, S.G. & Bruce, R.A. (1994). Determinants of innovative behavior: A path model of individual innovation in the workplace. *Academy of Management Journal, 37*, 580–607.

Skinner, E.A., Edge, K., Altman, J., & Sherwood, H. (2003). Searching for the structure of coping: A review and critique of category systems for classifying ways of coping. *Psychological Bulletin, 129*, 216–269.

Spector, P.E. (1992). A consideration of the validity and meaning of self-report measures of job conditions. In C.L. Cooper & I.T. Robertson (Eds), *International review and industrial and organizational psychology* (vol. 7, pp. 123–151). Chichester: Wiley.

Taggar, S. (2002). Individual creativity and group ability to utilize individual creative resources: A multilevel model. *Academy of Management Journal, 45*, 315–330.

Tooren, van den, M. & Jonge, de, J. (2010). The role of matching job resources in different demanding situations at work: A vignette study. *Journal of Occupational and Organizational Psychology, 83*, 39–54.

Tregaskis, O., Daniels, K., Glover, L., & Butler, P. (in press). High performance work practices and firm performance: A longitudinal case study. *British Journal of Management*.

West, M.A. (2002). Sparkling fountains or stagnant ponds: An integrative model of creativity and innovation implementation in work groups. *Applied Psychology: An International Review, 51*, 355–386.

Wrzesniewski, A. & Dutton, J. (2001). Crafting a job: Revisioning employees as active crafters of their work. *Academy of Management Review, 26*, 179–201.

Wrzesniewski A., Berg J.M., & Dutton J.E. (2010). Turn the job you have into the job you want. *Harvard Business Review, 88*, 114–117.

Zacharatos, A., Barling, J., & Iverson, R.D. (2005). High-performance work systems and occupational safety. *Journal of Applied Psychology, 90*, 77–93.

6 The Application of Diary Methods to Examine Workers' Daily Recovery During Off-Job Time

Carmen Binnewies and Sabine Sonnentag

Over recent years, studies using diary research methods have become more popular and have been applied to a broad range of research questions, such as how affective experiences influence workers' job satisfaction and behavior (Dalal *et al.*, 2009; Judge & Ilies, 2004) or how daily job stressors impact workers' well-being (Fuller *et al.*, 2003). In this chapter, we will first present an overview of diary research methods and how diary research methods can be used to examine a wide range of research questions. Second, after briefly describing how research on recovery from job stress is related to happiness, we will summarize diary research on recovery as an example of how diary research methods can be used to advance our theoretical and practical knowledge of how workers' happiness can be promoted on a daily basis.

The Nature and Core Features of Diary Studies

In a typical diary study, participants provide data over several days, sometimes also over several weeks (Fuller *et al.*, 2003; Teuchmann *et al.*, 1999). Often, diary studies realize several measurement occasions per day, allowing study participants to report events, affective states, and cognitions in close temporal proximity to the actual occurrence of these events, affective states, and cognitions. As a consequence, retrospection bias is reduced. In addition, diaries are often completed within participants' everyday environment – for instance, at their workplace or in their home – allowing for an ecologically valid assessment. The basic features of diary studies are very similar to typical features of experience-sampling studies. One distinction may be seen in the frequency of assessments: experience-sampling studies often have more frequent and more similar assessments during the course of a day (i.e. the same set of questions is asked at several measurement occasions during the day), whereas diary studies often ask different sets of questions at the various measurement occasions throughout a day (and repeat these sets of questions over several days). However, as there is a broad overlap between the experience-sampling methodology and the diary approach, the diary method may be seen as a specific type of experience-sampling method (Sonnentag *et al.*, in press). A data collection protocol that is similar to that of a diary study but uses longer intervals between the measurement occasions can be completed in a week-level study. Here, data collection takes place once or twice per week and is continued over a period of several weeks (e.g. Bakker & Bal, 2010; Sonnentag, Mojza *et al.*, 2008; Totterdell *et al.*, 2006).

Diary studies collect multiple measures per person. This allows for analysis of changes in variables of interest over time and in the examination of within-person variability. Moreover, internal validity of diary studies is stronger than in panel studies because in diary studies the temporal order of assumed cause and assumed effect can be tracked within very short time intervals, often supplemented by the statistical control of potential confounding variables. We will address different categories of research questions that can be addressed with diary studies in the next section.

Traditionally, diary data has been collected using paper-based instruments. More recently, researchers use electronic diaries. Such electronic diaries are either implemented on hand-held computers (Binnewies *et al.*, 2009) or smartphones (Courvoisier *et al.*, 2010; Song *et al.*, 2008), or are made available to study participants via the internet or the company's intranet (Ilies, Schwind, Wagner *et al.*, 2007; Ohly *et al.*, 2010). An important advantage of electronic diaries is that they automatically record the time when the diary was completed, thereby providing information about study participants' compliance (for a more detailed discussion, see Green *et al.*, 2006). Moreover, electronic diaries allow for flexible programming of survey questions so that tailored study interfaces can be presented to study participants. Although presenting specific questions contingent on participants' earlier answers are also feasible when using a paper-and-pencil method, they can be implemented in a more participant-friendly way within electronic diaries. Moreover, acoustic reminders can be incorporated into electronic diaries.

Which Kind of Research Questions Can Be Answered with Diary Designs?

Diary studies are conducted to examine different types of research question. Although all diary studies capture data over several days or weeks, researchers can analyze the data in very different ways to answer different research questions. According to Bolger *et al.* (2003), three different categories of research questions can be answered with diary studies: a) questions related to aggregated data over time, b) questions related to the time course of certain processes, and c) questions related to within-person processes. In the following, we will describe each category of research question, provide empirical examples, and discuss their relevance for research on happiness.

Concerning the first category of research questions examined with diary designs, studies focusing on aggregated data from diaries provide more generalized person-level data from multiple measurement occasions. Instead of relying on assessing workers' happiness at a single point of time, researchers can use a diary design to measure workers' happiness over several days and aggregate the daily happiness ratings to get an index of a person's average level of happiness. An advantage of such an approach is that retrospection bias and other situation-specific influences (e.g. the current state of mind) can be minimized (Reis & Gable, 2000). An example of a diary study using aggregated data is the study of Weiss, Nicholas, and Daus (1999). The authors assessed episodic affect by measuring affect randomly four times a day over a period of 16 working days. The authors then assessed overall job satisfaction only once in a final survey. In their analyses, they used the aggregated affect data from the 64 diary surveys to predict the overall job satisfaction rating in the final survey. The authors found that the average level of affect, specifically pleasantness, predicted overall satisfaction while controlling for a measure of dispositional happiness.

The second category of research questions investigated with diary studies involves studies focusing on the time course of processes. For example, researchers can examine the cyclical pattern of happiness over the course of a week. In addition, diary data can be used to investigate the trajectory of happiness over the week and identify factors that affect the slope of the trajectory, such as age or emotional stability. Beal and Ghandour (2011) recently examined stable and cyclical patterns in workers' work-related affect over a period of 21 days. The authors found that both positive and negative affect followed a consistent weekly pattern, such that positive affect was the lowest and negative affect the highest in the middle of the week. In addition, they identified individual differences in the amplitude of these weekly patterns.

Third, diary designs can be used to examine within-person variation and associated correlates (predictors and outcomes). Regarding the technical aspects, examining within-person variation requires centering of day-level (Level 1) data around the person mean (this approach corresponds to group-mean centering). The study of Ilies, Scott, and Judge (2006) is an example of a study on the correlates of daily positive affect and job satisfaction at work. Specifically, the authors revealed that workers showed a higher level of organizational citizenship behavior (OCB) at work on days when they experienced higher positive affect and when they were more satisfied with their job.

In addition, researchers can also examine the daily covariation of different constructs with diary designs. In this approach, day-level (Level 1) data are centered around the grand mean (i.e. grand-mean centering). Therefore, this approach takes both within- and between-variation into account. As day-level data capture both within- and between-person variance, it is important to control for between-person variables because otherwise the covariation of day-level constructs may be inflated by between-person differences, such as trait negative affect or different job conditions (see Kenny et al., 2002). For example, the study of Ohly and Fritz (2010) investigated the relationship between day-level job control and day-level time pressure on the one hand and day-level proactive behavior on the other hand. Controlling for the general level of job control and time pressure, they found that higher levels of daily job control and time pressure were associated with higher levels of daily proactive behavior.

One major advantage of diary designs is that both within- and between-variation in variables can be assessed. Consequently, researchers can both examine questions related to within-person (intra-individual) and between-person (inter-individual) relationships and even combine both perspectives. One type of research question which is often examined is the investigation of between-person variables moderating within-person relationships. Thus, the question here is whether the degree of association between two variables at the day level differs between persons (so-called "slopes as outcomes" models). For example, Ilies *et al.* (2006) proposed that workers' personality traits (between-person variables), specifically agreeableness and conscientiousness, moderate the within-person relationships of positive affect and job satisfaction with OCB. The authors found that the relationship between daily positive affect and OCB was stronger for disagreeable workers. Agreeable workers showed a high level of daily OCB independent of their daily positive affect, while the daily OCB of disagreeable workers was strongly affected by their level of positive affect on a given day.

Taken together, diary designs can be used to examine a wide range of research questions, disentangling both within-person and between-person processes and their interplay. From a theoretical perspective, diary designs are also useful for shedding more light on the temporal dynamics of processes – for example, how processes such as the experience of strain and recovery unfold over time (e.g. within a day, from one day to another, or over several weeks). Although longitudinal designs are also useful for detecting temporal dynamics, diary designs usually capture a larger amount of data per person and provide more accurate, real-time information, allowing researchers to study short-term processes over time rather than examining relationships between variables assessed at two or more (randomly) selected occasions (Bolger *et al.*, 2003; Reis & Gable, 2000). In the following sections, we will summarize how diary methods have been used in the field of research on recovery from work-related stress and how this work is related to happiness research.

Studying the Recovery of Workers Using Diary Studies

Most of the existing recovery research is conceptually closely linked to research on job stress. Based on numerous job-stress studies, there is rather consistent evidence that exposure to job stressors is associated with strain reactions in the organism exposed to the stressors. For example, hormones such as adrenaline or cortisol are released, heart rate and blood pressure increase, and more negative affective states are elicited (Ilies *et al.*, 2010; Zohar *et al.*, 2003). In other words, during and after exposure to stressors at work, it is difficult for many workers to stay happy and in a positive mood. Moreover, as affective states at work tend to spill over to the non-work domain (Ilies *et al.*, 2007; Song *et al.*, 2008), happiness and positive mood at home are likely to decrease after exposure to stressors at work.

In order to regain happiness and a positive affective state, recovery is needed. Recovery can be described as a process opposed to the strain process during which the organism returns to its baseline, pre-stressor state. Indicators of a successful recovery process are the deactivation of physiological systems, an increase in positive affective states, and a decrease in negative affective states (Geurts & Sonnentag, 2006).

In this section, we describe recovery processes as they are studied using diary designs from various perspectives. First, we concentrate on recovery during breaks at work. Second, we focus on recovery that takes place at home and that results in positive affective states. Third, we address predictors of recovery and ask how stressful experiences at work may interfere with a successful recovery process. Fourth, we examine how recovery experiences and outcomes may become beneficial at the work site. Thereby, we focus on work engagement and performance-related concepts as outcomes of recovery. Finally, we will take an individual-difference perspective and look at person characteristics that may influence recovery processes and outcomes.

Recovery During Work Breaks

Trougakos, Beal, Green, and Weiss (2008) examined recovery during the work breaks of cheerleading instructors. Participants completed records of their break activities and their emotional states during eight work sessions following the breaks. In addition, instructors' emotional expressions during these work sessions were video-recorded and, later, instructors' performance was rated by experts. Analyses showed that engaging in chore activities during breaks (e.g. practicing material, continuing to work with customers, preparing for upcoming work, running errands) predicted an increase in negative emotional states after the breaks. Engaging in respite activities (e.g. napping, relaxing, socializing) was related to positive emotional states after the breaks and inversely related to negative emotional states. Moreover, engaging in respite activities predicted high levels of emotional expressions during the after-break sessions. Overall, this study demonstrated that what happens during work breaks matters for emotions and behavior after breaks. Engaging in respite activities can put workers in a happier state, which also becomes evident in more positive emotional displays when interacting with others at work.

While the study by Trougakos *et al.* (2008) looked at immediate outcomes of work breaks, a study conducted by Sanz-Vergel, Demerouti, Moreno-Jiménez, and Mayo (2010) examined more medium-term outcomes. Specifically, by using data from a Spanish sample, these authors analyzed the relationship between recovery resulting from breaks during the day and vigor at night. Analysis indicated that the more workers felt re-vitalized from their breaks at work, the higher their level of vigor was at night, even after controlling for work pressure during the day and other variables that might influence vigor (e.g. positive emotions expressed at work and at home).

Daily Recovery at Home

After a stressful day at work, workers' happiness often is low; they experience elevated levels of negative affect and a high need for recovery (Ilies *et al.*, 2007;

Sonnentag & Zijlstra, 2006; Zohar et al., 2003). In order to restore positive affective states, recovery during after-work hours is needed. Research has looked at specific activities that may help recovery (e.g. sports and exercise), as well as at broader recovery experiences, such as relaxation or psychological detachment from work.

Typical diary studies on recovery activities and experiences at home have asked workers when coming home from work about their current affective states. Later during the evening – mostly at bedtime – workers have been asked to report recovery activities or experiences and their present affective states (Sonnentag & Bayer, 2005; Sonnentag & Zijlstra, 2006). Some studies also assessed affective states the next morning, before workers returned back to work (Sonnentag et al., 2008).

One of the first diary studies on recovery addressed the question of how teachers recover from a day at work, and examined off-job activities (Sonnentag, 2001). Analysis of diary data collected over the course of one working week showed that the amount of time spent on work-related activities during the time at home was negatively related to well-being at bedtime. Time spent on physical activities (i.e. sports), social activities (e.g. meeting friends), and low-effort activities (e.g. doing nothing, watching TV) was positively related to well-being at bedtime.

These findings were partially replicated by a study among flight attendants (Sonnentag & Natter, 2004). This study measured three well-being indicators: vigor, depression, and fatigue. Flight attendants reported an increased level of vigor and a decreased level of depression at bedtime (compared to vigor and depression immediately after work) after having spent time on sport activities. A diary study by Rook and Zijlstra (2006) with a sample from various occupational backgrounds confirmed the positive effect of sports activities. In this study, participants reported lower fatigue on days when they pursued sports activities.

The study with flight attendants also demonstrated that pursuing work-related activities during after-work hours marginally decreased vigor (Sonnentag & Natter, 2004). Interestingly, in this sample of flight attendants, depression increased after flight attendants had spent a lot of time on social activities. It might be that, because the job of a flight attendant is characterized by high social and emotional job demands and because, particularly after outbound flights, flight attendants often spend their free time with their co-workers, social activities lose their recovery potential. In addition to these findings on activities, this study identified that, when flight attendants experienced an activity as "recovering," their vigor level increased and their depression and fatigue levels decreased. Thus, this study provided the first empirical evidence that, beyond the specific activities pursued, the way these activities are experienced is also important for an improvement of mood during non-work time. Similarly, based on diary data from a sample of health-care workers, Sonnentag and Zijlstra (2006) reported that experiencing off-job activities in a positive way (assessed with items such as "Pursuing these activities was a positive experience for me," "Performing these activities made me feel good," "I was in a good mood after pursuing these activities") predicted serenity at bedtime, after controlling for the effect of the specific activities performed.

A more recent study by van Hooff, Geurts, Beckers, and Kompier (2011) addressed similar processes in university workers. These authors found that the more time university workers spent on active leisure (i.e. sports, social activities, creative activities) during after-work hours, the less fatigued they were at bedtime. Moreover, and in line with the Sonnentag and Zijlstra study, van Hooff and her colleagues reported that out-of-work pleasure predicted a decrease in fatigue and an increase in vigor during after-work hours – again beyond the effects of the activities per se. Interestingly, out-of-work job effort was related neither to fatigue nor to vigor at bedtime.

Sonnentag and Bayer (2005) also found that sport activities increased positive mood during after-work hours. Moreover, this study revealed that on days when people were psychologically detached from work during non-work time (i.e. gained a mental distance from their jobs), positive mood increased and fatigue decreased, in addition to the effects of the activities per se.

The diary studies presented so far have focused on improvement of mood during after-work hours until bedtime. An important question, however, is whether the positive effects of recovery persist until the next day. A diary study by Sonnentag, Binnewies, and Mojza (2008) addressed this question by asking a sample of public service workers to report their after-work recovery experiences at bedtime and their affective state the next morning before going to work. This study showed that psychological detachment from work during evening hours predicted low levels of fatigue and low levels of activated negative affect the following morning. Relaxation during the evening predicted morning serenity, and mastery experiences during the evening predicted activated positive affect in the morning. Moreover, good sleep quality was strongly related to low negative and high positive affective states in the morning. Overall, this study demonstrated that the way workers experience their after-work hours is strongly related to affective states the next morning. In other words, workers came to work in a happier (and a less unhappy) state when they mentally detached from work, relaxed, and had experienced some kind of mastery during their non-work time.

Spillover from Work to Private Life: Work-Related Experiences as Predictors of Non-Work Recovery

Over recent years, research applying diary designs has accumulated empirical evidence showing that daily experiences at work spill over into private life and impact on workers' daily well-being and recovery. Ilies, Schwind, and Heller (2007) developed a theoretical framework explaining how work events (e.g. job demands) influence workers' non-work experiences (e.g. well-being, marital satisfaction). Building on the affective events theory (Weiss & Cropanzano, 1996), the authors argued that work events impact experiences at work, particularly affective experiences and cognitions, and that these work experiences spill over from the work to the non-work domain, impacting non-work experiences (e.g. affective states at home, recovery processes).

In line with this framework, Sonnentag and Bayer (2005) investigated the relationships between day-specific and chronic workload and psychological detachment at home in a diary study. Results revealed that workers' psychological detachment at home was impaired on days when they worked longer work hours. In addition, they found that workers who suffered from a high level of chronic time pressure experienced less psychological detachment over the week. In sum, the study of Sonnentag and Bayer (2005) showed that both daily and chronic levels of workload affected daily detachment at work. From a theoretical perspective, these results imply that both intra-individual and inter-individual differences in workload influence workers' daily psychological detachment at home. A similar line of research conducted by Cropley and colleagues (Cropley *et al.*, 2006; Cropley & Purvis, 2003) showed in different diary studies that teachers in high-strain jobs (i.e. jobs characterized by high job demands and low job control) ruminate more about their job during off-job time and show a smaller decrease in rumination over the course of the evening.

In another diary study with police officers, Sonnentag and Jelden (2009) examined the effects of daily job stressors (situational constraints, time pressure, role ambiguity) on the daily pursuit of sport and low-effort activities. As described above, pursuing sports is a highly efficient recovery activity, while pursuing low-effort activities has not been found to be an effective recovery strategy in most studies (e.g. Rook & Zijlstra, 2006; Sonnentag & Zijlstra, 2006). In addition, the authors tested self-regulatory resources (energy) as a mediator. Results showed that, on days when police officers experienced a high level of situational constraints, they pursued fewer sports activities but more low-effort activities. Daily time pressure and daily role ambiguity were not significant predictors. Daily self-regulatory resources mediated the relationship between daily situational constraints and time spent on sports activities, but was not a mediator in the relationship with time spent on low-effort activities. This finding might imply that the depletion of self-regulatory resources impairs the pursuit of sport activities, but in itself does not promote low-effort activities; it might be that situational constraints increase negative affective states, to which people may respond with low-effort activities.

Additional support for the role of self-regulatory resources comes from the diary study of van Hooff, Geurts, Kompier, and Taris (2007). Using a sample of university staff, the authors found that persons who, over several days, indicated that they needed to invest high amounts of work-related effort (i.e. self-regulatory resources) during the day spent on average less time on active off-job time activities. Such active off-job activities include physical, social, and creative activities.

Going beyond subjective measures of recovery, Rau and Triemer (2004) investigated whether the experience of job stressors during a day is related to physiological indicators of recovery. Physiological recovery can be characterized by physiological parameters (e.g. heart rate, blood pressure) returning to the pre-stressor levels after a stressful workday. Rau and Triemer (2004) found that women who worked overtime showed higher levels of diastolic blood pressure during evening off-job time and before going to bed than women working regular hours. These differences were not found for men.

In sum, there is increasing empirical evidence that work-related events and experiences such as job stressors influence workers' non-work experiences and even their physiological recovery during off-job time. The depletion of self-regulatory resources seems to play an important role in these spillover processes. As described earlier, workers whose recovery is negatively affected often experience poorer well-being and less happiness.

Spillover from Home to Work Life: Work-Related Outcomes of Non-Work Recovery

As summarized above, recovery processes in the non-work domain are affected by work experiences. However, these spillover processes are not only unidirectional but bidirectional. In this section, we will describe how workers' recovery during off-job time also affects experiences and behaviors in the work domain.

In a diary study over one working week, Sonnentag (2003) investigated the role of recovery for work-related experiences and behavior. Specifically, she found that workers experienced more work engagement and engaged in more proactive behavior (personal initiative and learning activities) on days when they felt highly recovered in the morning.

The diary study of Binnewies, Sonnentag, and Mojza (2009) extended these findings by revealing that, on days that workers felt highly recovered in the morning, they showed higher levels of task performance, proactive performance, and helping behavior at work, and had to invest less work-related effort to fulfill their job tasks. The authors replicated these results in a week-level study, conducted over four working weeks (Binnewies *et al.*, 2010). In weeks when workers felt highly recovered after the weekend, they showed higher levels of task performance, proactive behavior, and helping behavior during the week, and had to invest less work-related effort than in weeks when workers felt less recovered after the weekend. In sum, these studies show that being highly recovered in the morning or after the weekend benefits daily work engagement and job performance.

Individual Differences as Moderators

Overall, the studies summarized so far have shown that recovery has positive effects for worker mood and work behavior. However, the degree to which workers benefit from recovery is not uniform for all people: Some gain more from recovery than others. For example, Sonnentag and Niessen (2008) examined workers' state of vigor at the end of the working day. Analyses showed that recovery accumulated over previous days was positively related to vigor at the end of the working day. Importantly, workers high on trait vigor benefitted more from accumulated recovery than workers low on trait vigor. This finding suggests that people who generally enjoy more positive affective experiences gain more from recovery than people who tend not to be so positive. It might be that people with a high level of trait vigor respond more quickly to the positive features of recovery experiences. Another study that tracked recovery experiences (particularly psychological detachment from work during non-work time) and affect over several weeks showed a similar pattern of results (Sonnentag et al., 2008): workers who were successful in detaching from work during the evening showed higher levels of positive affect on Friday afternoons. This positive association between psychological detachment and positive affect was particularly pronounced for workers who reported high levels of work engagement. Thus, people who are vigorous, dedicated to their work, and absorbed in their work remain in a more positive affective state when they detach from work while at home.

Theoretical And Practical Implications of Diary Designs

In this last section, we will provide an overview of the most important theoretical and practical implications researchers can draw from diary studies. First, diary designs enable researchers to examine both within-person and between-person processes and their interplay. Investigating within-person processes is distinct from investigating the same processes from a between-person perspective, although both approaches often lead to congruent empirical results (cf. Cervone, 2005; Ilies et al., 2011). Specifically, a within-person study on recovery investigates when and under which circumstances a person can better recover during the day. Between-person studies disentangle research questions, such as which personality traits or general job characteristics are associated with higher or lower recovery (i.e. which persons can better recover than others). Regarding practical implications, results from within-person studies give advice on how organizations and workers can intervene in the daily processes and thus promote daily recovery. Thereby, the practical implications concern the development of workers' daily behaviors (e.g. pursuing recovery activities) and the influence on daily work-related events (e.g. time pressure or conflicts at work), rather than giving advice on which workers should be selected for a job or how the workplace should be designed in general.

Moreover, within-person studies addressing short-term relationships between variables (typically on a daily basis) contribute to theory development as they cover a different time-frame than between-person studies (cf. Judge et al., 2009). While most cross-sectional and longitudinal studies focus on rather stable, chronic constructs and their relationships, diary studies often focus on state-like constructs and examine the short-term changes in these constructs. Therefore, diary designs addressing short-term processes add to the literature by shedding more light on the development of processes, such as strain reactions or recovery processes. Concerning the practical implications, knowledge on the development of strain and recovery processes enables us to develop organizational and personal interventions that aim at preventing negative strain effects and promoting recovery processes on a daily basis before workers experience chronic consequences, such as burnout or psychosomatic complaints, which are more difficult to counteract. For example, Hahn, Binnewies, Sonnentag, and Mojza (2011) showed that recovery experiences (e.g. psychological detachment, relaxation) can be promoted by a training intervention. The intervention included the identification of individual recovery strategies and the practice of techniques to promote recovery activities (e.g. goal setting, time management), as well as the presentation and discussion of activities that have been found to be effective for most workers (e.g. progressive muscle relaxation, sleep hygiene rules).

Taken together, diary designs enable researchers to examine a broad range of research questions concerning workers' experiences and behaviors in the work and non-work domain. As diary studies can be used to examine short-term, within-person relationships such studies can provide us with information on how organizations and workers can promote workers' well-being and happiness on a daily basis.

References

Bakker, A.B. & Bal, P.M. (2010). Weekly work engagement and performance: A study among starting teachers. *Journal of Occupational and Organizational Psychology, 83*, 189–206.

Beal, D.J. & Ghandour, L. (2011). Stability, change, and the stability of change in daily workplace affect. *Journal of Organizational Behavior, 32*, 526–546.

Binnewies, C., Sonnentag, S., & Mojza, E.J. (2009). Daily performance at work: Feeling recovered in the morning as a predictor of day-level job performance. *Journal of Organizational Behavior, 30*, 67–93.

Binnewies, C., Sonnentag, S., & Mojza, E.J. (2010). Recovery during the weekend and fluctuations in weekly job performance: A week-level study examining intra-individual relationships. *Journal of Occupational and Organizational Psychology, 83*, 419–441.

Bolger, N., Davis, A., & Rafaeli, E. (2003). Diary methods: Capturing life as it is lived. *Annual Review of Psychology, 54*, 579–616.

Cervone, D. (2005). Personality architecture: Within-person structures and processes. *Annual Review of Psychology, 56*, 423–452.

Courvoisier, D.S., Eid, M., Lischetzke, T., & Schreiber, W.H. (2010). Psychometric properties of a computerized mobile phone method for assessing mood in daily life. *Emotion, 10*, 115–124.

Cropley, M. & Purvis, L.J.M. (2003). Job strain and rumination about work issues during leisure time: A diary study. *European Journal of Work & Organizational Psychology, 12*, 195–207.

Cropley, M., Dijk, D.-J., & Stanley, N. (2006). Job strain, work rumination, and sleep in school teachers. *European Journal of Work and Organizational Psychology, 15*, 181–196.

Dalal, R.S., Lam, H., Weiss, H.M., Welch, E.R., & Hulin, C.L. (2009). A within-person approach to work behavior and performance: Concurrent and lagged citizenship-counterproductivity associations, and dynamic relationships with affect and overall job performance. *Academy of Management Journal, 52*, 1051–1066.

Fuller, J.A., Fisher, G.G., Stanton, J.M., Spitzmueller, C., Russell, S.S., & Smith, P.C. (2003). A lengthy look at the daily grind: Time series analysis of events, mood, stress, and satisfaction. *Journal of Applied Psychology, 88*, 1019–1033.

Geurts, S.A.E. & Sonnentag, S. (2006). Recovery as an explanatory mechanism in the relation between acute stress reactions and chronic health impairment. *Scandinavian Journal of Work, Environment & Health, 32*, 482–492.

Green, A.S., Rafaeli, E., Bolger, N., Shrout, P.E., & Reis, H.T. (2006). Paper or plastic? Data equivalence in paper and electronic diaries. *Psychological Methods, 11*, 87–105.

Hahn, V.C., Binnewies, C., Sonnentag, S., & Mojza, E.J. (2011). Learning how to recover from job stress: Effects of a recovery training program on recovery, recovery-related self-efficacy, and well-being. *Journal of Occupational Health Psychology, 16*, 202–216.

Ilies, R., Scott, B.A., & Judge, T.A. (2006). The interactive effects of personal traits and experienced states on intraindividual patterns of citizenship behavior. *Academy of Management Journal, 49*, 561–575.

Ilies, R., Schwind, K.M., & Heller, D. (2007). Employee well-being: A multilevel model linking work and nonwork domains. *European Journal of Work and Organizational Psychology, 16*, 326–341.

Ilies, R., Schwind, K.M., Wagner, D.T., Johnson, M.D., DeRue, D.S., & Ilgen, D.R. (2007). When can employees have a family life? The effects of daily workload and affect on work–family conflict and social behaviors at home. *Journal of Applied Psychology, 92*, 1368–1379.

Ilies, R., Dimotakis, N., & De Pater, I.E. (2010). Psychological and physiological reactions to high workloads: Implications for well-being. *Personnel Psychology, 63*, 407–436.

Ilies, R., Johnson, M.D., Judge, T.A., & Keeney, J. (2011). A within-individual study of interpersonal conflict as a work stressor: Dispositional and situational moderators. *Journal of Organizational Behavior, 32*, 44–64.

Judge, T.A. & Ilies, R. (2004). Affect and job satisfaction: A study of their relationship at work and at home. *Journal of Applied Psychology, 89*, 661–673.

Judge, T.A., Woolf, E.F., & Hurst, C. (2009). Is emotional labor more difficult for some than for others? A multilevel, experience-sampling study. *Personnel Psychology, 62*, 57–88.

Kenny, D.A., Bolger, N., & Kashy, D.A. (2002). Traditional methods for estimating multilevel models. In D.S. Moskowitz & S.L. Hershberger (Eds), *Modeling intraindividual variability with repeated measures data: Methods and applications* (pp. 1–24). Mahwah, NJ: Erlbaum.

Ohly, S. & Fritz, C. (2010). Work characteristics, challenge appraisal, creativity, and proactive behavior: A multi-level study. *Journal of Organizational Behavior, 31*, 543–565.

Ohly, S., Sonnentag, S., Niessen, C., & Zapf, D. (2010). Diary studies in organizational research: An introduction and some practical recommendations. *Journal of Personnel Psychology, 9*, 79–93.

Rau, R. & Triemer, A. (2004). Overtime in relation to blood pressure and mood during work, leisure, and night time. *Social Indicators Research, 67*, 51–73.

Reis, H.T. & Gable, S.L. (Eds) (2000). *Event-sampling and other methods for studying everyday experience*. New York, NY, US: Cambridge University Press.

Rook, J.W. & Zijlstra, F.R.H. (2006). The contribution of various types of activities to recovery. *European Journal of Work and Organizational Psychology, 15*, 218–240.

Sanz-Vergel, A.I., Demerouti, E., Moreno-Jiménez, B., & Mayo, M. (2010). Work–family balance and energy: A day-level study on recovery conditions. *Journal of Vocational Behavior, 76*, 118–130.

Song, Z., Foo, M.-D., & Uy, M.A. (2008). Mood spillover and crossover among dual-earner couples: A cell phone event sampling study. *Journal of Applied Psychology, 93*, 443–452.

Sonnentag, S. (2001). Work, recovery activities, and individual well-being: A diary study. *Journal of Occupational Health Psychology, 6*, 196–210.

Sonnentag, S. (2003). Recovery, work engagement, and proactive behavior: A new look at the interface between nonwork and work. *Journal of Applied Psychology, 88*, 518–528.

Sonnentag, S. & Bayer, U.-V. (2005). Switching off mentally: Predictors and consequences of psychological detachment from work during off-job time. *Journal of Occupational Health Psychology, 10*, 393–414.

Sonnentag, S. & Jelden, S. (2009). Job stressors and the pursuit of sport activities: A day-level perspective. *Journal of Occupational Health Psychology, 14*, 165–181.

Sonnentag, S. & Natter, E. (2004). Flight attendants' daily recovery from work: Is there no place like home? *International Journal of Stress Management, 11*, 366–391.

Sonnentag, S. & Niessen, C. (2008). Staying vigorous until work is over: The role of trait vigour, day-specific work experiences and recovery. *Journal of Occupational and Organizational Psychology, 81*, 435–458.

Sonnentag, S. & Zijlstra, F.R.H. (2006). Job characteristics and off-job activities as predictors of need for recovery, well-being, and fatigue. *Journal of Applied Psychology, 91*, 330–350.

Sonnentag, S., Binnewies, C., & Mojza, E.J. (2008). "Did you have a nice evening?" A day-level study on recovery experiences, sleep, and affect. *Journal of Applied Psychology, 93*, 674–684.

Sonnentag, S., Mojza, E.J., Binnewies, C., & Scholl, A. (2008). Being engaged at work and detached at home: A week-level study on work engagement, psychological detachment, and affect. *Work & Stress, 22*, 257–276.

Sonnentag, S., Binnewies, C., & Ohly, S. (in press). Event-sampling studies in Occupational Health Psychology. In B. Sinclair, L. Tetrick & M. Wang (Eds), *Research methods in occupational health psychology*. New York, NY: Routledge.

Teuchmann, K., Totterdell, P., & Parker, S.K. (1999). Rushed, unhappy, and drained: An experience sampling study of relations between time pressure, perceived control, mood, and emotional exhaustion in a group of accountants. *Journal of Occupational Health Psychology, 4*, 37–54.

Totterdell, P., Wood, S., & Wall, T. (2006). An intra-individual test of the demands-control model: A weekly diary study of psychological strain in portfolio workers. *Journal of Occupational and Organizational Psychology, 79*, 63–84.

Trougakos, J.P., Beal, D.J., Green, S.G., & Weiss, H.M. (2008). Making the break count: An episodic examination of recovery activities, emotional experiences, and affective delivery. *Academy of Management Journal, 51*, 131–146.

van Hooff, M.L.M., Geurts, S.A.E., Kompier, M.A.J., & Taris, T.W. (2007). Workdays, in-between workdays and the weekend: A diary study on effort and recovery. *International Archives of Occupational and Environmental Health, 80*, 599–613.

van Hooff, M.L.M., Geurts, S.A.E., Beckers, D.G.J., & Kompier, M.A.J. (2011). Daily recovery from work: The role of activities, effort and pleasure. *Work & Stress, 25*, 55–74.

Weiss, H.M. & Cropanzano, R. (1996). Affective Events Theory: A theoretical discussion of the structure, causes and consequences of affective experiences at work. In B.M. Staw & L.L. Cummings (Eds), *Research in organizational behavior* (Vol. 18, pp. 1–74). Greenwich, CT: JAI Press.

Weiss, H.M., Nicholas, J.P., & Daus, C.S. (1999). An examination of the joint effects of affective experiences and job beliefs on job satisfaction and variations in affective experiences over time. *Organizational Behavior and Human Decision Processes, 78*, 1–24.

Zohar, D., Tzischinski, O., & Epstein, R. (2003). Effects of energy availability on immediate and delayed emotional reactions to work events. *Journal of Applied Psychology, 88*, 1082–1093.

7 Experience-Sampling and Event-Sampling Research

Nikolaos Dimotakis and Remus Ilies

In recent years, an emerging focus on studying within-person processes and phenomena has started to complement traditional between-person research streams that explain how and why construct scores co-vary among individuals (Ilies, Schwind, & Heller, 2007; Ilies *et al.*, 2010). This emerging focus has been aided by the introduction of frameworks that include an episodic conceptualization of work events and occurrences in order to explain variations in affective states, attitudes, and behaviors within people and across time (see Weiss & Cropanzano, 1996; Beal *et al.*, 2005). That is, this within-person focus aims to examine the effects of workplace episodes, dynamically experienced states, and temporally fluctuating factors in order to investigate phenomena and research questions that cannot be adequately addressed with between-individual approaches (Alliger & Williams, 1993; Sheldon *et al.*, 1996). Specifically, between-person designs consider variations in construct scores across time as transient error, as they can only investigate the "trait-like" or stable component of the variables being examined.

Within-person designs, on the other hand, are primarily focused on explaining these very variations across time. In other words, within-person designs examine how some individual characteristics can vary or fluctuate across measurement periods as a result of external or internal influences. Between- and within-person designs can thus be seen as complementary to each other, with each providing important investigations on specific components of the total variance in construct scores (composed of the sum of between- and within-person variance); their combination can ultimately provide a more complete understanding of the phenomena being examined. Moreover, within-person investigations can be used to construct between-person and cross-level models as well, depending on the constructs investigated or the aggregation processes followed by researchers, thus being able to provide a comprehensive examination of the research question at hand. Such comprehensiveness becomes even more important when considering that the significance and magnitude of between- and within-person effects and processes can vary considerably (and can even be in opposite directions), necessitating the use of dual research approaches or methods that can address both sides of the "temporal coin."

Within-person approaches have a long history, with some initial investigations taking place as early as 1925 (Scollon *et al.*, 2003). However, recent innovations and improvements in technological, analytical, and conceptual areas have helped the field expand rapidly, spurring a greatly increased interest in this research approach. One of the most important of these innovations has been the introduction of the Experience-Sampling Method (ESM; Larson & Csikszentmihalyi, 1983). ESM, in broad terms, aims to utilize a multiple measurement schedule over a set period of time in order to explain fluctuations in episodic experiences (e.g. affective states) and the dynamic antecedents and outcomes of these fluctuations. More specifically, ESM approaches include using a random- or fixed-event or signal-contingent schedule in order to measure the dependent and independent variables at multiple points during an individual's day, typically over a period of multiple days. Data from ESM designs are then commonly used as input in within-person or cross-level multivariate, mediational, or moderational multilevel regression models, using statistical techniques such as Hierarchical Linear Modeling (HLM; Raudenbush & Bryk, 2002).

In order to contribute to this emerging stream of research, this chapter aims to outline and discuss the basic features of ESM and to examine the advantages and disadvantages of implementing these features in ESM research designs. Moreover, we provide illustrative examples of various types of these designs. We also provide suggestions for future research utilizing ESM in various ways to examine within-person research questions.

The Basic Features of Experience-Sampling Methodology

ESM, as originally conceptualized by Larson and Csikszentmihalyi (1983), represents a general research procedure that requires study participants to respond to (a) multiple daily questionnaires, delivered to them at (b) random or fixed signal-contingent timing schedules or (c) event-contingent times throughout the subjects' day, and (d) to continue to do so for a number of days, with data collection typically lasting a week or longer. Extant ESM designs have commonly utilized some variation of the above features to a greater or lesser extent; naturally, ESM designs are best served by utilizing a customized combination of the aforementioned features in order to optimally examine the specific research question at hand. Below, we discuss each of these four basic ESM features, the advantages and disadvantages involved with utilizing them in psychological or organizational research investigations, and provide examples of past research and suggestions for future research aimed at investigating within-person research questions.

Multiple Daily Measurements

ESM designs typically involve multiple measurement points throughout each day of the study. In other words, participants are asked to fill out multiple surveys each day, with each survey containing some combination of the dependent and independent, moderating and mediating variables of the study. The primary purpose of these multiple measurements is to provide a more complete and comprehensive picture of an individual's day, in order to best capture the totality of the phenomena being investigated. Depending on the research question being examined, the number of daily surveys can vary from very frequent, such as the study by van Eck, Nicolson, and Berkhof (1998), who sampled participants ten times each study day, to more sparse, such as the study by Foo, Uy, and Baron (2009), which only sampled participants twice per study day.

ESM designs utilizing frequent sampling can be advantageous in a number of ways. First of all, as mentioned above, multiple surveys allow researchers to capture a more complete picture of individuals' daily experience, including their affective states, thoughts, and behaviors throughout the workday. This benefit can be particularly important in cases where the variables or phenomena being examined are fleeting (such as emotional responses; Frijda, 1994) or relatively rare (such as workplace aggression) in nature, or where retrospective accounts are for any reason problematic (for example, due to recall processes; see Bower, 1981; Robinson & Clore, 2002). In other words, a study utilizing a more frequent daily measurement schedule is more likely to provide a distribution of observations that is temporally closer to the phenomenon being investigated, thus providing a more clear assessment of the same. Even in cases in which these multiple observations are ultimately aggregated at the data analysis stage to create higher-level response scores (e.g. daily scores), having multiple day-level observations can still provide a more reliable and complete picture of an individual's daily experience compared to single day-level measurements. Therefore, depending on the way data is aggregated, more frequent sampling can be of help in investigations of variance at various levels of analysis. Dimotakis, Scott, and Koopman (2011), for example, utilized this approach by measuring their dependent and mediating variables (workplace social interaction characteristics and affective states, respectively) at three points throughout the workday, and then aggregating these to the level of the day to predict a day-level dependent variable (also see Ilies et al., 2010, for a more complex example of multiple daily measurements being aggregated into day-level variables).

Second, having multiple daily surveys allows for the separation of the dependent and independent variables in the study, thus helping to alleviate common method variance concerns (Podsakoff et al., 2003). For example, in a study predicting organizational citizenship behaviors (Organ, 1997) from variations in individuals' experienced affective state during work, researchers can separate the measurement of affective states from the measurement of behavior utilizing two or more daily surveys. In the study by Ilies, Dimotakis, and De Pater (2010), the researchers used a ten-day study design involving five daily observations, and capitalized on the advantage of multiple daily surveys by using the first three surveys to measure their independent variable (workload), the fourth to measure their proposed mediators (affective stress and systolic blood pressure), and the final survey to measure their dependent variables (emotional exhaustion and experienced strain used as indicators of low subjective well-being).

Furthermore, multiple measurements can enable researchers to perform additional analyses to be used as robustness checks, to account for temporal effects, or to provide additional evidence for the causal ordering of the relationships included in this study. For example, the aforementioned study by Dimotakis *et al.* (2011) utilized this advantage to present additional evidence of causality by presenting a series of lagged analyses that utilized the lag of the independent variables to predict the dependent variables of the study (and vice versa); the results of these analyses provided some additional support for the validity of the hypothesized causal order of the study variable relationships. Similarly, other research designs could benefit from having multiple daily measurements by estimating how the temporal distance between two measured variables affects the magnitude of their relationship (see, for example, Judge and Ilies, 2004). Similar to the study by Judge and Ilies (where the authors examined how the time elapsed between the measurement of affect and job satisfaction influenced the relationship among the two), a study investigating the relationship between stressful events and individual well-being could estimate temporal effects on the magnitude of this relationship, by predicting well-being measured at increasingly more distant temporal frames from a given experienced event (or by alternatively predicting the independent variables measured at a fixed point in time by increasingly temporally distant event-level observations). A similar design could provide an additional contribution by investigating more nuanced relationships between variables, such as cumulative effects (for example, by investigating how persistently high effects of workload across days can affect employee well-being).

Finally, in research designs focusing on the level of the event (that is, measuring both dependent and independent variables concurrently and predicting the relationship among them at multiple points throughout the day), utilizing multiple day-level observations can greatly increase a study's within-person statistical power. Although multilevel power analyses (see Snijders & Bosker, 1993, 1999) need to be conducted to assess how much within- versus between-person statistical power is necessary to address the goals of the study, increasing the frequency of day-level observations can be a simple and expedient way to increase statistical power to the required level.

Of course, utilizing a research design that involves multiple daily observations also carries some risks and disadvantages. The primary and potentially most harmful of these is the risk of participant fatigue. Having to fill out multiple surveys each day can quickly result in participants being tired or annoyed at the volume of the workload required by the study, which can in turn result in hasty responses, higher levels of missing responses, and ultimately increasing the risk of collecting low-quality or untrustworthy data. While this problem can potentially be alleviated to some extent by, for example, cultivating a strong positive relationship with the research subjects that can increase their motivation to participate, utilizing surveys of shorter individual length, or by statistically checking for differences among data collected at the beginning and later on in the study (using some combination of t-tests and tests for equality of variance, such as Levene's [1960] test), participant fatigue will remain an issue of concern in studies utilizing frequent daily measurement and will need to be taken into consideration.

A similar disadvantage faced by studies involving multiple daily measures is their potential to exert a reactive effect on study participants. That is, requiring participants to fill out measurement schedules too frequently can actually interfere with their daily experiences, affective states, and behaviors. Reactive effects can be as simple as taking up participant time that they would have otherwise spent on behaviors of interest to the study, or they can be more subtle, such as focusing participant attention on states and experiences that they would have otherwise not noted or considered (for discussions on participant reactivity, see Hufford *et al.*, 2002; Korotitsch & Nelson-Gray, 1999). The common characteristic of these issues of concern is that they can alter the very phenomena that the study aims to examine, which means that reactive effects must be taken into consideration when considering the number of daily observations that will be included in the study. While a full investigation of participant reactivity is beyond the scope of this chapter, such issues need to be taken on board.

Finally, implementing a more frequent daily sampling design can force specific tradeoffs to be made that might compromise other aspects of the study. For example, increased daily measurement frequency might force a shorter overall study length to counteract study fatigue, or it might prohibit the measurement of all the variables that researchers would like to include. For example, the very frequent daily measurement schedules utilized by Marco and Suls (1993) and van Eck *et al.* (1998) were balanced by short overall study lengths, while Kuppens, Oravecz, and Tuerlinckx (2010) opted instead for utilizing a very brief instrument to counteract their own very frequent daily sampling design. Therefore, care must be taken to ensure that the daily measurement schedule ultimately selected is optimal and appropriate to the research question at hand.

Event- and Signal-Contingent Delivery Schedules

Researchers conducting studies using ESM designs can also utilize both event- and signal-contingent delivery schedules. Event-contingent delivery schedules refer to designs that assess the study variables after some specified event (or class of events) has taken place; for example, by delivering questionnaires to participants after they experience an event that involves workplace conflict or the successful accomplishment of a task; these surveys are thus most commonly participant initiated, as the study participants typically need to indicate when the focal workplace event has taken place (unless the technological sophistication of the study is high enough to allow for automatic survey initiation). On the other hand, signal-contingent delivery schedules assess the study variables at specified fixed times (or during specified time blocks) during the day, with the measurement being initiated by the researchers through the programming of the signaling device used in the study.

Naturally, researchers can also utilize a mix of the two delivery schedules, assessing participant experiences or feeling states at some times of the day and also after the occurrence of some event of interest to the study. It is also worth noting that sometimes the distinction between the two can be mostly conceptual rather than operational. For example, Sonnentag and Bayer (2005), in a within-person study of psychological detachment, asked participants to fill in two questionnaires each day, at two specific "events" (end of the workday and before sleeping). Depending on the stability of a participant's day, this event-contingent schedule could be operationally equivalent to a customized signal-based schedule (with measurements being initiated at 5:00 pm and 11:30 pm, for example). It should also be noted that signal-based survey delivery methodologies can be further paired with a fixed or random time delivery schedule, a topic we will discuss further in the next section.

These delivery schedules are each optimally suited to investigating different types of research questions, and might also work better or worse depending on the specific context in which the research study is taking place. First, in cases where the research focus is on participant reactions to specific episodes or workplace experiences, event-contingent sampling allows researchers to assess participants' reactions at an optimal and deliberate temporal distance from the event, instead of relying on chance. The specific event to be studied is still, however, of interest in making this decision; when studying commonplace events or episodes (such as, for example, commonplace social interactions in the workplace; see Basch & Fisher, 2000), an event-sampling study might lead to participants being deluged with questionnaires during their workday as a result, which can lead to participant fatigue or reactive effects as previously discussed. Moreover, since, as mentioned above, most event-contingent studies depend on the participant to initiate the measurement, tying surveys on some common event can result in a decreasing level of participant compliance.

On the other hand, signal-contingent delivery schedules are best suited to capturing a general overview of participants' daily experiences. That is, these schedules allow for assessing participants at sufficient points in time throughout each day of the study, without needing to depend on external episodes or events to initiate measurement; this can provide a higher level of control over the specifics of measurement on the part of the researchers conducting the study and allows for sophisticated survey delivery scheduling, customization, and fine-tuning. For example, participant affective states can be assessed at a fixed interval every two hours or randomly within four two-hour time blocks that cover the entire workday. This approach was used by Ilies, Schwind, Wagner, Johnson, DeRue, and Ilgen (2007), who utilized a signal-contingent delivery schedule to measure participant affect twice daily at work and once daily at home, in order to capture a general overview of daily experienced states. Signal-contingent schedules are thus optimal in investigations of commonplace workplace occurrences, demands, and behaviors because they can be customized to assess what a typical or commonplace workday is like for a particular person.

The particular organizational context can also be of value in informing the choice of signal-contingent or event-contingent delivery schedules. In cases where the study participants have to follow a complex yet predictable daily schedule as a result of their job or task responsibilities (such as might be the case with teachers, drivers, or certain types of factory workers), signal-contingent schedules can be designed to ensure that the survey does not interfere with participants' work tasks, yet still measure the study variables in an appropriate manner. For example, Huth, Ryan, Ilies, and Dimotakis (2008), in a ten-day within-person investigation using a sample of 57 public and parochial school teachers, utilized a signal-contingent schedule to ensure that measurement would only be initiated during these times that participants would be able to fill out the questionnaires without interrupting their job tasks. On the other hand, if there are fewer contextual constraints (as might be with typical administrative or clerical office workers), then the choice between event- or signal-contingent delivery schedules depends to a greater degree on what the optimal choice is for the research question at hand.

Fixed and Random Delivery Schedules

In signal-contingent designs, ESM studies can deliver survey instruments to participants utilizing either fixed or random delivery schedules. Simply stated, fixed delivery schedules refer to administering surveys at fixed times during each survey day based on a timetable defined before the beginning of the study by researchers. Most commonly, this schedule is held constant throughout this study (for example, surveying participants every day at 11:00 am and 3:00 pm), but can also be held to vary across days or weeks of the study (by, for example, surveying participants every day at 9:00 am and 1:00 pm for the first week of the study, and then surveying them at 10:00 am and 2:00 pm for the second week). An example of a fixed delivery schedule is the study by Judge and Ilies (2004) on mood and job satisfaction; in this study, 74 working individuals were instructed to complete surveys at 9:00 am, 12:00 pm, and 3:00 pm on each workday. On the other hand, a random delivery schedule involves administering surveys at varying periods of time during the days of the study, or at varying times within specified temporal periods within each study day. For example, this approach can involve delivering three daily measurements at random points in time each study day, or sampling participants randomly in the morning and afternoon, thus randomizing the distribution of surveys within specified time blocks throughout the workday. This latter approach was followed by Ilies, Dimotakis, and De Pater (2010), who measured daily workload using three daily surveys, delivered randomly during the workday within three two-hour time blocks (specifically, 9:30 am to 11:30 am, 12:00 pm to 2:00 pm, and 2:30 to 4:30 pm).

Fixed and random delivery schedules can of course also be used concurrently in a research study, in order to combine their advantages and mitigate their shortcomings. In the aforementioned Ilies *et al.* (2010) study, for example, while workload was measured with randomly delivered surveys, the study mediators (affective stress and systolic blood pressure) were measured with surveys administered with a fixed delivery schedule (every day at 4:45 pm). Similarly, a dual fixed and random delivery schedule was followed by Weiss, Nicholas, and Daus (1999), who surveyed their study participants four times a day, with two of these assessments being randomly triggered (within two one-hour blocks in the morning and afternoon) and two being delivered at set times (when arriving at and leaving the workplace).

Moreover, fixed delivery schedules can be made to tolerate a specific amount of randomness in the actual response time by allowing a wider or narrower response window for participants after the survey has been administered to them. For example, the data collection procedures in the studies of Dimotakis et al. (2011) and the aforementioned Ilies et al. (2010) allowed individuals a narrow ten-minute window in which they were allowed to respond to a signaled survey, after which the survey became unavailable. Other studies have used a wider response window; for example, Judge and Ilies (2004) allowed participants a one-hour window in which to provide their responses. The difference between fixed and random delivery schedules can thus be thought of as more of a continuum rather than a dichotomy, allowing researchers to provide an additional degree of fine-tuning to their study designs.

In general, delivery schedules with a higher degree of randomness can allow for a higher degree of protection against systematic bias, in cases where this might be a concern due to contextual factors. For example, delivering the study questionnaires at two random time blocks during the workday (one in the morning and one in the afternoon) can help ensure that the questionnaires do not consistently sample participants at an invariant point of their day that is not representative of the whole day (e.g. lunch time, beginning and end of the workday, or after the daily staff meeting); such an approach was followed in the Ilies et al. (2010) study discussed above. Obviously, this is much more of a concern in workplaces and contexts in which systematic event or time effects are likely and such effects are not a focus of the study.

At the same time, the inclusion of a higher degree of randomness in a study (when using the proper measurement and recording technologies) can allow for more nuanced examinations of the relationships among experienced events and the outcome variables included in the study. Since the time between experiencing an event and responding to the administered survey will vary to some extent with a random delivered schedule, this temporal distance can become an interesting control, independent, or moderating variable of the study. For example, a random schedule can enable researchers to investigate how affective reactions to workplace events persist or fade out based on the temporal distance between experiencing the event and the actual measurement. Of course, such frameworks require an adequate level of within-person sample size to ensure adequate variance in the temporal distance between the event that triggered the measurement and the administration of the measurement.

The potential benefits of using randomly delivery schedules can also present researchers with a few potential problems, however. The very unpredictability inherent in these random schedules, by definition, results in reduced control over the study on the part of the research administrators. That is, attempting to assess participants at random times means that there is an increased possibility that the surveys will be delivered at times where participants are unable or unwilling to complete them (e.g. lunchtime, workplace meetings, and so on). Similarly, random signaling increases the chances that unrelated events and workplace episodes that can be a threat to the internal validity of the study might occur before the start of the measurement (see Kerlinger & Lee, 2000; Nunnally & Bernstein, 1994; Rosenthal & Rosnow, 1991).

Study Length

The final feature of ESM that must be taken into consideration by researchers designing within-person studies relates to the total length of the study, or the number of days over which the study will be running. While deciding on the length of the study seems to be a straightforward decision, it represents the final balancing decision aimed at optimizing the study design and best addressing the research question at hand. Past ESM studies have ranged from fairly long study lengths, as with the 20-day study conducted by Seo and Ilies (2009) and the 28-day study conducted by Foo *et al.* (2009), to fairly short ones, such as the five-day study conducted by Sonnentag, Binnewies, and Mojza (2008) and the two three-day intensive measurement periods utilized by Kamarck, Schwartz, Shiffman, Muldoon, Sutton-Tyrell, and Janicki (2005) and Kamarck, Shiffman, Smithline, Goodie, Paty, Gnys, and Jong (1998). Moreover, it is technically possible to have single-day ESM studies in cases where the assessment methods can be frequent and robust enough to sufficiently address the research question; for instance, the ambulatory blood pressure measurement methods utilized in the Kamarck *et al.* (1998, 2005) studies, combined with some sufficiently brief survey instruments, can result in levels of power sufficient to successfully examine some study hypotheses within a single day.

Longer study lengths have advantages similar to those of frequent daily measurement schedules discussed above. Studies of longer length naturally result in higher levels of power (see Cohen, 1992; Snijders & Bosker, 1999), providing a higher probability of detecting the effects being investigated. Similarly, they allow researchers to conduct many of the same classes of additional analyses mentioned before, such as models utilizing lagged variables and temporal effects; increased study length directly corresponds to more observations that can be lagged or otherwise shifted across time as needed, and to a greater time span that allows for a greater variety of temporal investigations (such as growth or seasonally adjusted models). Additionally, however, longer study lengths can also assist with external validity concerns; Wheeler and Reis (1991), for example, argued that a two-week period provides a stable and generalizable window into individuals' daily lives. In essence, a longer study period helps insure that an atypical or extraordinary day experienced by study participants will not contaminate the results and conclusions of the research study.

On the other hand, longer study lengths can also have many of the disadvantages of more frequent daily measurement schedules. For example, participant fatigue is still an issue, with longer studies being more likely to result in participant fatigue at some point during the study. Moreover, depending on the technological delivery method utilized (such as handheld digital devices without internet access), a longer study length can increase the likelihood of technological failure or data corruption, as was the case in the Ilies *et al.* (2010) study discussed above, which resulted in a number of participants being removed from the final sample due to technological failures.

Constructing Balanced ESM Research Designs

The decisions of whether to include event- or signal-contingent scheduling, and random or fixed delivery schedules, as well as the decisions of how often to sample participants and for how long, therefore, become a balancing issue between the potential benefits of each approach and their potential downsides, a situation with which researchers are of course not unfamiliar with. In order to make the best possible decision, researchers need to be aware of the constraints of their research context and the needs of their research question, in order to design a balanced and optimal research design. Above, we described the basic features of ESM, their advantages and disadvantages, and we briefly discussed the various ways in which they can be combined to design studies aimed at optimally examining the research question at hand.

Since the introduction of ESM, however, researchers have been actively adding to the basic features of the method with a variety of conceptual, operational, and technological innovations aimed at enhancing its advantages and mitigating the impact of some of its disadvantages. Below, we outline some of these innovations and briefly discuss the ways in which they can help design and execute within-person research studies. We focus on three broad areas: the use of multiple rating sources, the use of novel and modern technological survey delivery options, and the use of multiple measurement techniques.

Multiple Rating Sources

The use of multiple rating sources is, of course, not a novel development. In fact, researchers have long utilized multiple raters in an effort to reduce or alleviate the effects of common methods variance (Podsakoff *et al.*, 2003). The use of multiple raters in ESM designs, however, is relatively new, but can provide solid benefits to researchers that integrate such a feature into their within-person designs. For example, such a choice can allow researchers to avoid having to deliver too many daily surveys to participants; instead of separating measurements of dependent and independent variables in time to avoid common methods bias concerns, researchers can instead measure their independent and dependent variables using more than one source of ratings. Alternatively, multiple rating sources can be used in conjunction with measures assessed at some other point in time to allow for alleviating bias concerns even further. For example, Ilies *et al.* (2007) utilized an additional rating source by assessing employee social behaviors at home using ratings provided by the study participants' partners. Similar approaches can be adopted in examinations of workplace behaviors or performance (using supervisors and peers as raters), affective states (using partners, peers, or other associates inside and outside the workplace), and a variety of other variables in diverse settings. That being said, the potential benefits of avoiding common methods variance need to be weighed against the additional requirements that a multi-source investigation entails (for a discussion, see Spector, 2006).

On the other hand, using multiple rating sources can create additional operational complications and difficulties. For example, recruiting additional rating sources can increase the overall cost of the study, since additional people need to be identified, recruited, and possibly compensated for their efforts; in any case, more surveys will have to be delivered to participants, thus directly increasing study costs. Moreover, including additional ratings sources can make the recruitment of the primary participants more difficult, as not all research participants will be willing and able to participate in study designs involving multiple raters. Apart from the complexity and cost of recruiting an additional rating source, there are also issues of confidentiality that will need to be addressed, in order to keep the additional sources' responses secret from the primary study participants. Nonetheless, including additional rating sources can be of value in cases of certain research designs or research questions.

Technological Survey Delivery Options

Technological advancements have also provided a wealth of new options in terms of delivering surveys and instruments to participants. Earlier ESM studies depended on participants filling out paper questionnaires when signaled by a device (such as a digital wristwatch) provided to them by researchers (see Marco & Suls, 1993, for an example of such an approach). While innovative for their time and economical in terms of equipment costs, the lack of technological sophistication of such studies prohibited researchers from utilizing more complex delivery schedules and made it harder to ensure subject compliance (by, for example, ensuring that subjects filled out the questionnaire at the proper time instead of later on in the study).

The increasing sophistication and availability of electronic delivery options, therefore, has provided researchers with a wealth of additional options. Surveys can now be delivered to subjects over the web (see Judge & Ilies, 2004), on Personal Digital Assistant devices provided to participants (see Ilies *et al.*, 2010), or even on the participants' own mobile phones (see Song *et al.*, 2008). While potentially more costly than paper surveys, these technological options excel at ensuring subject compliance (since responses can be made unavailable to participants outside the designated response windows and can be time and date stamped automatically as well). Moreover, continuing developments in technology will doubtless provide more novel choices on how and when to deliver survey instruments to participants in the future; for example, researchers might utilize the location services embedded in new generation smartphones as the triggering event in ESM studies, with measurements being initiated based on whether the participant has arrived or departed a particular location (home or work) or based on whether they recently were in the vicinity of another study participant (as might be the case with a study examining workplace interactions among employees or among employees and supervisors).

Of course, higher levels of technological sophistication will never become a substitute for designing research studies in a careful and deliberate manner; all established study design principles will still need to be taken into consideration no matter what the technological approach adopted for a study might be. Nevertheless, technological advances and innovations will continue to offer researchers additional options in administering surveys to participants, and these additional options can potentially provide a host of potential benefits.

Multiple Measurement Techniques

An additional advance in ESM research, standing in the crossroads of multiple ratings sources and technological innovation, is the adoption of multiple measurement techniques to assess the variables included in the study. For example, the improved portability and accuracy of physiological measurement devices (such as blood pressure and heart rate monitors, sleep measurement accelerometers, and so on) has enabled researchers to include a variety of objective or alternative outcomes in their investigations that are accurate, reliable, and less subject to measurement bias concerns. For example, Ilies, Dimotakis, and Watson (2010) utilized wrist-worn automated blood pressure monitors to collect blood pressure and heart rate data in a ten-day within-person study, using these measures as a complement to participant affective stress ratings that were measured with more traditional survey instruments.

Future approaches can therefore benefit by utilizing a host of alternative or additional measurement techniques. For example, ESM approaches can easily be combined with techniques such as the Implicit Association Test (IAT; Greenwald *et al.*, 1998) to measure implicit attitudes within people, or with tests of cognition and creativity, such as the Remote Associates Test (RAT; Mednick & Mednick, 1967). These techniques can allow for robust and creative assessment of the study variables that are less subject to common methods bias concerns.

Conclusion

ESM represents a powerful methodology that can provide important contributions to research and practice when implemented well, thus facilitating within-person approaches that can complement traditional between-person research efforts. This chapter attempted to outline the basic features of ESM, their advantages and disadvantages, as well as some more recent additions to previously used ESM techniques.

ESM has already been of great value to a variety of topic areas within the organizational literature, and its contribution is expected to increase in years to come as conceptual and technological improvements continue to accumulate. It is our hope that the discussion presented in this chapter can be of value to researchers conducting within-person studies, by assisting in the development of novel and robust research programs.

References

Alliger, G.M. & Williams, K.J. (1993). Using signal-contingent experience sampling methodology to study work in the field: A discussion and illustration examining task perceptions and mood. *Personnel Psychology, 46*, 525–549.

Basch, J. & Fisher, C.D. (2000). Affective events-emotions matrix: A classification of work events and associated emotions. In N.M. Ashkanasy, C.E. Härtel, & W.J. Westport (Eds), *Emotions in the workplace: Research, theory, and practice* (pp. 36–48). Westport, CT: Quorum Books/Greenwood Publishing Group, Inc.

Beal, D.J., Weiss, H.M., Barros, E., MacDermid, S.M. (2005). An episodic process model of affective influences on performance. *Journal of Applied Psychology, 90*, 1054–1068.

Bower, G.H. (1981). Mood and memory. *American Psychologist, 36*, 129–148.

Cohen, J. (1992). A power primer. *Psychological Bulletin, 112*, 155–159.

Dimotakis, N., Scott, B.A., & Koopman, J. (2011). An experience sampling investigation of workplace interactions, affective states, and employee well-being. *Journal of Organizational Behavior, 32*, 572–588.

Foo, M.D., Uy, M.A., & Baron, R.A. (2009). How do feelings influence effort? An empirical study of entrepreneurs' affect and venture effort. *Journal of Applied Psychology, 94*, 1086–1094.

Frijda, N.H. (1994). Varieties of affect: Emotions and episodes, moods, and sentiments. In P. Ekman & R.J. Davidson (Eds), *The nature of emotion* (pp. 59–67). New York: Oxford University Press.

Greenwald, A.G., McGhee, D.E., & Schwarz, J.L.K. (1998). Measuring individual differences in implicit cognition: The Implicit Association Test. *Journal of Personality and Social Psychology, 74*, 1464–1480.

Hufford, M.R., Shields, A.L., Shiffman, S., Paty, J., & Balabanis, M. (2002). Reactivity to ecological momentary assessment: An example using undergraduate problem drinkers. *Psychology of Addictive Behaviors, 16*, 205–211.

Huth, M., Ryan, A.M., Ilies, R. & Dimotakis, N. (2008). *School staff job demands, stress and work family conflict – an experience sampling study.* Presented at the 2008 Work, Stress and Health Conference, Washington DC.

Ilies, R., Schwind, K.M., & Heller, D. (2007). Employee well-being: A multi-level model linking work and non-work domains. *European Journal of Work and Organizational Psychology, 16*, 326–341.

Ilies, R., Schwind, K.M., Wagner, D.T., Johnson, M., DeRue, D.S., & Ilgen, D.R. (2007). When can employees have a family life? The effects of daily workload and affect on work–family conflict and social activities at home. *Journal of Applied Psychology, 92*, 1368–1379.

Ilies, R., Dimotakis, N., & De Pater, I.E. (2010). Psychological and physiological reactions to high workloads: Implications for well-being. *Personnel Psychology, 63*, 407–436.

Ilies, R., Dimotakis, N., & Watson, D. (2010). Mood, blood pressure and heart rate at work: An experience-sampling study. *Journal of Occupational Health Psychology, 15*, 120–130.

Judge, T.A. & Ilies, R. (2004). Affect and job satisfaction: A study of their relationship at work and at home. *Journal of Applied Psychology, 89*, 661–673.

Kamarck, T.W., Shiffman, S.M., Smithline, L., Goodie, J.L., Paty, J.A., Gnys, M., & Jong, Y.K. (1998). Effects of task strain, social conflict, and emotional activation on ambulatory cardiovascular activity: Daily consequences of recurring stress in a multiethnic adult sample. *Health Psychology, 17*, 17–29.

Kamarck, T.W., Schwartz, J.E., Shiffman, S., Muldoon, M.F., Sutton-Tyrell, K. & Janicki, D.L. (2005). Psychosocial stress and cardiovascular risk: What is the role of daily experience? *Journal of Personality, 73*, 1749–1774.

Kerlinger, F.N. & Lee, H.B. (2000). *Foundations of behavioral research*. Forth Worth, TX: Harcourt.

Korotitsch, W.J. & Nelson-Gray, R.O. (1999). An overview of self-monitoring research in assessment and treatment. *Psychological Assessment, 11*, 415–425.

Kuppens, P., Oravecz, Z., & Tuerlinckx, F. (2010). Feelings change: accounting for individual differences in the temporal dynamics of affect. *Journal of Personality and Social Psychology, 99*, 1042–1060.

Larson, R. & Csikszentmihalyi, M. (1983). The experience sampling method. *New Directions for Methodology of Social and Behavioral Science, 15*, 41–56.

Levene, H. (1960). Robust tests for equality of variances. In I. Olkin, S.G. Ghurye, W. Hoeffding, W.G. Madow, & H.B. Mann (Eds), *Contributions to Probability and Statistics: Essays in Honor of Harold Hotelling,* (pp. 278–292). Menlo Park, CA: Stanford University Press.

Marco, C.A. & Suls, J. (1993). Daily stress and the trajectory of mood: spillover, response assimilation, contrast, and chronic negative affectivity. *Journal of Personality and Social Psychology, 64*, 1053–1063.

Mednick, S.A. & Mednick, M.T. (1967). *Examiner's manual: Remote Associates Test.* Boston: Houghton Mifflin.

Nunnally, J.C. & Bernstein, I.H. (1994). *Psychometric theory.* New York, NY: McGraw Hill.

Organ, D.W. (1997). Organizational citizenship behavior: It's construct clean-up time. *Human Performance, 10*, 85–97.

Podsakoff, P.M., MacKenzie, S.B., Lee, J., & Podsakoff, N.P. (2003). Common method biases in behavioral research: A critical review of the literature and recommended remedies. *Journal of Applied Psychology, 88*, 879–903.

Raudenbush, S.W. and Bryk, A.S. (2002). *Hierarchical linear models: applications and data analysis methods.* Newbury Park: SAGE Publications.

Robinson, M.D. & Clore, G.L. (2002). Beliefs, situations, and their interactions: Towards a model of emotion reporting. *Psychological Bulletin, 128*, 934–960.

Rosenthal, R. & Rosnow, R.L. (1991). *Essentials of behavioral research: Methods and data analysis.* New York, NY: McGraw Hill.

Scollon, C.N., Kim-Prieto, C., & Diener, E. (2003). Experience sampling: Promises and pitfalls, strengths and weaknesses. *Journal of Happiness Studies, 4*, 5–34.

Seo, M. & Ilies, R. (2009). The role of self-efficacy, goal, and affect in dynamic motivational self-regulation. *Organizational Behavior and Human Decision Processes, 109*, 120–133.

Sheldon, K.M., Ryan, R.M., & Reis, H.T. (1996). What makes for a good day? Competence and autonomy in the day and in the person. *Personality and Social Psychology Bulletin, 22*, 1270–1279.

Snijders, T.A.B. & Bosker, R.J. (1993). Standard errors and sample sizes for two-level research. *Journal of Educational Statistics, 18*, 237–259.

Snijders, T.A.B. & Bosker, R.J. (1999). *Multilevel analysis: An introduction to basic and advanced multilevel modeling.* London, England: Sage Publishers.

Song, Z., Foo, M.D., & Uy, M.A. (2008). Mood spillover and crossover among dual-earner couples: A cell phone event sampling study. *Journal of Applied Psychology, 93*, 443–452.

Sonnentag, S. & Bayer, U. (2005). Switching off mentally: Predictors and consequences of psychological detachment from work during off-job time. *Journal of Occupational Health Psychology, 10*, 393–414.

Sonnentag, S., Binnewies, C., & Mojza, E.J. (2008). "Did you have a nice evening?" A day-level study on recovery experiences, sleep and affect. *Journal of Applied Psychology, 93*, 674–684.

Spector, P.E. (2006). Method variance in organizational research: Truth or urban legend? *Organizational Research Methods, 9*, 221–232.

Van Eck, M., Nicolson, N.A., & Berkhof, J. (1998). Effects of stressful daily events on mood states: Relationship to global perceived stress. *Journal of Personality and Social Psychology, 75*, 1572–1585.

Weiss, H.M. & Cropanzano, R. (1996). Affective events theory: A theoretical discussion of the structure, causes, and consequences of affective experiences at work. *Research in Organizational Behavior, 18*, 1–74.

Weiss, H.M., Nicholas, J.P., & Daus, C.S. (1999). An examination of the joint effects of affective experiences and job beliefs on job satisfaction and variations in affective experiences over time. *Organizational Behavior and Human Decision Processes, 78*, 1–24.

Wheeler, L. & Reis, H.T. (1991). Self-recording of everyday life events: Origins, types, and uses. *Journal of Personality, 59*, 339–354.

8 Reconstruction Methods

Using Episodic Memory Traces to Capture Experiences at Work Efficiently

Guido Hertel and Christian Stamov-Roßnagel

For many years, job-related experiences have been predominantly captured with aggregate ratings, which reflect general differences *between* individuals. In the last years, however, work and organizational psychologists have become increasingly interested in momentary feelings and thoughts "in situ" or "on the job" that vary *within* individuals across time and different job situations (Roe, 2008). In fact, this growing interest in within-person differences is one of the major paradigmatic trends today in work and organizational psychology. This new perspective requires detailed measures of subjective experiences at work which reflect workers' feelings and thoughts *while* working on their jobs; these measures are often described as *specific* or *experience-based* (e.g. Csikszentmihalyi & LeFevre, 1989; Hormuth, 1986).

Apart from yielding more detailed data, experienced-based measures systematically diverge from global or attitudinal rating scales, as has been initially shown both in non-work contexts (e.g. Schwarz *et al.*, 2009) and in work contexts (e.g. Fisher, 2002; Ilies & Judge, 2004). For instance, attitudinal and experience-based measures of job satisfaction have been shown to be only moderately intercorrelated and to predict different outcomes. In a study using a signal-based experience-sampling measure, Fisher (2002) found that attitudinal job satisfaction, but not experience-sampled affect, predicted turnover intention, whereas the reverse held for helping behavior. The correlations of experience-sampled affect and job satisfaction measured with a traditional global rating scale were only 0.30 and –0.29 for positive and negative affect, respectively. Similarly, Ilies and Judge (2004) found a correlation of 0.36 between an attitudinal and an experience-sampling measure of job satisfaction.

Explanations of such divergence rest on theories of recall and judgment processes. Global rating measures implicitly assume that participants recollect relevant experiences (e.g. of job satisfaction) before they aggregate these recollected experiences to an average judgment (e.g. a global job satisfaction rating). However, in addition to biases of such recall processes (e.g. memory distortions, current emotional states, overestimation of extreme experiences; see Schwarz & Strack, 1999), persons often are "cognitive misers," who simply recall complete judgments from earlier occasions instead of taking the effort to compute a new judgment (e.g. Hastie & Park, 1986; Hertel & Bless, 2000). These recalled global judgments (e.g. about job satisfaction) often do not overlap with momentary experiences. Therefore, methods that reflect momentary experiences more directly are important complements of – or even alternatives to – global measures, depending on the focused research question.

In the last 25 years, various methods have been developed to capture momentary experiences "in situ." For instance, experience-sampling techniques have been designed to measure thoughts and affect immediately when they occur (e.g. Hormuth, 1986; Csikszentmihalyi & LeFevre, 1989; Grandey et al., 2002; see Dimotakis & Ilies, this volume). In a similar way, diary methods have been introduced to picture the ups and downs of individuals' experiences in different settings (e.g. Ohly et al., 2010; see also, Binnewies & Sonnentag, this volume). Although both approaches have provided important research results, they are relatively invasive and time-consuming, which limits their use, particularly in work settings. Moreover, with these approaches, it is difficult to address job events that are rare or hard to predict (e.g. conflicts with customers or supervisors).

In this chapter, we introduce reconstruction methods as an approach to measure momentary thoughts and feelings at work. This approach is less invasive and time-consuming than diary or event-sampling methods. At the same time, reconstruction methods enable the assessment of both general experiences at work as well as specific job events. We start by outlining the rationale of reconstruction methods, followed by a more detailed description of two variants – that is, the Day Reconstruction Method (DRM) and the Event Reconstruction Method (ERM). Next, as examples of applying reconstruction methods, we outline how research on work motivation and on innovative work behavior could benefit from using reconstruction methods, in particular from event reconstruction. In the final section, we discuss both limitations of reconstruction methods as well as a potential combination of reconstruction methods with other assessment approaches.

The Rationale of Reconstruction Methods

The general idea of reconstruction methods is to use episodic memory traces in order to access momentary experiences without interfering with a person's ongoing activities (see Kahneman et al., 2004a). Participants are instructed to vividly re-experience recent episodes, focusing on *what* exactly has happened rather than *why* things have happened. This vivid re-experience of specific episodes re-activates thoughts and emotions people had during this episode, an effect that is often utilized as mood induction technique (e.g. descriptions of a happy or sad life event; cf. Bless et al., 1990; Schwarz & Clore, 1983). For the re-experiencing to come as close as possible to the original experience, participants are asked a series of specific questions about the target episode (see Appendix for an example). These questions serve as recall cues that aim to re-instantiate as many aspects in memory as possible, thereby allowing access to episodic memory traces (Robinson & Clore, 2002). In contrast to semantic memory, episodic memory includes direct access to thoughts or feelings during the concrete episode. After re-experiencing a specific episode or event, participants are asked to assess their thoughts and feelings on rating scales, just like they would in an experience-sampling study.

Reconstruction methods come in whenever the accuracy of experience sampling is needed and traditional experience sampling is not feasible. Although a large variety of traditional experience-sampling options is available, ranging from paper-based diaries to smartphone solutions (e.g. Bolger *et al.*, 2003; Christensen *et al.*, 2003; Klumb *et al.*, 2009; Raento *et al.*, 2009), we have four occasions in mind when reconstruction methods might be most useful. First, and most important, traditional experience sampling can be invasive and interfere with regular job duties. This might, for instance, be a problem in time-pressured jobs, such as production-line jobs. Even if workers agreed to fill out measures under these circumstances, they might experience additional pressure from this task, which might in turn bias their affect ratings. In a similar way, in more complex jobs (e.g. R&D positions), having to stop working in order to rate momentary experiences might alter the way work tasks are carried out and therefore also influence the affect ratings. Second and related, experience sampling can be quite cumbersome when high sampling frequencies are needed, requiring high participant commitment to avoid substantial drop-out (e.g. Stone *et al.*, 2002). Third, experience-sampling methods may be difficult to implement in large samples if they rely on smartphones, handheld computers, or paper-and-pencil questionnaires, if only for budget constraints. Finally, given that traditional experience sampling usually collects job experiences randomly, it is difficult to capture specific and rare job events, such as conflicts with supervisors or customers or positive feedback by colleagues.

Reconstruction methods can be an elegant way of addressing these issues because they blend near-experience sampling accuracy with global measure ease of use. Global measures capture *memories of affect*, rather than the momentary experience of affect. Reconstruction methods, in contrast, *make affect re-happen* in order to capture it. An obvious benefit of reconstruction methods, and the main difference from experience-sampling techniques, is that momentary thoughts and feelings are assessed in a post-hoc fashion. This greatly facilitates participating in a study without interfering with participants' ongoing activities (e.g. at work). Reconstruction thus grants "near real-time," non-invasive access to momentary thoughts and feelings. Also, no costly devices are needed as most data can be collected with traditional questionnaires, paper-and-pencil as well as online surveys. In this regard, reconstruction methods are similar to traditional attitudinal measures, meeting with participants' expectations of what surveys "usually are like," which, if at all, influences participation positively. Finally, reconstruction methods can address very specific job events, as will be described in more detail below.

Two variants of reconstruction methods have been developed to date, which differ in the duration and recency of their reference period, and thus their applications. We describe these variants, the day reconstruction and event reconstruction methods, in detail in the following section.

The Day Reconstruction Method

The *Day Reconstruction Method* (DRM) was introduced by Kahneman *et al.* (2004a). It combines elements of experience sampling and diary methods, and is designed specifically (but not exclusively) to facilitate accurate emotional recall. As a first step, participants produce a diary comprising a sequence of episodes to re-instantiate the previous day into working memory. Such episodic re-instantiation facilitates retrieval from autobiographical memory and attenuates biases commonly observed in retrospective reports (e.g. Robinson & Clore, 2002; Schwarz & Oyserman, 2001). These initial diaries are confidential and allow participants to use idiosyncratic notes, including details they may not want to share. Participants then draw on their confidential diaries to reconstruct the previous day in terms of the research question at hand. They complete a structured (usually self-administered) questionnaire asking them to describe key features of the episodes in the diaries, including (1) when the episode began and ended, (2) what they were doing (by selecting activities from a provided list), (3) where they were, (4) whom they were interacting with, and (5) how they felt on a variety of affect dimensions. Participants usually report the intensity of their momentary experiences "in situ" on a scale (e.g. from 0 "Not at all" to 6 "Very much"). Affect categories are specified by descriptors, mostly mood adjectives (for a detailed documentation of the DRM instrument, see Kahneman *et al.*, 2004b).

According to initial studies, participants bring up 14 episodes per day on average and take between 45 and 75 minutes to complete all materials (Kahneman *et al.*, 2004b). Compared to concurrent experience-sampling methods, the DRM requires less time and does not disturb everyday activities. Compared to traditional diary methods, the DRM focuses more explicitly on experiences "in situ" by activating episodic memory traces with a specific instruction. While traditional diary methods merely capture memories of events, reconstruction methods try to make events *re-happen* in order to capture cognition and affect during these events.

Using the DRM as a measure of subjective well-being, Kahneman *et al.* (2004a) demonstrated that the DRM leads to very similar results as traditional but more costly experience-sampling methods, despite its reliance on "post-hoc" memory processes. For instance, in a study with 909 working women, Kahneman *et al.* (2004a) observed that hourly variation in ratings of "being tired" in the DRM were very similar to ratings from an independent experience-sampling study. For instance, both studies showed tiredness to reach a minimum around noon. Moreover, the incidence of negative emotions (e.g. "angry," "hostile") was relatively rare in both studies as compared to positive emotions (e.g. "happy").

From the perspective of research in work contexts, the DRM has several advantages over traditional experience sampling in terms of participant burden and of interference with work behaviors. Yet, with completion times of up to 75 minutes, the DRM is still time-consuming for regular employee surveys, and not very different from traditional diary methods (see Binnewies & Sonnentag, this volume). Moreover, events that do not occur on a daily basis are difficult to address with the DRM. A solution to these problems is provided in the Event Reconstruction

Method (ERM); a method that originally was also envisioned by Kahneman et al. (2004a).

The Event Reconstruction Method

The ERM focuses on the most recent occurrence of specific, discrete events (e.g. interaction with customers, conversation with the supervisor), rather than on an entire day (Grube et al., 2008). Like the DRM, the ERM is non-invasive as events are reconstructed post-hoc. Also, the ERM rests on the same cognitive principles and is intended to systematically access workers' *episodic* memory of specific work events by guided re-experience. The context of the event in focus (e.g. "Your latest interaction with a customer") is evoked in the ERM by recall cues ("Where were you?", "Who else was there with you?", etc.) that have been shown to be effective in recalling daily life events (Wagenaar, 1986). Beyond facilitating access to episodic memory, this technique helps to minimize recall errors and biases. Limiting reconstruction to a short and recent reference period further increases the probability of precise recall (Schwarz & Oyserman, 2001). Finally, describing how the events evolved instead of explaining why things happened facilitates the re-experience of affect and emotions (see Appendix for an example instruction of the ERM). In addition to single job events, the ERM can be used to look at several job events, allowing for within-person comparisons.

Initial research (Grube et al., 2008) yielded two important findings. First, ERM ratings of job satisfaction were distinct from attitudinal job satisfaction. Grube et al. (2008) reported a correlation of 0.34 between attitudinal and experience-based job satisfaction, dropping to 0.01 after controlling for affect (see also Rauschenbach & Hertel, 2011, for similar data for strain measurements). Second, this ERM study yielded virtually the same data patterns as an earlier study using traditional experience sampling (Fisher, 2002). Similar to Fisher (2002), Grube et al. (2008) found that more general and strategic job concerns, such as turnover intentions, were more strongly related to attitudinal job satisfaction. However, experience-based job satisfaction turned out as a better predictor of more spontaneous behavior at work, such as helping. Moreover, multilevel analyses showed that about 75 percent of the variance in ERM affect and ERM job satisfaction ratings was within-person variance, suggesting that the ERM is a sensitive instrument to measure intra-individual differences.

Comparing Day Reconstruction and Event Reconstruction Methods

Very little research has compared the DRM and ERM directly. The evidence available to date suggests, however, that both methods yield converging results. Schwarz, Kahneman, and Xu (2009) report a comparison of affect ratings for a set of 14 daily activities as diverse as commuting, child care, housework, relaxing, watching TV, or work. With the exception of three activities (commuting from work, computer work, and housework), DRM and ERM-based affect ratings were virtually identical. Although the differences between DRM and ERM clearly await further research, the following criteria might provide initial guidance for the selection of the type of reconstruction method.

By making participants re-experience the job events in focus, both reconstruction methods allow for reliable answers to questions about workers' feelings and thoughts during specific job events. With its focus on entire days, the day reconstruction method is of a similar nature as diary methods and experience sampling. Day reconstruction allows for assessing the time course of, for instance, work-related stress during an average working day. The DRM might therefore be a good choice whenever time-course data are required and traditional experience sampling is not an option. The ERM, on the other hand, focuses on specific events, offering the opportunity to examine rather infrequent events that may not be typical of the average working day but have high impact on behavioral outcomes (e.g. conflicts with a superior). As the work events in question may be chosen by the participant, the ERM is particularly suitable to assess *rare* job events that are difficult to target with random experience-sampling methods or the DRM.

Using Reconstruction Methods in Work and Organizational Psychology Research

Reconstruction methods are a new development and have been rarely adopted in work and organizational psychology yet. In their seminal DRM study, Kahneman *et al.* (2004a) collected DRM and attitudinal data on satisfaction with one's work as a function of job characteristics as diverse as, for instance, required qualifications, social contact at work, or time pressure. Consistent with the findings of divergence between attitudinal and experience-based measures, they found that DRM measures of affect related more strongly than attitudinal job satisfaction to context variables (time pressure, the opportunity to chat with co-workers, etc.). In a similar way, the ERM has been applied successfully in initial studies on global and experience-based job satisfaction (e.g. Grube *et al.*, 2008) and perceived strain at work (Rauschenbach & Hertel, 2011). Moreover, Hertel, Grube, Schroer, and Hentzschel (2007) explored whether experience-based affect at work and global job satisfaction are more aligned for older as compared to younger workers. This hypothesis was derived from Socioemotional Selectivity Theory (Carstensen, 2006), which states that aging and related decreases of future (work) time perspective lead to higher values for positive affective experiences. In contrast, concerns for future prospects, such as learning goals and career opportunities, should decrease with age and fewer years of expected future (work) time. Therefore, older workers' overall job satisfaction should be more strongly determined by their momentary affect at work, whereas younger workers' overall job satisfaction should also include prospects of future gains and opportunities. In line with this hypothesis, convergence of global and experience-based judgments was higher for older than for younger workers.

Other applications of the ERM have yet to be explored. Next, we outline potential benefits of reconstruction methods in research on work motivation and innovative work behavior as examples for applying ERM to a wider range of topics.

Work Motivation

Demographic change has refueled research interest in work motivation as the successful retention of older workers becomes crucial and fewer young workers enter the workforce (e.g. Alley & Crimmins, 2007). This requires a profound understanding of age-related changes in work motivation, defined as the set of "energetic forces that . . . determine . . . form, direction, intensity, and duration of work-related behaviors" (Pinder, 1998, p. 11). At least two things make work motivation a promising topic for ERM research.

First, several researchers have called for research on work motivation on a more momentary level, as opposed to motivation on a more attitudinal level (Weiss *et al.*, 2005; Kanfer, 2009). Consistent with these perspectives, Stamov-Roßnagel and Hertel (2010) argued that discrete work tasks rather than the entire job are the most useful level of analysis when assessing age differences in motivation. Tasks are defined by a work-related goal and are a regular part of one's work. Any one worker usually performs a variety of tasks during his or her daily work. Tasks vary in the level of demands they place on that worker – and so does the level of motivation for each of the tasks.

Second, variations in motivation arise as a result of selection, optimization, and compensation processes (SOC; Baltes & Baltes, 1990) so that increased motivation in some tasks might compensate for motivation decline in other tasks (e.g. Stamov-Roßnagel & Hertel, 2010). Compensation is functional for positive affect regulation that gains importance as people grow older (Carstensen, 2006). Work tasks might be classified as predominantly supporting, for instance, worker's information-related goals (e.g. acquiring new skills or knowledge) or emotion-related goals (e.g. acting as a mentor). As a consequence of age-related shifts in goal priorities, older workers would be expected to show higher levels of motivation for emotion-related tasks, relative to information-related tasks. Consistent with these propositions, Grube and Hertel (2011) found that older workers place higher value on generativity values (helping others, passing on knowledge, etc.), whereas younger workers judge knowledge acquisition as more important. Moreover, an exploratory study (Stamov-Roßnagel *et al.*, 2009) showed that workers in the age group 51–65 years showed higher motivation for emotion-related tasks than for information-related tasks, while there was no task difference for younger workers. In all age groups, higher levels of motivation were associated with higher levels of job satisfaction and positive affect, and with lower levels of negative affect. Age moderated this motivation–affect link so that the association between motivation and affect became stronger with age.

Reconstruction methods provide interesting opportunities for further research along these lines. In a traditional questionnaire approach, workers would rate their level of motivation per task type (emotion-related tasks, information-related tasks, etc.) and complete an overall measure of work-related affect. In such an approach, it would be difficult to assess affect separately for different task types. Using the ERM, participants would go back to a specific event when s/he was working on the task, re-instantiate this event into working memory, and indicate current feelings and affect. Thus, participants would get as close as possible to their affective experience during the task type in question without interfering with their work. An ERM approach would furthermore accommodate the fact that a worker might only work on a subset of tasks her/his job comprises on any one day. Therefore, s/he would be instructed separately for each task type in question to recall the most recent opportunity of working on this task type.

Innovative Work Behavior

Innovative work behavior is another important area of research that might benefit from reconstruction methods. Innovative work behavior rests on creativity – that is, the generation of ideas, insights, or problem solutions that are novel and potentially useful (e.g. Amabile, 1983). It comprises the intentional introduction and application within a role, group, or organization of ideas, processes, products, or procedures that are new to the relevant unit of adoption and designed to significantly benefit the individual, the work team, or the organization (West & Farr, 1990). In many jobs, innovative work behavior is part of everyday performance and may be achieved by workers on any organizational level. For instance, recent research has investigated innovative work behavior in nurses (Ohly *et al.*, 2006), service technicians (Gilson *et al.*, 2005), and machine operators (Axtell *et al.*, 2000).

Similar to work motivation, there are two primary reasons why innovative work behavior could fruitfully be studied with reconstruction methods. First, mood and affect are important predictors of creativity, but the exact nature of the mood–creativity relationship is not yet well understood (Baas *et al.*, 2008). Some studies yielded evidence of greater creativity in positive mood (see Ashby *et al.*, 1999), others found that negative mood promotes creative performance (e.g. Adaman & Blaney, 1995; Carlsson *et al.*, 2000; Clapham, 2001); still others show creativity to be rather impeded by negative affect (e.g. Mikulincer *et al.*, 1990; Vosburg, 1998). Second, most of the aforementioned research is laboratory research for which implications for work settings have not been established. Almost none of the studies that did focus on work settings, in turn, considered affect.

The benefits of a reconstruction approach for innovative work behavior, and of the ERM in particular, are similar to those described for work motivation. Obviously, the event to reconstruct would be a recent occasion when a worker was involved in any of the phases of an innovation (cf. Daniels, this volume). First of all, having participants re-experience the episode could yield close insight into the role of mood and affect in that situation. In addition, the role of other proximal contingencies (e.g. task characteristics, concrete leadership behaviors) could be investigated accurately. More generally, and comparable to work motivation, the ERM can be an important tool in teasing apart the relative roles of more distal determinants (e.g. personality characteristics, work attitudes) and more proximal variables (e.g. mood, social interaction). As compared to experience-sampling methods that might interfere with ongoing work activities, reconstruction would be more easily applicable. Diary methods, on the other hand, would not create much of an interference problem but might not address the momentary work experiences as focused as the guided retrieval process in reconstruction methods. Moreover, repeated measurements (same type of event or different types) over a longer period of time might be an issue both in terms of companies' resistance to granting data access and in terms of participant commitment. In such cases, event reconstruction methods can be a promising solution.

Applications, Limitations, and Future Research Directions

One promising application of reconstruction methods is their systematic combination with attitudinal measures to explore work-related judgments. We have outlined above that attitudinal and experience-based measures of job satisfaction are differentially related to outcomes such as turnover intention and helping behavior (e.g. Fisher, 2002; Grube et al., 2008). Future research could use designs that combine attitudinal and experience-based measures to explore other sets of outcome variables and determine whether global measures are best seen as predictors of more strategic and distal outcomes (e.g. personnel turnover), whereas experience-based measures are suitable for more proximal outcomes, such as work-related stress or health behaviors. Interesting in this regard are age-related differences. Initial evidence suggests that the contribution of momentary affect to global job satisfaction covaries with age (Hertel et al., 2007). Future studies might address the more general issue of whether experience-based and global measures are differentially aligned as a function of workers' age.

Beyond research, reconstruction methods have interesting application potentials, for instance, when used as part of training evaluations or organizational development interventions. In particular, if interventions address the daily experience of workers (e.g. health management), experience-based measures seem to be more appropriate than global assessments of stress, satisfaction, anger, frustration, etc. While the latter are often biased by general beliefs and self-presentation concerns, the former might be more valid indicators of success or failure of organizational training and interventions. Also, the ERM can show whether trained skills are being used even if the application of skills is rare. This can hardly be addressed with standard questionnaire-based training evaluation. Of course, these assumptions need to be tested empirically, most desirably in longitudinal designs. However, we are optimistic that the high efficiency and low invasiveness of reconstruction methods facilitate their use for evaluation of applied trainings and HR interventions.

When using reconstruction methods, it is noteworthy that autobiographical memory processes are not identical for all workers. For instance, Levine, Svoboda, Hay, Winocur, and Moscovitch (2002) found that older adults produced fewer internal details (e.g. who, what, when, and where details) and more external details (e.g. semantic information, other external events, repetitions) than did younger adults when recalling past autobiographical events (see also Addis et al., 2008). These findings suggest that cognitive aging adversely affects episodic recall accuracy. This has implications for reconstruction-based studies with older workers since the quality of reconstruction data depends on detailed, vivid re-instantiations of the days or events to reconstruct.

Affective memory biases are a second important age difference. Older adults tend to orient away from negative stimuli and toward positive stimuli. As a consequence, recall of negative information might be reduced (Gruhn *et al.*, 2005) and/or memory for positive information might be enhanced (Mather & Carstensen, 2005). In a recent diary study on younger (< 37 years of age) and older (> 65 years of age) participants, Ready, Weinberger, and Jones (2007) asked participants to report their daily affect at the end of every day. In addition, participants at the end of the study recalled their affect over varying time-frames within the four-week diary period (i.e. past few days, past week, past month). Accuracy of recall was assessed by comparing retrospective reports to the diary ratings. The authors hypothesized that older adults would recall recent experiences as more positive and less negative than had actually been reported in their daily diaries. Indeed, recall bias differed as a function of participant age and of the reference period. Younger adults were significantly more accurate than older adults for positive affect over *the past few days*, while age-group differences disappeared for ratings on the past week or the past month. Moreover, older adults tended to overestimate positive affect more than younger adults. While the age-related reduction of recall specificity and the increase of affective bias do not invalidate data from reconstruction methods, it is important to take these into account in future research designs.

Generally speaking, since recall is far more constrained than the typical recall of events in autobiographical memory research, the influence of bias should be much more limited than in more narrative recall. Moreover, reconstruction-based research, as well as applications of reconstruction methods in HR settings (e.g. diagnostic steps in consulting or coaching programs, evaluation of HR interventions, etc.), focuses on very recent events. Ideally, reference periods include only a few days, although future research will have to determine what actually counts as "recent" if bias is to be minimized (Schwarz *et al.*, 2009). These findings on specificity and bias emphasize the importance of thoroughly re-instantiating an event into working memory. As a general rule, bias and specificity reduction effects will be more limited when more cues are utilized to re-instantiate a given event. Moreover, in field research projects, the time constraints often imposed by companies should not lead to a reduction in the number of recall cues; in studies comprising the reconstruction of several events, it might be a better option to drop an entire event, rather than to reduce the number of cues per event.

Concluding Remarks

We have presented reconstruction methods as a relatively new alternative to obtain efficient and valid access to persons' momentary affect and cognitions during work settings. It is important to note that reconstruction methods should be viewed as an extension of our repertoire of methods, rather than as an alternative to existing techniques. One way to structure the relationship between the different methods discussed is that of a spectrum with experience sampling on the one end and global or attitudinal measures on the other end. Experience sampling perhaps provides the closest possible access to momentary experiences, while global or attitudinal scales capture overarching aggregated constructs. Reconstruction methods are, similar to diary methods, aimed at the experience-sampling side and are particularly useful when an efficient procedure is warranted that enables focused access to work-related experiences based on a guided retrieval process. Moreover, there are no principal constraints to combine reconstruction approaches with other methods. For instance, the ERM might be part of a diary-type study with five consecutive questionnaires over a working week focusing on specific work events in each working day. In any case, utilizing current research results on memory and retrieval processes is a promising avenue for the further refinement of our measures to assess momentary and ongoing experiences at work.

Appendix

Sample instruction for the Event Reconstruction Method (ERM) adapted from Rauschenbach and Hertel (2011)

Dear participant, we would like to ask you now to recall specific job events from your last work days. Please try to reconstruct each of these job events as vividly as possible in your memory. It is important that you recall the specific job event in the exact way it happened.

When you have recalled a specific job event, we would like to know what you felt and what you thought during this specific event. Thus, for each of the recalled job events, we will ask a few questions on what you were doing, and what you were feeling and thinking at that time.

Please recall now a job event that was particularly stressful for you. Please recall this job event now into your memory, and remember who was with you, what exactly you were doing, and what you were feeling and thinking in this situation. Please take a few moments to put yourself in this situation again.

Please answer now the following scales . . .

References

Adaman, J.E. & Blaney, P.H. (1995). The effects of musical mood induction on creativity. *Journal of Creative Behavior, 29*, 95–108.

Addis, D.R., Wong, A.T., & Schacter, D.L. (2008). Age-related changes in the episodic simulation of future events. *Psychological Science, 19*, 33–41.

Alley, D. & Crimmins, E. (2007). The demography of aging and work. In K.S. Shultz & G.A. Adams (Eds), *Aging and work in the 21st century* (pp. 7–24). Mahwah, New Jersey: Lawrence Erlbaum Associates.

Amabile, T.M. (1983). The social psychology of creativity: A componential conceptualization. *Journal of Personality and Social Psychology, 45*, 357–376.

Ashby, F.G., Isen, A.M., & Turken, A.U. (1999). A neuropsychological theory of positive affect and its influence on cognition. *Psychological Review, 106*, 529–550.

Axtell, C.M., Holman, D.J., Unsworth, K.L., Wall, T.D., & Waterson, P.E. (2000). Shopfloor innovation: Facilitating the suggestion and implementation of ideas. *Journal of Occupational and Organizational Psychology, 73*, 265–285.

Baas, M., De Dreu, C.K.W., & Nijstad, B.A. (2008). A meta-analysis of 25 years of mood–creativity research: Hedonic tone, activation, or regulatory focus? *Psychological Bulletin, 134*, 779–806.

Baltes, P.B. & Baltes, M.M. (1990). Psychological perspectives on successful aging: The model of selective optimization with compensation. In P.B. Baltes & M.M. Baltes (Eds), *Successful aging: Perspectives from the behavioral sciences* (pp. 1–34). New York: Cambridge University Press.

Bless, H., Bohner, G., Schwarz, N., & Strack, F. (1990). Mood and persuasion: A cognitive response analysis. *Personality and Social Psychology Bulletin, 16*, 331–345.

Bolger, N., Davis, A., & Rafaeli, E. (2003). Diary methods: Capturing life as it is lived. *Annual Review of Psychology, 54*, 579–616.

Carlsson, I., Wendt, P.E., & Risberg, J. (2000). On the neurobiology of creativity. Differences in frontal activity between high and low creative subjects. *Neuropsychologia, 38*, 873–885.

Carstensen, L.L. (2006). The influence of a sense of time on human development. *Science, 312*, 1912–1915.

Christensen, T.C., Barrett, L.F., Bliss-Moreau, E., Lebo, K., & Kaschub, C. (2003). A practical guide to experience-sampling procedures. *Journal of Happiness Studies, 4*, 53–78.

Clapham, M.M. (2001). The effects of affect manipulation and information exposure on divergent thinking. *Creativity Research Journal, 13*, 335–350.

Csikszentmihalyi, M. & LeFevre, J. (1989). Optimal experience in work and leisure. *Journal of Personality and Social Psychology, 56*, 815–822.

Fisher, C.D. (2002). Antecedents and consequences of real-time affective reactions at work. *Motivation and Emotion, 26*, 3–30.

Gilson, L.L., Mathieu, J.E., Shalley, C.E., & Ruddy, T.M. (2005) Creativity and standardization: Complementary or conflicting drivers of team effectiveness? *Academy Of Management Journal, 48*, 521–531.

Grandey, A.A., Tam, A.P., & Brauburger, A.L. (2002). Affective states and traits in the workplace: Diary and survey data from young workers. *Motivation and Emotion, 26*, 31–55.

Grube, A. & Hertel, G. (2011). *Age differences in work values and related goal orientation.* Manuscript under editorial review.

Grube, A., Schroer, J., Hentzschel, C., & Hertel, G. (2008). The Event Reconstruction Method: An efficient measure of experience-based job satisfaction. *Journal of Occupational and Organizational Psychology, 81*, 669–689.

Gruhn, D., Smith, J., & Baltes, P.B. (2005). No aging bias favoring memory for positive material: Evidence from a heterogeneity–homogeneity list paradigm using emotionally toned words. *Psychology and Aging, 20*, 579–588.

Hastie, R. & Park, B. (1986). The relationship between memory and judgment depends on whether the judgment task is memory-based or on-line. *Psychological Review, 93*, 258–268.

Hertel, G. & Bless, H. (2000). 'On-line' und erinnerungsgestützte Urteilsbildung: Auslösefaktoren und empirische Unterscheidungsmöglichkeiten ['On-line' versus memory-based judgments: Triggering conditions and empirical methods for differentiation]. *Psychologische Rundschau, 51*, 19–28.

Hertel, G., Grube, A., Schroer, J., & Hentzschel, C. (2007). *Age differences in global and experience-based job satisfaction ratings.* Unpublished data, University of Würzburg.

Hormuth, S.E. (1986). The sampling of experiences in situ. *Journal of Personality, 54*, 262–293.

Ilies, R. & Judge, T.A. (2004). An experience-sampling measure of job satisfaction and its relationships with affectivity, mood at work, job beliefs, and general job satisfaction. *European Journal of Work and Organizational Psychology, 13*, 367–389.

Kahneman, D., Krueger, A.B., Schkade, D.A., Schwarz, N., & Stone, A.A. (2004a). A survey method for characterizing daily life experience: The day reconstruction method. *Science, 306*, 1776–1780.

Kahneman, D., Krueger, A.B., Schkade, D.A., Schwarz, N., & Stone, A.A. (2004b). The Day Reconstruction Method (DRM): Instrument Documentation. http://sitemaker.umich.edu/norbert.schwarz/files/drm_documentation_july_2004.pdf.

Kanfer, R. (2009). Work motivation: Identifying use-inspired research directions. *Industrial and Organizational Psychology, 2*, 77–93.

Klumb, P., Elfering, A., & Herre, C. (2009). Ambulatory assessment in industrial/organizational psychology: Fruitful examples and methodological issues. *European Psychologist, 14*, 120–131.

Levine, B., Svoboda, E., Hay, J.F., Winocur, G., & Moscovitch, M. (2002). Aging and autobiographical memory: Dissociating episodic from semantic retrieval. *Psychology and Aging, 17*, 677–689.

Mather, M. & Carstensen, L.L. (2005). Aging and motivated cognition: The positivity effect in attention and memory. *Trends in Cognitive Science, 9*, 496–502.

Mikulincer, M., Kedem, P., & Paz, D. (1990). Anxiety and categorization – 1. The structure and boundaries of mental categories. *Personality and Individual Differences, 11*, 805–814.

Ohly, S., Sonnentag, S., & Pluntke, F. (2006). Routinization, work characteristics and their relationships with creative and proactive behaviors. *Journal of Organizational Behavior, 27*, 257–279.

Ohly, S., Sonnentag, S., Niessen, C., & Zapf, D. (2010). Diary studies in organizational research. *Journal of Personnel Psychology, 9*, 79–93.

Pinder, C.C. (1998). *Work motivation in organizational behavior.* Upper Saddle River, NJ: Prentice Hall.

Raento, M., Oulasvirta, A., & Eagle, N. (2009). Smartphones: An emerging tool for social scientists. *Sociological Methods & Research, 37*, 426–454.

Rauschenbach, C. & Hertel, G. (2011). Age differences in strain and emotional reactivity to stressors in professional careers. *Stress and Health, 27*, e48–e60.

Ready, R.E., Weinberger, M.I., & Jones, K.M. (2007). How happy have you felt lately? Two diary studies of emotion recall in older and younger adults. *Cognition and Emotion, 21*, 728–757.

Robinson, M.D. & Clore, G.L. (2002). Belief and feeling: Evidence for an accessibility model of emotional self-report. *Psychological Bulletin, 128*, 934–960.

Roe, R.A. (2008). Time in applied psychology. The study of "what happens" rather than "what is". *European Psychologist, 13*, 37–52.

Schwarz, N. & Clore, G.L. (1983). Mood, misattribution, and judgments of well-being: Informative and directive functions of affective states. *Journal of Personality and Social Psychology, 45*, 513–523.

Schwarz, N. & Oyserman, D. (2001). Asking questions about behavior: Cognition, communication, and questionnaire construction. *American Journal of Evaluation, 22*, 127–160.

Schwarz, N. & Strack, F. (1999). Reports of subjective well-being: Judgmental processes and their methodological implications. In D. Kahneman, E. Diener, & N. Schwarz (Eds), *Well-being: The foundations of hedonic psychology* (pp. 61–84). New York: Sage

Schwarz, N., Kahneman, D., & Xu, J. (2009). Global and episodic reports of hedonic experience. In R. Belli, D. Alwin, & F. Stafford (Eds), *Using calendar and diary methods in life events research* (pp. 157–174). Newbury Park, CA: Sage.

Stamov-Roßnagel, C. & Hertel, G. (2010). Older workers' motivation: Against the myth of general decline. *Management Decision, 48*, 894–906.

Stamov-Roßnagel, C., Biemann, T., & Kinscher, M. (2009). Wege aus dem Teufelskreis [Ways out of the vicious circle]. *Personal, 61*, 48–50.

Stone, A.A., Shiffman, S., Schwartz, J.E., Broderick, J.E., & Hufford, M.R. (2002). Patient non-compliance with paper diaries. *British Medical Journal, 324*, 1193–1194.

Vosburg, S.K. (1998). The effects of positive and negative mood on divergent-thinking performance. *Creativity Research Journal, 11*, 165–172.

Wagenaar, W.A. (1986). My memory: A study of autobiographical memory over six years. *Cognitive Psychology, 18*, 225–252.

Weiss, H.M., Ashkanasy, N.M., & Beal, D.J. (2005). Attentional and regulatory mechanisms of momentary work motivation and performance. In J.P. Forgas, K.D. Williams, & S.M. Laham (Eds), *Social motivation: Conscious and unconscious processes* (pp. 314–331). New York, NY: Cambridge University Press.

West, M.A. & Farr, J.L. (1990). Innovation at work. In M.A. West & J.L. Farr (Eds), *Innovation and creativity at work: Psychological and organizational strategies*. Chichester: Wiley.

9 Latent Growth Modeling Applied to Diary Data
The Trajectory of Vigor Across a Working Week as an Illustrative Example

Sven Gross, Laurenz L. Meier, and Norbert K. Semmer

Emma and Harry both work in the service sector. They have normal jobs and spend five days a week, from Monday to Friday, at their workplace. It is Monday morning and they are about to start their working week. Emma has fully recovered from the weekend and, in light of the forthcoming interesting day at work, feels vigorous and lively. This is also true for Harry, but during the course of the week, he becomes increasingly less vigorous and he reaches a low in terms of energy on Wednesday. Thursday morning, however, is a turning point for Harry. In sight of the weekend, he starts to feel more vigorous again. His cheerfulness and spirits rise as he eagerly awaits the hockey game on Saturday night. His vigorous feelings steadily increase and reach a peak on Sunday. While Harry evinces a drop in vigor across his working week, Emma does not. In contrast, her energetic mood increases slightly as the week proceeds. The inspiring and supportive team at work makes her feel increasingly more energetic as the days pass. Furthermore, she looks forward to hiking with her friends on the upcoming weekend.

The example of Emma and Harry depicts two possible patterns of change with regard to vigor across a working week. This example suggests that for both Emma and Harry, intra-individual variability in vigor is time-structured, but that they also differ in their progress across the week: Harry's vigor has a U-shaped pattern, whereas Emma's follows a linear pattern. One might ask whether a typical pattern of change with regard to vigor exists. Supervisors, for instance, could use this knowledge to determine how the workload should be structured in order to maintain stable levels of performance. Alternatively, this information could be used to gauge when would be best to express esteem for employee motivation. Furthermore, one might ask why Emma and Harry differ in their patterns. What are the personal and situational factors explaining different patterns of change across the week? Knowledge about differences in employees' vigor trajectories could also be beneficial for daily "micro-interventions." Conceptually, such questions refer to the issue of time-structured intra-individual variability (Ram & Gerstorf, 2009) and of inter-individual differences in these intra-individual processes.

These questions can be tackled using latent growth models[1] (LGMs; Bollen & Curran, 2006; Singer & Willet, 2003). LGMs provide a potentially powerful approach to longitudinal data requiring analysis of changes, including both decreases and increases, in a latent construct across time. The basic idea of LGMs is that a set of repeated measures is systematically related to time. For instance, a positive linear growth in vigor would mean that vigor increases systematically from day to day for an average individual. In contrast to traditional methods such as ANOVA or ordinary least square (OLS) regressions, LGMs estimate growth curves that are allowed to vary across individuals. Thus, variance in the estimated growth curves is regarded as meaningful variance (i.e. differences in growth between individuals) rather than error variance. Hence, LGMs simultaneously take into account the form (e.g. linear, curvilinear) and rate of the change, as well as interindividual differences in the rate of change. LGMing has a number of additional advantages, such as its increased statistical power, compared to traditional methods (see McArdle, 2009).

The idea of growth is incorporated into various theoretical frameworks in industrial and organizational (I/O) psychology. For instance, health problems are thought to develop as a result of stressors at work (Semmer *et al.*, 2005). Motivation is thought to grow because of appropriate resources at work (Schaufeli & Bakker, 2010). Intellectual flexibility is thought to increase with fewer job restrictions (Schooler *et al.*, 1999), while conflicts are thought to escalate due to inappropriate conflict management (De Dreu, 2005). This suggests a clear need to study time-structured change (e.g. development) in the field of industrial/organizational psychology (I/O) psychology. Despite this need, it has rarely been investigated how relevant variables develop over time and what the important factors are that initiate or alter development.

A review of the literature regarding I/O psychology reveals that very few studies have applied LGMs. We are aware of 27 such studies that have been published in peer-reviewed journals. The earliest study is by Ployhart and Hakel (1998), who investigated time-structured intra-individual variability in job performance. Later studies using LGMs touch upon a broad range of topics, including the development of attitudes and health-related variables in particular phases of an individual's working life (e.g. organizational entry; Jokisaari & Nurmi, 2009). Other studies report the effect of work stressors on the development of well-being or attitudes (Garst *et al.*, 2000; Grech *et al.*, 2009), or the effects of job resources on the development of job-related flow (Mäkikangas *et al.*, 2010).

The rather low number of studies using an LGM approach may be partly explained by the fact that the majority of studies are still cross-sectional in nature and therefore do not allow intra-individual processes to be taken into account. However, this argument does not accommodate the recently observed increase in diary studies being published (Ohly *et al.*, 2010). Diary studies are short-term longitudinal studies through which short-term growth processes can be investigated. In spite of this, LGMs are rarely applied to diary data. Most studies with a focus on growth span months or years. Therefore, they cover long-term developmental processes. However, there is evidence of relevant short-term variability that is time-structured (e.g. fatigue within and across consecutive working days; Grech *et al.*, 2009). Another reason for the low number of studies that have applied LGMs may be that researchers are not yet familiar with this rather new methodology and may not always realize that their research question could be tackled elegantly through the application of LGMs.

Taken together, LGMs are regarded as a powerful analytical framework for studying change processes. The few studies that have applied LGMs have focused on long-term developmental processes. Given this state of affairs, and the increasing interest in and availability of data to study short-term intra-individual processes, the goal of this chapter is to give a step-by-step example of the application of LGMs to diary data. Specifically, we will use the pattern of vigor across a working week as an illustrative example in order to give a non-technical introduction to LGMs within a structural equation modeling (SEM) framework. For this reason, we will briefly introduce vigor as a state concept, present our data and summarize some basic conceptual issues regarding change in relation to our example. We will continue by discussing a central prerequisite to conducting latent growth modeling (i.e. longitudinal measurement invariance) and how to test for it. We then will compute a basic LGM that captures time-dependent change in vigor across a working week. Finally, we will show, as an example, how to analyze inter-individual differences in a LGM. In this chapter, we aim to inspire other researchers to study the broad field of growth-related research questions in general and short-term growth in particular.

State Vigor

The construct of vigor has recently received a great deal of attention from various scholars, who have described it as a central facet of work engagement (Bakker *et al.*, 2008), as a multi-dimensional construct (Shraga & Shirom, 2009), or as a mood facet (Cranford *et al.*, 2006). Upon reviewing the literature, it becomes apparent that efforts have been made to relate vigor to other important constructs in the workplace. Meta-analytic results, for instance, show that vigor is related to resources at work (e.g. feedback), to a lesser extent to demands (e.g. work–family conflict), and to important outcomes such as performance (Halbesleben, 2010).

Most studies conceptualize vigor as a rather stable construct; however, vigor can also be regarded as a state concept (Cranford *et al.*, 2006). In this sense, feeling vigorous refers to a state of positive energy that, according to an interview study, lasts a few minutes to a maximum of a few days (Shraga & Shirom, 2009). The question is whether these changes in vigor are systematically related to time. More specifically, does vigor follow a certain pattern of change across a working week? Descriptive results from a recent study by Cranford *et al.* (2006) support the idea of systematic weekly changes in levels of vigor. An inspection of the average vigor trajectory of 164 graduate students (Figure 2 in Cranford *et al.*, 2006) suggests that vigor embodies a U-shaped pattern over the course of a week, in a similar way to the example of Harry. In the remainder of this chapter, we will examine whether or not such a pattern is apparent in our example data drawn from the working population.

The Example Data

For illustrative purposes, we will use data from a diary study of 116 employees (64 percent females) working in various organizations. Mean age of the participants was 34.0 ($SD = 12.7$). Before the diary study started, the participants completed a general questionnaire, including trait measures, general measures of their work situation (e.g. job resources), and demographic variables. After this, the participants were asked to fill in diaries before work, after work, and before sleeping, for two weeks, including weekends. Thus, most participants filled in three diary entries per day for 14 days. For reasons of simplicity, we will focus only on the morning diary entries from one week (seven days). In the morning diary, we included a scale to measure state vigor. This scale was developed by Cranford *et al.* (2006). It consists of three items and is based on the Profile of Mood States (McNair *et al.*, 1992). Every morning, the participants had to indicate the extent to which they felt vigorous, cheerful, and lively (1 = *not at all*; to 5 = *extremely*) at that moment in time.

Change Versus Variability

LGMs are a means by which to analyze change within individuals. Change in vigor can be analyzed using different time scales that correspond to the different conceptualizations of change in the literature. For instance, one could be interested in how trait vigor changes across the lifespan (for an analogous research question regarding self-esteem, see Orth *et al.*, 2010). However, a complementary perspective to this long-term approach (i.e. development) is the investigation of short-term, relatively rapid, and more or less reversible change processes (i.e. daily variability in energetic resources). Most diary studies focus on this kind of change. Highlighting the differentiation between these two types of change, Nesselroade (1991, p. 215) has termed the former *intra-individual change*, which is defined as "more or less enduring changes that are construed as developmental." The latter type is termed *intra-individual variability*, which refers to "relatively short-term changes that are construed as more or less reversible and that occur more rapidly than the former."

Moreover, Ram and Gerstorf (2009) suggest that intra-individual variability can be further differentiated. They highlight that there is intra-individual variability that is unstructured in relation to time. For instance, the occurrence of success at work is not usually ordered in time (i.e. it is equally likely to occur in the morning or in the afternoon, and on Monday or Friday). Ram and Gerstorf (2009, p. 779) use the term *net intra-individual variability* to refer to "short-term within-person changes that are analyzed as being unstructured in relation to time." In contrast, *time-structured intra-individual variability* is defined as "changes that are systematically ordered in time." The circadian rhythm is an example of the second kind of variability. This latter distinction is important for the purpose of this chapter. In asking whether or not there is a typical pattern of change in vigor over a working week, we are implicitly asking whether vigor follows a time-dependent pattern of change or whether variability in vigor is randomly fluctuating with regard to time. Analytically, we will answer this question by comparing different models that assume vigor to be either: (a) a construct that varies within person, while variance is treated as unrelated to time (i.e. the state model); (b) a construct consisting of a stable part (i.e. trait) and a variable part that is unrelated to time (i.e. the state-trait model); or (c) a construct with intra-individual variance that is related to time (i.e. LGMs). Before we do this, we need to discuss measurement invariance, which is an important prerequisite to modeling longitudinal data.

Importance of Measurement Invariance When Investigating Longitudinal Data

In longitudinal research, it is crucial to ensure that the same construct is measured at each point in time (i.e. measurement invariance or factorial invariance). For an unambiguous interpretation of change in a construct, this change needs to happen at the level of the construct (i.e. latent variable) and not at the level of the observed variables that measure the construct (Ferrer *et al.*, 2008). Possible threats to measurement invariance are changes regarding the interpretation of item content or a change in the level of items that cannot be explained by a change in the latent construct. For instance, the extensive repetition of measurements within a short time interval might be a cause for concern in diary studies. In response to previous assessments, participants subjectively redefine the constructs of interest so that they are no longer comparable between states.

In addition to invariance in terms of configuration (i.e. the same indicators and latent constructs must be specified at each point of measurement), three levels of factorial invariance can be distinguished (e.g. Widaman & Reise, 1997). Weak factorial invariance occurs when the factor loadings of each indicator are invariant over time. Strong factorial invariance requires, in addition to equal factor loadings, the intercept of each indicator to be invariant over time (i.e. the relative contribution of each intercept to the scale mean should be the same over time). Finally, strict factorial invariance also requires the unique variance (i.e. error variance) of each indicator to be equal over time. In practice, strict factorial invariance is unlikely to occur, and violations of this assumption can be tolerated (e.g. Sayer & Cumsille, 2001). Hence, before modeling change at the latent level, it is necessary to test for and to establish the presence of (at least) strong factorial invariance.

The Basic LGM

The general principle of an LGM is that a given set of repeatedly measured constructs is functionally related to time. The model depicted in Figure 9.1 represents a basic second-order LGM (Ferrer *et al.*, 2008; Sayer & Cumsille, 2001; for an introduction to first-order LGMs, see: Bollen & Curran, 2006). This second-order LGM consists of: (a) a measurement part (confirmatory factor analyses [CFA] for longitudinal data), where multiple observed variables (i.e. items; in this case, three items: X; Y; W) are used as indicators of a latent construct (i.e. first-order factor; f) at each measurement point; and (b) a structural part, where the growth in the latent construct over time is modeled through a second-order intercept factor (f_0) and a slope factor (f_s). Thus, the growth parameters capture time-dependent variation among the latent true scores. More specifically, the intercept represents a constant value of the construct for any given individual across time. This is apparent from the factor loadings of the intercept factor, which are fixed to 1. The latent slope factor captures the rate of change across time for any given individual. In order to estimate the intercept and slope of the growth curve, not only must the covariance structure of the data be taken into account (as in ordinary cross-lagged models, for instance), but the mean structure must be as well. This is because, in LGMs, both the relationships between variables and changes in the intercepts of the variables are of interest. The factor loadings ($\beta_1 - \beta_t$) determine the shape of the curve. For instance, if we assume that the measurement points are equally spaced (such as daily measures), and that there is consecutive linear growth from the first day onwards, the factor loadings would then have numerical values of $\beta_0 = 0$ for the first day, $\beta_1 = 1$ for the second day, $\beta_2 = 2$ for the third day, and so forth. Later in the chapter, we will discuss how non-linear (e.g. quadric) growth can be modeled. In general, thorough theoretical and empirical consideration is required concerning questions of how to incorporate time into LGMs and how to decide upon the level of complexity of the change trajectory. For an in-depth treatment of issues relating

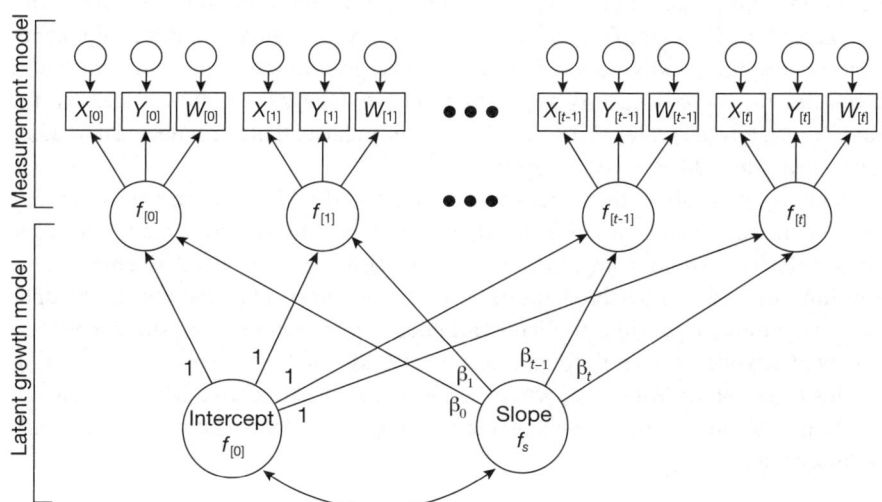

Figure 9.1 Simplified path diagram of a second-order linear LGM

Note
Latent variables are represented by circles and manifest variables by squares. Not depicted in this figure are the intercepts of the manifest and latent variables, the covariances among the same manifest variables at adjacent measurement points, and the variances of the latent variables.

to time and the complexity of LGMs, we recommend that the interested reader consult Bollen and Curran (2006), Blozis and Cho (2008), or Ram and Grimm (2007).

In order to illustrate the basic LGM shown in Figure 9.1, we will apply it to our data. We measured vigor with three items (vigorous, cheerful, and lively), which represent the manifest indicators X, Y, W in Figure 9.1. By means of CFA, these items were used to "build" a latent construct of vigor at each of the seven measurement points. The growth (i.e. time-structured intra-individual variability) of these latent true scores was then modeled through a second-order latent intercept and latent slope. For reasons of simplicity, let us assume at this stage that we specified a linear growth process as described above. The mean of the latent intercept represents the average vigor score of the sample on Monday, while the variance of the latent intercept captures the amount of inter-individual difference in vigor on Monday. The mean of the latent slope represents the average rate of change in vigor per day of the sample. A positive mean implies an increase and a negative mean a decrease over time. Finally, the variance of the latent slope represents inter-individual differences in the rate of change.

The Basic Analytical Steps When Building an LGM

Analytically, building an LGM is a three-stage procedure. First, measurement invariance is tested by fitting a CFA for longitudinal data. Second, individual growth trajectories are fitted to the latent construct, which is measured on multiple occasions. Note that, at this point, we model the within-individual aspects of the LGM, resulting in a sample-mean growth trajectory including variance components that capture inter-individual differences in the growth curve. It is imperative at this stage to correctly specify a growth trajectory that is theoretically meaningful and empirically accurate. Third, variables are introduced that are expected to predict inter-individual differences in growth.

Now, we will follow these steps and build an LGM with our sample data. First, we test measurement invariance, and then we compare the different models in order to decide: (a) whether an LGM for vigor scores over a week is empirically meaningful; and (b) how the shape of the curve should best be specified. In the final step, we introduce possible predictor variables (i.e. the amount of positive feedback received at work, trait vigor) for the specified LGM. Analyses were conducted using Mplus (Version 6; Muthén & Muthén, 1998–2010). Annotated Mplus syntax of all the models specified in this chapter can be downloaded from http://science.cloud-solutions.net.

First Step: Testing Measurement Invariance

In order to test for measurement invariance, we follow the procedure recommended by Ferrer *et al.* (2008). We start with an unrestricted longitudinal CFA model (CFA1). In this model, the first item is used as a reference indicator at each point of measurement. Accordingly, its factor loading is fixed to 1. Furthermore, all seven factors (i.e. the latent scores for vigor from Monday to Sunday) are allowed to correlate with each other, and the uniqueness of individual indicators (i.e. measurement error) is modeled as being correlated over time in order to account for consistency in item-specific variance. In the next model, we fix the factor loadings of each indicator to be equal across time (CFA2) and compare this model with the CFA1 model. Next, we also fix the intercepts of each indicator to be equal over time (CFA3) and compare this model with the CFA2 model. If the more constrained model does not yield a worse fit than the less constrained model, then the constraints are empirically justified. This can be tested by using the X^2-difference test and by comparing the sample-size adjusted Bayesian information criterion (ABIC). More specifically, if the more restricted model does not show a significant increase in X^2, the restriction is justified. Moreover, the ABIC should be lower in the restricted model. To evaluate the overall goodness of fit, we also use the indices suggested by Ferrer et al. (2008), namely the X^2 statistic, the root mean square error of approximation (RMSEA), the comparative fit index (CFI), and the Tucker–Lewis index (TLI).

Table 9.1 summarizes the results of these tests with our sample data. In general, all three measurement models show good fit indices (see Hu & Bentler, 1999). In terms of measurement invariance, neither the restriction of invariant factor loadings (ΔX^2 (12) = 5.7, p = 0.93) nor the restriction of invariant indicator intercepts (ΔX^2 (12) = 17.4, p = 0.14) led to a relevant loss of information. Moreover the ABIC decreases as the model becomes more restricted. Thus, there is evidence for strong factorial invariance in our measure of vigor. At this point, we can be confident that potential changes across time are "true" changes in the construct and not changes at the level of the observed variables. This is crucial for the interpretation of an LGM (see Ferrer et al., 2008). The final measurement model (CFA3) can be regarded as a latent state model with invariant factor loadings and intercepts for each indicator. For the remainder of the chapter, we will refer to this as the state model.

Table 9.1 Fit indices of the measurement models tested

Model	X^2	df	RMSEA	90%-CI	TLI	CFI	ABIC
Tests of measurement invariance							
Unconstrained model (CFA1)	120.5	105	0.036	0.000–0.062	.99	.99	4764
Invariant factor loadings (CFA2)	126.2	117	0.026	0.000–0.055	.99	.99	4751
Difference of 2 and 1	5.7	12					
Invariant intercepts (CFA3)	143.6	129	0.031	0.000–0.057	.99	.99	4749
Difference of 3 and 2	17.4	12					

Notes
RMSEA = root mean square error of approximation; 90%-CI = confidence interval for RMSEA; TLI = Tucker–Lewis index; CFI = comparative fit index; ABIC = Bayesian information criterion, adjusted for sample size.

Second Step: Specification of the Form of Change

In this section, we will answer two consecutive questions. First, is the daily intra-individual variability in vigor time-structured over the week (i.e. is it possible to fit an LGM model to our vigor data)? Second, what is the form of this time-structured variability (i.e. what does the average vigor trajectory over the course of a week look like)? Again, we will achieve this by comparing alternative models with each other. The ultimate goal of comparisons such as these is to find a model that is theoretically meaningful and parsimonious without losing important information which is "hidden" in the data. Thus, empirically speaking, the final model should show an acceptable goodness of fit and should be as parsimonious as possible. We evaluate the overall goodness of fit using the X^2 statistic, the RMSEA, the CFI, and the TLI. In order to compare alternative models, we use, in addition to the ABIC, the Akaike information criterion (AIC). This gives us a broader basis for decision-making than the ABIC alone. Both indices provide information on the fit of a model while also considering the parsimony of the model (i.e. including a penalty function as the amount of parameters to estimate increases). Thus, when comparing two models, the smaller the information criteria, the better the fit.

In practice, it is common to directly specify different LGMs (e.g. linear LGM, curvilinear LGM) and compare these models with each other, in order to determine the shape of the trajectory. For illustrative purposes, however, we will also consider a state-trait model of vigor that acts as an intermediate step between the state model and the LGMs. All in all, this is a somewhat more rigorous test to determine whether a growth-based approach is more appropriate than simply comparing different LGMs to one another.

It is worth noting that vigor may not only have a state component, but also a trait component. Thus, variance in state vigor may not be exclusively intrapersonal but also interpersonal. Different individuals may fluctuate at different levels. Indeed, calculations with our sample data show that 43 percent of the total variance in vigor is intrapersonal, whereas 57 percent is interpersonal[2]. Conceptually, this could indicate a latent state-trait model (STM), where the covariances among the first-order factors are structured through a second-order trait factor (see Figure 4 in the supplemental material at http://science.cloud-solutions.net). The variance in the first-order factors that cannot be explained by the trait factor can be interpreted as "pure" state variance. Specifying a basic STM, like a basic state model, is based on the assumption that variance is not time-dependent. The trait factor, by definition, captures only interpersonal variance and hence cannot be related to time. As for the state part of the model, time has not been incorporated as a structuring element.

This constitutes an important difference between an STM and a LGM. By including a slope factor in the LGM, we proceed on the assumption that intra-individual changes in vigor over the course of a week have a certain pattern that is related to time. Moreover, in the case of daily diary data and a construct that includes state and trait components such as vigor, one can assume that the intercept of the growth model captures mostly the trait component. One frequently specified

Latent Growth Modeling Applied to Diary Data 123

trajectory with regard to LGMs is a linear trajectory. In addition, with regard to vigor, it seems plausible that there is a linear pattern across the week. To clarify, assuming a linear growth does not mean that the average trajectory of the sample has to increase or decrease across the week. It might be that, on average, the linear slope is zero, which would imply that aggregating all of the individual linear slopes would result in no change across the week. However, the slope may feature a significant amount of variance between individuals, meaning that some individuals show an increase while others show a decrease, resulting in a zero slope at the aggregated level. As a linear LGM is often a starting point from which to specify the form of a growth process, we will specify a linear LGM as a third model.

As mentioned above, the study by Cranford *et al.* (2006) suggests that vigor has a curvilinear pattern over the course of a week. Specifically, it seems that, on average, vigor decreases from Monday to mid-week and then increases again until Sunday (U-shape). This suggests that a quadratic slope factor should be included in the model. Figure 9.2 illustrates this specification. The growth process is now defined by three factors: an intercept, a linear slope, and a quadratic slope. The factor loadings for the quadratic slope are set as the squares of the linear terms. For each of the factors, the mean, the variance, and the three covariances between them are estimated. Thus, a quadratic LGM is the fourth model that we will test against the others.

The application of these four models to our sample data shows that the STM and the linear LGM yield a poorer fit to the data compared to the state model (Table

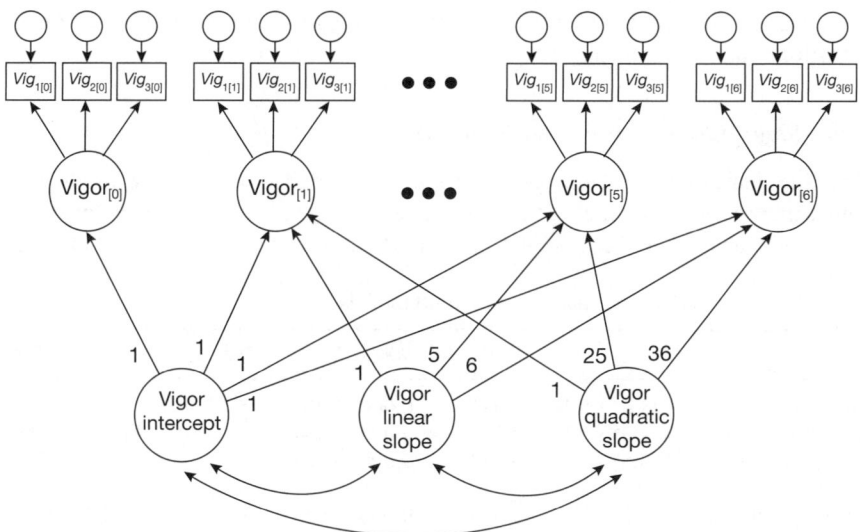

Figure 9.2 Simplified path diagram of the second-order quadratic LGM for vigor

Note
Latent variables are represented by circles and manifest variables by squares. Not depicted in this figure are the intercepts of the manifest and latent variables, the covariances among the same manifest variables at adjacent measurement points, and the variances of the latent variables.

9.2). Even though the values of RMSEA, TLI, and CFI suggest a good overall fit of these two models, the X^2 values do not. Moreover, compared to the state model, the STM shows an increase of the AIC and ABIC, while the linear LGM exhibits an increase of the ABIC. This suggests that the higher parsimony of the STM and the linear LGM, in comparison to the state model, is too "costly" in terms of decreased fit. In contrast, the quadratic LGM shows a good overall fit (X^2, RMSEA, CFI, TLI) and the lowest AIC and ABIC values compared to the other models. This suggests that the quadratic LGM fits the data best. According to these results, we can answer the questions raised at the beginning of this section, by stating that vigor does have a time-structured pattern across the week. This pattern is best described using a linear and a quadratic growth factor.

Table 9.3 summarizes the parameter estimates for this quadratic LGM (see LGM without time-invariant covariates [TICs]; we will explain the LGM with TICs below). The mean of the intercept (μ_{fo}; estimated average vigor value on Monday) is significantly different from zero and varies significantly between individuals (σ^2_{fo}; estimated variance of the vigor score on Monday). Furthermore, on average, vigor neither increases nor decreases over the course of the week. The mean of the linear slope (μ_{fl}) and the mean of the quadratic slope (μ_{fq}) are not statistically different from zero. More important, however, is the significant inter-individual variability in the slopes (σ^2_{fl}, σ^2_{fq}) of the model. This suggests that some individuals show increases or decreases in vigor across the week and that these changes are curvilinear. For the multivariate study of LGM, the latter result is crucial. Even if the mean intra-individual change is low, the variability in intra-individual change should be significant, in order to justify an investigation of potential predictors of growth factors.

Third Step: Adding Covariates to the LGM

Once the shape of the growth curve is correctly specified, covariates (i.e. predictors) can be incorporated into the LGM. The inclusion of covariates into the model results in a conditional LGM because the fixed and random parts of the model are then

Table 9.2 Fit indices of the specified structural models

Model	X^2	df	RMSEA	90%-CI	TLI	CFI	AIC	ABIC
State model	143.6	129	0.031	0.000–0.057	.99	.99	4800	4749
State-trait model	172.3*	143	0.042	0.004–0.064	.98	.98	4801	4756
Linear growth model	183.5*	152	0.042	0.009–0.063	.98	.99	4794	4753
Quadratic growth model	163.1	148	0.030	0.000–0.054	.99	.99	4782	4739

Notes
RMSEA = root mean square error of approximation; 90%-CI = confidence interval for RMSEA; TLI = Tucker–Lewis index; CFI = comparative fit index; AIC = Akaike information criterion; ABIC = Bayesian information criterion, adjusted for sample size.
* $p < .05$, ** $p < .01$.

Table 9.3 Parameter estimates for the quadratic LGMs of vigor with and without TICs

Model	LGM without TICs		LGM with TICs	
	Coef.	SE	Coef.	SE
Fixed effects				
Mean of intercept (μ_{fo})	2.882**	0.090	2.879**	0.091
Mean of linear slope (μ_{fl})	−0.035	0.046	−0.037	0.044
Mean of quadratic slope (μ_{fq})	0.012†	0.008	0.013†	0.007
Random effects				
Variance of intercept (σ^2_{fo})	0.527**	0.113	0.359**	0.092
Variance of linear slope (σ^2_{fl})	0.104**	0.037	0.084*	0.035
Variance of quadratic slope (σ^2_{fq})	0.003**	0.001	0.003**	0.001
TICs				
Effects on intercept				
Trait vigor			0.75**	0.16
Positive feedback			−0.09	0.06
Effects on linear slope				
Trait vigor			−0.09	0.09
Positive feedback			0.10**	0.03
Effects on quadratic slope				
Trait vigor			0.02	0.02
Positive feedback			−0.01*	0.01

Notes
All values are maximum likelihood estimates from Mplus. *Coef.* = unstandardized coefficient; *SE* = standard error. Further information about the two models (Mplus syntax and figures) can be found at http://science.cloud-solutions.net.
†$p < .10$, *$p < .05$, **$p < .01$.

dependent on the covariates. Basically, there are two different types of predictor. One type is TICs. These are (relatively) stable predictors that do not vary over time, such as demographic variables (i.e. gender), trait variables (i.e. trait vigor) or stable work conditions (i.e. general job resources). Typically, these variables are used to explain inter-individual variance in the LGM. Thus, they are incorporated as predictors of the intercept and the slope factors. For instance, one might investigate whether a certain TIC is associated with a higher initial value (intercept) or with a steeper increase over time (slope). The other type of covariate is referred to as time-variant covariates (TVC). These are variables that vary across time and are repeatedly assessed (i.e. sleep quality the night before or goal attainment the previous day). TVCs are incorporated into the LGM in a different way: they directly predict the latent true scores (f_s in Figure 9.1), while controlling for the influence of the growth factors. As a result, the repeated latent true scores are simultaneously predicted by the specified growth factors and the TVCs at that point in time. Due to limitations in the scope of this chapter, we will only illustrate how TICs can be included in LGMs. Readers who are interested in TVCs are referred to Bollen and Curran (2006) for the treatment of this topic within an SEM framework and to Singer and Willet (2003) for the applications in a multilevel framework.

In order to illustrate the inclusion of TICs, we will use trait vigor and the amount of positive feedback generally received at work. We chose these variables because they should predict different parts of our quadratic LGM. Stable inter-individual differences in vigor (i.e. trait vigor) should mainly be related to the level of the weekly vigor trajectory (i.e. intercept factor). The amount of positive feedback received at work is also more likely to influence the rate of change (i.e. slope factors). Positive feedback is an important job resource (Grebner et al., 2010) that is associated with vigor (Halbesleben, 2010). Frequent positive feedback throughout the week should energize and motivate employees (Kluger & DeNisi, 1996), and should consequently prevent a drop in vigor over time. This reasoning leads to the assumption that the general amount of positive feedback an employee receives from his/her supervisor may positively influence the level of vigor as well as the pattern of change with regard to vigor over the week.

In order to investigate whether trait vigor and the general amount of positive feedback received at work can explain inter-individual differences in time-dependent changes in vigor, we include these two variables as TICs in the quadratic LGM. Trait vigor and the general amount of positive feedback were assessed using the general questionnaire that was completed before the diary study began. Trait vigor was measured with the same three items which were used to measure state vigor, but the instructions asked the participants to indicate the extent to which they had felt vigorous, cheerful, and lively in the past 30 days. The general amount of positive feedback from the supervisor was assessed with a single item. The participants had to indicate how often they received positive feedback from their supervisor (1 = *never* to 5 = *constantly*). Hence, in the quadratic LGM, we use a CFA to build a latent true score of trait vigor, which is modeled to predict the intercept, the linear slope, and the quadratic slope of vigor. The amount of positive feedback is introduced as a manifest variable that also predicts the intercept, linear, and quadratic slope.

Table 9.3 summarizes the results of this model (LGM with TICs). Trait vigor is positively associated with the intercept, but not with the slope factors of the LGM. Thus, trait vigor seems to influence the general level of weekly vigor, but not the linear or quadratic rates of change. In contrast, the general amount of positive feedback received at work only explains variance in the slope factors but not in the intercept factor. The effect of a TIC on a slope factor can be regarded as a two-way interaction between time and the TIC. Thus, positive feedback moderates the association between time and vigor. Analogously to the interpretation of interactions in an OLS regression, plotting vigor trajectories for different conditional values of positive feedback is one way to interpret the pattern of the interaction (Preacher *et al.*, 2006). Following the advice of Aiken and West (1991), we chose values that are one standard deviation below and above the sample mean. Figure 9.3 depicts vigor trajectories for participants who received infrequent (−1 *SD*) and frequent (+1 *SD*) positive feedback from their supervisors. Individuals who generally receive frequent positive feedback have an almost linear trajectory that increases as the week advances. In contrast, employees who receive little positive feedback followed a U-shaped pattern, with a low in the middle of the week. These results suggest that the general amount of positive feedback received from one's supervisor influences the pattern of change with regard to vigor over a working week. In other words, frequent positive feedback can prevent energetic lows or even increase vigor from day to day. More generally, these results confirm the importance of appreciation at work (see Semmer *et al.*, 2007).

It should be noted that the main purpose of this analysis was to illustrate the ways in which an LGM can be applied to diary data and how TICs can be incorporated into a previously specified LGM. For reasons of clarity and comprehensibility, we focused on a time-frame of one week and therefore simplified our analysis accordingly. As the pattern of change in vigor from one week to the next is likely to be a cyclic phenomenon, more than one week should be taken into account. For instance, our results could be cross-validated with data from the second week, or an LGM for two weeks could be modeled with cyclic functions (see Beal & Ghandour, 2011). Nevertheless, our simplified example allowed us to show the potential of LGMs in diary research and to provide a step-by-step application for a possible research question. In the remainder of the chapter, we will highlight possible extensions of our example.

Further Applications of LGMs in the Analysis of Diary Data

We showed that vigor follows a time-dependent pattern of change across a working week. However, we also noted that Emma and Harry follow different patterns. Thus, one may be interested not only in the typical pattern of time-dependent changes in vigor, but also in the question of whether different types (classes) of patterns exist. An extension of LGM called growth mixture modeling (GMM) addresses such research questions and helps to identify unobserved subpopulations

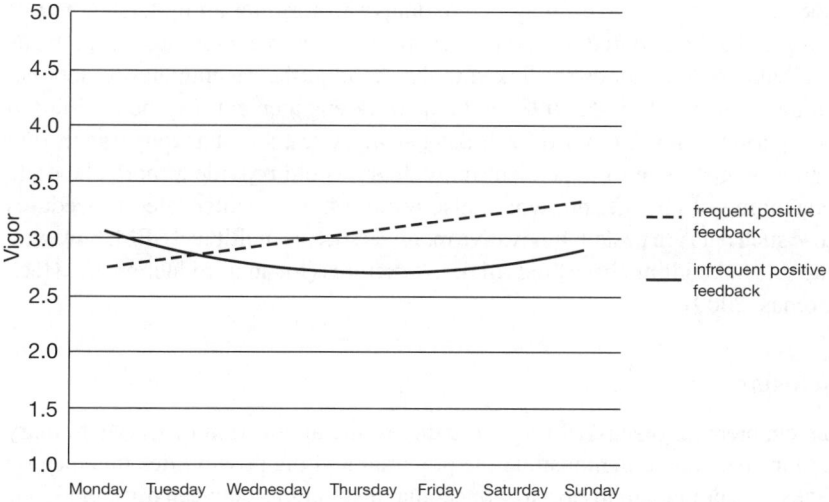

Figure 9.3 Trajectory of vigor as a function of positive feedback at work

(classes) with similar patterns of change. For example, Mäkikangas *et al.* (2010) investigated classes of change in job resources and how these are related to flow. GMM is, therefore, an interesting way to examine whether different classes of change exist, how frequent such classes are, and how these classes are related to other variables, such as work or personal characteristics. A non-technical introduction to GMM is presented by Wang and Bodner (2007).

In our empirical example, we conceptualized state vigor as an outcome of other variables (trait vigor and feedback). Slope variables, however, may also be used as predictors. For example, the pattern of change in vigor from Monday to Friday may predict the need for recovery and recovery-related activities during the weekend. Moreover, patterns of change can simultaneously be used as an outcome and a predictor, providing opportunities to test mediation models (e.g. work characteristics shape the trajectory of vigor during the working week, which has an impact on recovery activities at the weekend).

In the present chapter, we restricted our focus to a univariate trajectory. However, combining two or more trajectories is possible and may shed light on the parallel changes in two or more variables. For example, does a change in job resources go hand-in-hand with a change in vigor, and vice versa (Bakker, 2010)? Bivariate LGMs can provide information about parallel intra-individual changes over time, but they do not provide a basis for drawing conclusions regarding whether or not one of the variables predicts subsequent changes in the other variable because the parameters of the curves are based on an identical time interval. In order to investigate a temporal sequence of two or more variables, bivariate latent difference score (LDS) analyses are more appropriate (see McArdle, 2009; for an application, see Orth *et al.*, 2008).

Finally, we limited our discussion to individual patterns of change and neglected the fact that employees often work in teams and live with a partner. Considering the social context, however, may be conducive to forming an understanding of patterns of change in outcomes such as vigor. For example, previous research has shown that people's moods are linked to the mood of their teammates (emotional contagion; Totterdell *et al.*, 1998) and that work engagement may be transferred to one's partner at home (crossover; Bakker *et al.*, 2005). Simultaneously analyzing the patterns of change of dependent individuals would provide a more elaborate understanding of change, but would also require more sophisticated procedures because such data are nested. Innovative methods such as multilevel SEM, however, are capable of handling these kinds of data structures (for an introduction, see Heck & Thomas, 2009).

Conclusion

In this chapter, we discussed issues relating to the application of LGMs to diary data. Our goal was to demonstrate the potential and the possibilities this method provides. We pointed to important conceptual distinctions between different kinds of intra-individual change, providing a framework for the application of LGMs.

We discussed measurement invariance as a crucial prerequisite when modeling longitudinal data, including diary data. We built a quadratic LGM with TICs in a step-by-step process and illustrated this process with sample data. Overall, we hope that our introduction to this promising method will inspire many I/O researchers to apply it to a variety of research topics and that it will ultimately lead to happy days in the lives of many researchers.

Notes

1 In the literature, different terms are used to refer to this method. Alternative terms include latent curve analysis and latent trajectory modeling, among others. In this paper, we have adopted the term "latent growth model" because it is probably the most commonly used term. Researchers who prefer names which do not include the word "growth" explain this by referring to the fact that this framework can also be applied to cases where, on average (i.e. sample average), no increase or decrease is observed (e.g. Curran & Hussong, 2003). As we will discuss later on, LGMs can often be advantageous when a variable shows zero average growth over time but enough heterogeneity in change between individuals is observed (i.e. some individuals increase while others decrease).
2 In order to estimate the proportions of intra-individual and inter-individual variance, we calculated the intraclass correlation according to Hox (2010) using the program HLM version 6.04 (Raudenbush *et al.*, 2004).

References

Aiken, L.S. & West, S.G. (1991). *Multiple regression: Testing and interpreting interactions.* Newbury Park: Sage Publications Inc.
Bakker, A.B. (2010). Engagement and job crafting: Engaged employees create their own great place to work. In S. Albrecht (Ed.), *Handbook of employee engagement: Perspectives, issues, research and practice* (pp. 229–244). Glos, UK: Edward Elgar.
Bakker, A.B., Demerouti, E., & Schaufeli, W.B. (2005). The crossover of burnout and work engagement among working couples. *Human Relations, 58*, 661.
Bakker, A.B., Schaufeli, W.B., Leiter, M.P., & Taris, T.W. (2008). Work engagement: An emerging concept in occupational health psychology. *Work & Stress, 22*, 187–200.
Beal, D.J. & Ghandour, L. (2011). Stability, change, and the stability of change in daily workplace affect. *Journal of Organizational Behavior, 32*, 526–546.
Blozis, S. & Cho, Y. (2008). Coding and centering of time in latent curve models in the presence of interindividual time heterogeneity. *Structural Equation Modeling: A Multidisciplinary Journal, 15*, 413–433.
Bollen, K. & Curran, P. (2006). *Latent curve models: A structural equation approach.* Hoboken, NJ: Wiley.
Cranford, J., Shrout, P., Lida, M., Rafaeli, E., Yip, T., & Bolger, N. (2006). A procedure for evaluating sensitivity to within-person change: Can mood measures in diary studies detect change reliably? *Personality and Social Psychology Bulletin, 32*, 917–929.
Curran, P. & Hussong, A. (2003). The use of latent trajectory models in psychopathology research. *Journal of Abnormal Psychology, 112*, 526–544.
De Dreu, C.K.W. (2005). A PACT against conflict escalation in negotiation and dispute resolution. *Current Directions in Psychological Science, 14*, 149–152.
Ferrer, E., Balluerka, N., & Widaman, K. (2008). Factorial invariance and the specification of second-order latent growth models. *Methodology, 4*, 22–36.

Garst, H., Frese, M., & Molenaar, P. (2000). The temporal factor of change in stressor-strain relationships: A growth curve model on a longitudinal study in East Germany. *Journal of Applied Psychology, 85*, 417–438.

Grebner, S., Elfering, A., & Semmer, N.K. (2010). The success resource model of job stress. In P.L. Perrewé & D.C. Ganster (Eds), *New developments in theoretical and conceptual approaches to job stress (Research in occupational stress and well-being,* Vol. 8, pp. 61–108). Bingley, UK: Emerald Group Publishing Limited.

Grech, M., Neal, A., Yeo, G., Humphreys, M., & Smith, S. (2009). An examination of the relationship between workload and fatigue within and across consecutive days of work: Is the relationship static or dynamic? *Journal of Occupational Health Psychology, 14*, 231–242.

Halbesleben, J. (2010). A meta-analysis of work engagement: Relationships with burnout, demands, resources, and consequences. In A.B. Bakker & M.P. Leiter (Eds), *Work engagement: A handbook of essential theory and research* (pp. 102–117). New York: Psychology Press.

Heck, R. & Thomas, S. (2009). *An introduction to multilevel modeling techniques* (2nd ed.). New York: Routledge.

Hox, J. (2010). *Multilevel analysis. Techniques and applications* (2nd ed.). New York: Routledge.

Hu, L. & Bentler, P.M. (1999). Cutoff criteria for fit indexes in covariance structure analysis: Conventional criteria versus new alternatives. *Structural Equation Modeling, 6(1)*, 1–55.

Jokisaari, M. & Nurmi, J. (2009). Change in newcomers' supervisor support and socialization outcomes after organizational entry. *The Academy of Management Journal, 52*, 527–544.

Kluger, A. & DeNisi, A. (1996). Effects of feedback intervention on performance: A historical review, a meta-analysis, and a preliminary feedback intervention theory. *Psychological Bulletin, 119*, 254.

McArdle, J.J. (2009). Latent variable modeling of differences and changes with longitudinal data. *Annual Review of Psychology, 60*, 577–605.

McNair, D., Lorr, M., & Droppleman, L. (1992). *Edits manual for the profile of mood states.* San Diego, CA: Educational and Industrial Testing Service.

Mäkikangas, A., Bakker, A.B., Aunola, K., & Demerouti, E. (2010). Job resources and flow at work: Modelling the relationship via latent growth curve and mixture model methodology. *Journal of Occupational and Organizational Psychology, 83*, 795–814.

Muthén, L.K. & Muthén, B.O. (1998–2010). *Mplus user's guide* (6th ed.). Los Angeles, CA: Muthén & Muthén.

Nesselroade, J. (1991). Interindividual differences in intraindividual change. In L.M. Collins & J.L. Horn (Eds), *Best methods for the analysis of change: Recent advances, unanswered questions, future directions* (pp. 92–105). Washington, DC: American Psychological Association.

Ohly, S., Sonnentag, S., Niessen, C., & Zapf, D. (2010). Diary studies in organizational research. *Journal of Personnel Psychology, 9*, 79–93.

Orth, U., Berking, M., Walker, N., Meier, L., & Znoj, H. (2008). Forgiveness and psychological adjustment following interpersonal transgressions: A longitudinal analysis. *Journal of Research in Personality, 42*, 365–385.

Orth, U., Trzesniewski, K., & Robins, R. (2010). Self-esteem development from young adulthood to old age: A cohort-sequential longitudinal study. *Journal of Personality and Social Psychology, 98*, 645–658.

Ployhart, R. & Hakel, M. (1998). The substantive nature of performance variability: Predicting interindividual differences in intraindividual performance. *Personnel Psychology, 51*, 859–901.

Preacher, K.J., Curran, P.J., & Bauer, D.J. (2006). Computational tools for probing interactions in multiple linear regression, multilevel modeling, and latent curve analysis. *Journal of Educational and Behavioral Statistics, 31*, 437–448.

Ram, N. & Gerstorf, D. (2009). Time-structured and net intraindividual variability: Tools for examining the development of dynamic characteristics and processes. *Psychology and Aging, 24*, 778–791.

Ram, N. & Grimm, K. (2007). Using simple and complex growth models to articulate developmental change: Matching theory to method. *International Journal of Behavioral Development, 31*, 303.

Raudenbush, S.W., Bryk, A., Cheong, Y.F., & Congdon, R. (2004). *HLM 6: Hierarchical linear and nonlinear modeling* [computer software]. Chicago: Scientific Software International.

Sayer, A. & Cumsille, P. (2001). Second-order latent growth models. In L.M. Collins & A.G. Sayer (Eds), *New methods for the analysis of change* (pp. 177–201). Washington, DC: American Psychological Association.

Schaufeli, W.B. & Bakker, A.B. (2010). Defining and measuring work engagement: Bringing clarity to the concept. In A.B. Bakker & M.P. Leiter (Eds), *Work engagement: A handbook of essential theory and research* (pp. 10–24). New York: Psychology Press.

Schooler, C., Mulatu, M.S., & Oates, G. (1999). The continuing effects of substantively complex work on the intellectual functioning of older workers. *Psychology and Aging, 14*, 483–506.

Semmer, N., McGrath, J., & Beehr, T. (2005). Conceptual issues in research on stress and health. In C.L. Cooper (Ed.), *Handbook of stress medicine and health* (2nd ed., pp. 1–43). Boca Raton: CRC Press.

Semmer, N.K., Jacobshagen, N., Meier, L.L., & Elfering, A. (2007). Occupational stress research: The "Stress-as-Offense-to-Self" perspective. In J. Houdmont & S. McIntyre (Eds), *Occupational health psychology: European perspectives on research, education and practice, Vol. 2* (pp. 43–60). Castelo da Maia, Portugal: ISMAI Publishing.

Shraga, O. & Shirom, A. (2009). The construct validity of vigor and its antecedents: A qualitative study. *Human Relations, 62*, 271.

Singer, J. & Willet, J. (2003). *Applied longitudinal data analysis: Modeling change and event occurrence*. New York: Oxford University Press.

Totterdell, P., Kellett, S., Teuchmann, K., & Briner, R. (1998). Evidence of mood linkage in work groups. *Journal of Personality and Social Psychology, 74*, 1504.

Wang, M. & Bodner, T. (2007). Growth mixture modeling. *Organizational Research Methods, 10*, 635.

Widaman, K. & Reise, S. (1997). Exploring the measurement invariance of psychological instruments: Applications in the substance use domain. In K.J. Bryant, M. Windle & S.G. West (Eds), *The science of prevention: Methodological advances from alcohol and substance abuse research* (pp. 281–324). Washington, DC: American Psychological Association.

10 Using Qualitative Diary Research to Understand Emotion at Work

Kathryn Waddington

This chapter addresses the role of qualitative diary research as a method for documenting subjective experiences and emotions at work. Qualitative diary research can yield rich insights into relationships, processes, events, and settings, and diaries more generally are a means by which to 'capture the particulars of experience in a way that is not possible using traditional designs' (Bolger *et al.*, 2003, p. 579). The chapter gives an overview and discussion of key aspects involved in the design and conduct of qualitative diary research. More specifically, it aims to:

- provide a background to the development of diary research and its use, strengths, and limitations in organizational research;
- highlight ethical and methodological principles underpinning qualitative diary research design;
- discuss the role of qualitative diaries in interdisciplinary research into emotion at work.

The chapter draws upon empirical data from organizational psychology research into work-related gossip and emotion to provide practical examples of using diary research methods, data analysis, and working reflexively. Importantly, researchers are not immune to emotion in and about their work. Therefore, the role and use of diaries in reflective and reflexive research practice are also discussed using illustrative material from three researchers' diaries and field notes.

The chapter is structured as follows. First, key issues in the historical development and use of diaries as a research tool provide a context within which to consider principles of qualitative diary research design. This is followed by a practical research example of a diary study drawing upon empirical material from a study of work-related gossip and emotion in nursing and healthcare organizations. The role of diaries is discussed in regard to interdisciplinary research and as a means of linking workplace emotions with organizational processes and outcomes. The chapter ends with consideration of the role of diaries as a tool for reflexive research practice and a way of thinking about researchers' emotional experiences and engagement with research processes and transitions.

The Development of Diary Research

Diaries are a familiar feature of everyday life, used to record social engagements as well as activities and events, thoughts, and feelings. Commentators and politicians from Samuel Pepys's (1633–1703) time onwards have written diaries as a memoir for posterity through archives and more recently profit through publication. Pepys's diaries provide an account of his personal life and work (which concerned the civil administration of the British Royal Navy), and are replete with emotions of marital rage and professional jealousies (Pepys, 1985/2003). More recently, Mullin (2010) suggests that 'the most successful political diarists are people who have occupied the lower foothills . . . because they have had time to look around and observe details' (p. 2). Diaries are used in qualitative research for precisely the same reasons, to observe and document the details of everyday experience. Researcher-led diaries, often referred to as solicited diaries, can be used to collect both qualitative and quantitative data, transforming private, subjective intrapersonal processes into public data open to scrutiny and interpretation.

Allport's *The Use of Personal Documents in Psychological Science* is frequently cited as one of the earliest discussions on the use of diaries as a research tool. For Allport, familiarity with the 'particulars of life' is the foundation of all psychological knowledge: 'Psychology needs to concern itself with life as it is lived, with significant total-processes of the sort revealed in consecutive and complete life documents' (Allport, 1942, p. 56; cited in Bolger *at al.*, 2003, p. 580). Diaries have been used in research in a broad range of areas, including occupational stress, personal identity, text messaging, organizational culture and change, and patients' reactions to the diagnosis and experience of serious illness (e.g. Clarkson & Hodgkinson, 2007; Patterson, 2005; Plowman, 2010; Willig, 2009). Diaries can vary enormously in terms of structure and flexibility in the ways in which information is captured and recorded – for example, using an electronic personal digital assistant (PDA), audio diary recording, and paper-and-pencil records. Alaszewski's (2006) analysis of the role of diaries in social research notes their use in a wide range of different research designs, including experimental, social survey, historical, ethnographic, and naturalistic research.

Diaries are particularly suited to naturalistic research as they enable the collection of 'real-time' data, recorded as subjective experiences occurring in their natural, spontaneous context. Used in this manner, diaries can access and reveal taken-for-granted activities and insights into how individuals ascribe meanings to actions and social interactions. Qualitative diaries can elicit rich emotional data, as illustrated in the extract below, written by Carla Willig (2009), about her experience of being diagnosed and treated for cancer.

> I suddenly realized (and it was a sudden insight, something which 'came to me', effortlessly and unexpected at this point) that there was only one way in which I could cope with what was happening to me, and that was to confront my mortality head-on. Later that day, I wrote the following diary entry:

> *I realize that the only way I can deal with this is by engaging with the experience and by confronting my mortality – and not to pretend that it isn't happening or to try to escape from it in some way. Attempts to avoid or escape from the experience only increase my anxiety and the sense of lurking horror. By contrast, the thought of embracing and fully entering this experience does not. If this is going to happen to me, I want to 'be there', and not try to be somewhere else.*
>
> I was struck by just how powerful an effect these thoughts had on my mood. The realization that I could choose to accept, to stay with, this situation rather than having to find ways of escaping from it, relieved my anxiety greatly. I felt calm, even relaxed.
>
> (Willig, 2009, p.184; emphasis to diary entry added)

This is a powerful example of qualitative diary data which reveals, in this instance, strong emotions and insight into subjective experiences.

Plowman's (2010) 'diary project' used qualitative diaries, participant dialogue, and interviews in an investigation into gendered organization, power, and change in a South African non-governmental organization. The diary project revealed aspects of organizational life that would have otherwise remained hidden and silenced. Plowman's study is noteworthy for two reasons. First, it illustrates a potentially significant role for qualitative diary designs in linking subjective experience with organizational processes, and the interface between the informal and formal, personal and professional/organizational practices. Second, the methodology, which allows for intervention as well as study, is highly relevant to researchers interested in designing and evaluating employee engagement because:

> The diary project methodology is also experienced as being both useful and *energising*. In the process of bringing staff together across formal and informal hierarchies and divisions, the diary project creates space for shared reflection and ideas for change. The methodology as an *intervention* also gives opportunity for thinking about and taking steps to build inclusive organisational cultures.
>
> (Plowman, 2010, p. 44; emphasis added)

Strengths and Limitations of Qualitative Diaries

Diaries are useful in capturing subjective responses to events in real time and are a means of uncovering and digging deep into everyday processes and events which may otherwise be neglected, hidden, or silenced. The quality and quantity of data is likely to be different to that available through questionnaire or retrospective interviews and can provide a more comprehensive and nuanced picture. Data based on human experience, as we have seen, are powerful and more compelling than quantitative data alone, and diaries can also be designed to collect quantitative and qualitative data at the same time. They can capture events close to when they unfold with the potential to trace events over time, providing a record of ever-changing individual and organizational landscapes. Diaries allow researchers to track contemporaneous public and private events, require relatively little of the researcher's time, and, in paper-and-pencil form, are relatively cheap to administer. According to Bolger *et al.* (2003), electronic diaries such as Personal Digital Assistants (PDAs) have advantages for the conduct of diary studies, such as their ability to allow for signalling and the provision of time stamps. However, there are some disadvantages associated with PDAs and electronic diaries, primarily relating to cost, maintenance, and training participants in how to use them.

Other limitations of qualitative diaries more generally are that researchers are reliant upon diarists' conscientiousness, honesty, self-awareness, and insight. Knowledge that diaries will be read, analysed, and interpreted may result in diarists' censoring entries to avoid embarrassment, although self-consciousness tends to decrease over time (Milligan *et al.*, 2005). However, studies that require participation over a long period of time may also result in high attrition or less complete or accurate data towards the end, requiring gentle reminders in the form of visits, telephone calls, texts, or e-mails from the researcher.

Designing Qualitative Diary Research

When designing qualitative diary research, it is important to recognize that the approach is deliberately open and flexible. A variety of free response techniques can be used to enable participants to recall and record personally meaningful events and interactions which have emotional resonance. For example, qualitative diaries can also be used in a number of different ways, including descriptive experience sampling, audio diaries, recording of critical incidents, and creative reflective journals (Chell, 2004; Clarkson & Hodgkinson, 2007; Duncan, 2004; Heavey *et al.*, 2010; Theodosius, 2006). Because of this diversity, there are no specific typologies or standardized approaches to follow; therefore, a recap of the principles of rigorous and ethical research practice is given as a starting point.

Generic methodological and ethical principles of designing and doing qualitative research (e.g. Silverman, 2009; Willig & Stainton-Rogers, 2008) can be applied to qualitative diary research. This relates to overarching principles of good research design, with a clearly stated rationale for using qualitative diaries and how this is justified in terms of the research question. There should be congruence between method and psychological/interdisciplinary theoretical perspectives and a clearly articulated and consistent epistemological approach. However, flexibility of approach is also necessary in order to tailor the research design to the different ways that diaries may be used (e.g. audio diaries vs. creative reflective journals).

Ethical Issues

Ethical issues are important in all research designs/approaches, yet they are frequently neglected, or simply implied, in guidance for the design and practice of diary research. For example, Bolger *et al.*'s (2003) frequently cited review of diary methods makes no mention of ethical issues at all. Symon (2004), on the other hand, does acknowledge the need to assure respondents of the confidentiality of completed diary records and the importance of ensuring anonymity in the reporting of findings, but there is little detailed discussion. Clearly, researchers are required to work within ethical codes of practice, and research proposals receive ethical scrutiny by funding bodies and committees. These are the professional and procedural ethical considerations, but there are also other considerations relating to 'ethics in practice' and researcher reflexivity (Guillemin & Gillam, 2004, p. 261).

Diaries written for personal use are private documents; solicited diaries written for research purposes are public documents. Ethically, the rights and privacy of 'absent' third parties – for example, individuals or organizations who may appear in a diary record – need to be acknowledged and protected. Furthermore, research participants may reveal information about illegal activities, moral judgments, or gossip about other people or organizations. Researchers' own diaries may be used to reflect on ethical dilemmas raised by information given during their research and the following questions can be used to promote 'ethical reflexivity'. Consider, for example: (i) How are you going to act ethically? (ii) Are any adjustments required by you or your research design in order to be sensitive to participants or third parties? (iii) If a research diary record was inadvertently found by someone not involved in the study, what might be the outcome?

Diary data, like all research data, must be confidential and secure, and participants and researchers need to give careful consideration to storage and accessibility, particularly in the field site and in transit (e.g. data used/stored on laptops and USB storage devices). In the, albeit unlikely, event that an individual or organization taking part in a research study is involved in litigation, diary data may be subject to disclosure. For example, in the UK under Rule 31 of the Civil Procedure Rules, any record of information may be required to be disclosed (www.justice.gov.uk/courts/procedure-rules/civil/rules/part31#IDAAKICC, accessed 31 August 2012). This extends from hand-written notes, letters, and correspondence through e-mails, to computer discs, photographs, and any other way of permanently recording information. Researchers also need to ensure their practice is compliant with relevant legislation regarding data protection, and give accurate information to participants regarding how any personal information will be stored and used.

Practical Considerations

Qualitative diaries are likely to involve either paper-and-pencil or digital media methods of data collection, and sampling decisions may need to take account of participants' IT skills, literacy, self-awareness, insight, and any training needs, for instance, in using digital media recording devices, or PDAs. Ethically, participants will need to know: (i) how the information they provide will be used, and give consent for their data to be used in reports and publications; (ii) realistic estimations of how much of their time will be taken up completing diaries; (iii) how to contact the researcher and what to do should they have concerns about the conduct of the study; and (iv) what support is available should any aspect of participation cause distress.

Qualitative diary records may be unstructured, or lightly structured, but all will need to have clear and unambiguous instructions for completion, and pilot studies can yield useful feedback here. The instructions used to *guide*, rather than prescribe, diary entries will clearly depend upon the research question. Face-to-face introductory briefing sessions, either individually or in groups, are crucial to establish rapport and trust, and to clarify the practical requirements of diary keeping. They also provide an opportunity to raise concerns about the overall conduct of the study or any specific ethical concerns (Plowman, 2010). Qualitative interviews may also be incorporated into the design after the completion of diaries to clarify meaning and understanding, as well as probe further to elicit deeper insights. Additional qualitative data should also be collected by researchers in the form of detailed field notes of observations, emotions and insights, as well as a research diary to aid their reflexive research practice (Nadin & Cassell, 2006).

Data Analysis

Qualitative data analysis is fundamentally an iterative process which may, to a lesser or greater extent, be guided by the methodological approach adopted – for example, grounded theory or interpretive phenomenological analysis (Willig & Stainton-Rogers, 2008). Iteration is not a repetitive mechanical task, rather it is a reflexive process which involves: 'visiting and revisiting the data and connecting them with emerging insights, progressively leading to refined focus and understandings' (Srivastava & Hopwood, 2009, p. 77). An overarching principle is the requirement for a clear rationale and articulation of an analytic framework/approach, and accurate and complete descriptions of analytic procedures, processes, and audit trail. If more than one source and/or type of data are collected, the framework should also include the process/es for combining and integrating data and findings. The development and use of such a framework is described next in an illustrative research example of the practical use of diary methods.

Using Diaries to Study Work-Related Gossip

This section summarizes key aspects of a multi-method research study into work-related gossip which used qualitative and quantitative diary methods. The focus here was predominantly upon methodological issues and qualitative aspects, but for further details of quantitative diary design, see Waddington (2005).

Research Design

The overall research design combined qualitative and quantitative methods of data collection, analysis, and inference across three phases. This approach was a product of the 'pragmatist paradigm', rejecting the incommensurate paradigm view of qualitative and quantitative research, and the 'either/or' choice between methods

(Teddlie & Tashakkorie, 2009; Waddington & Fletcher, 2005). The final phase diary study built upon findings from two earlier phases which had used repertory grids, a 20-statements method, critical incident analysis, and in-depth qualitative interviews. The aim was to examine further the emotions expressed in gossip, the nature of the gossiper–gossipee interpersonal relationships, and wider organizational factors. However, gossip is notoriously difficult to define and highly resistant to categorization and conventional research approaches (Michelson *et al.*, 2010; Waddington, 2012). In this study, the following 'attributes of gossip', drawn from the literature, were used to determine what constituted a 'gossip event': (i) gossip is informal talk; (ii) occurring between small groups of two or more people; (iii) which concerns the verbal exchange of information; (iv) about work-related issues.

Sample: A convenience sample of 20 was chosen because, in qualitative research, sample sizes tend to be smaller. Additionally, this was the final phase of a larger study, and the respondents were a subset of an overall sample of 96 participants, and diary data were analysed in a wider context (see Figure 10.2 on p. 140). Respondents were all experienced nurses working in a variety of clinical, managerial, and educational roles in South East England.

Ethical considerations: The instructions to participants were carefully worded thus: 'Please note, for reasons of confidentiality and research purposes, I am interested in individual and organizational factors in incidents of gossip, rather than the specific content of what was said.' This was to avoid inappropriate disclosure of names/identities or organizations, which is crucial when collecting gossip-related data, particularly if it is negative, judgmental, or distorts and trivializes the experience of others.

Data collection: The diary records were structured in such a way as to enable the collection of qualitative and quantitative data about incidents of gossip experienced over a two-week/ten-day time period. Practically, and ethically, this meant that, on the whole, diary entries were made at the end of the day to avoid disruption to participants' clinical/managerial/educational responsibilities. Quantitative data is not considered in detail here, but it related primarily to: (i) the number of people involved in an incident of gossip and how long it lasted; (ii) who initiated the gossip; and (iii) the nature of the gossip and associated emotions. Briefly, the number of people involved in an incident of gossip was typically small, on average 2.6 people (including the respondent) and the average amount of time spent gossiping was six minutes per incident. The total number of incidents reported over the ten-day period of diary recording was 273. Qualitative data regarding the nature of gossip and associated emotions were collected in the form of paper-and-pencil diary records and detailed textual accounts of critical incidents of gossip (see Figure 10.1). Follow-up telephone interviews explored contextual and emotional aspects of these, and other, diary-recorded incidents.

DIARY RECORD SHEET

Date .... Time .... am/pm Length of time of incident
approx .... minutes

No of people involved ....Females/ ....Males

Where the incident took place:

Nature of your interpersonal relationship with the person(s) involved
(please circle)

Work relationship only/friends at work/friends outside of work/partner/family member/other – please specify

I disclosed	very little	1	2	3	4	5	6	7	a great deal
Others disclosed	very little	1	2	3	4	5	6	7	a great deal
Social integration	I didn't feel part of the group	1	2	3	4	5	6	7	I felt part of the group
Quality	unpleasant	1	2	3	4	5	6	7	very pleasant
Initiation	I initiated	1	2	3	4	5	6	7	others initiated

*What did you gossip about?

*How did you feel at the time the above took place?

A CRITICAL INCIDENT
*Please describe in your own words details of one significant incident of work-related gossip which occurred during the data collection period indicating:
1. Why you chose this particular incident
2. How you felt at the time
3. Where, when and who was involved (do not give names, if necessary use pseudonyms)
4. The nature of the gossip (again do not give names or inappropriate detail)
5. Any organizational factors which contributed to the occurrence of this particular incident

Figure 10.1 Diary record sheet and critical incident instructions

Note
The actual record sheets allowed much more space for textual qualitative description.

The Analytical Framework and Coding Template

Quantitative and qualitative data were analysed on two levels using quasi-statistical, template, and immersion/crystallization styles of analysis, as outlined in the framework in Figure 10.2.

Quasi-statistical analysis was used in the first level of analysis; template analysis was used in both first and second levels of analysis, and the template developed, for example, by extending or deleting codes, as data were analysed and integrated. Immersion/crystallization and second-level analysis were, in practice, an iterative cycle rather than a linear relationship. Figure 10.3 provides an extract from the diary study coding template relating to emotional expression and outcome.

The template defined higher-order codes that were both theory and data driven, arising from the literature review and preliminary phases of the research. The template was amended by adding/combining/removing lower-order codes as engagement with new data occurred and analysis progressed. There were some complex issues evident; for example, engaging in gossip may either: (i) enable the expression of concern, for example, *about* another person's health; or (ii) result in feelings of concern *for* the third party being gossiped about. Concern for self was expressed in terms of anxiety and worry: *'Glad to put the experience into words as it had been quite unusual and worrying.'*; *'I felt slightly anxious.'*

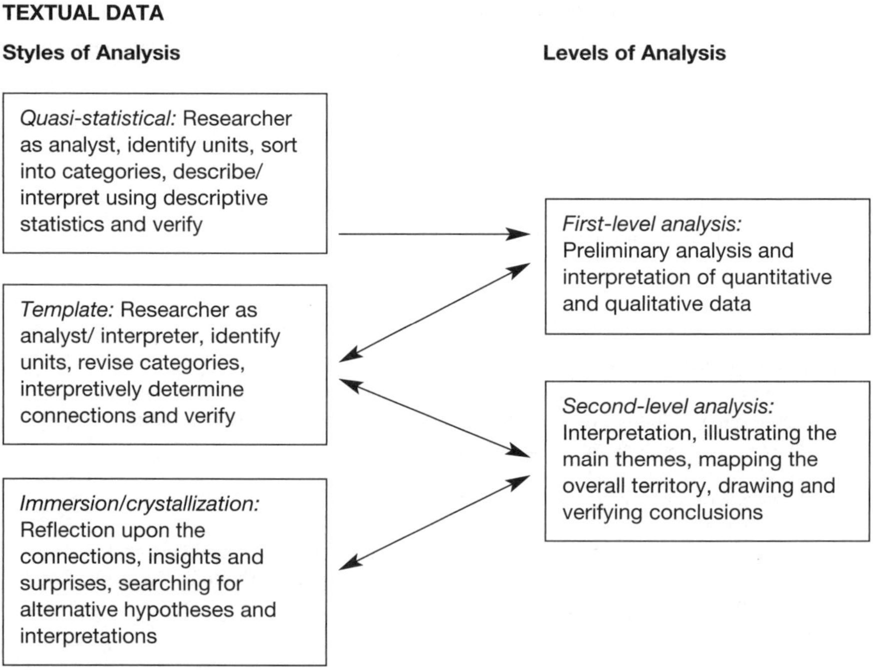

TEXTUAL DATA

Styles of Analysis

Quasi-statistical: Researcher as analyst, identify units, sort into categories, describe/interpret using descriptive statistics and verify

Template: Researcher as analyst/ interpreter, identify units, revise categories, interpretively determine connections and verify

Immersion/crystallization: Reflection upon the connections, insights and surprises, searching for alternative hypotheses and interpretations

Levels of Analysis

First-level analysis: Preliminary analysis and interpretation of quantitative and qualitative data

Second-level analysis: Interpretation, illustrating the main themes, mapping the overall territory, drawing and verifying conclusions

Figure 10.2 Framework for combining and integrating qualitative and quantitative data
Note
Adapted from Waddington (2005).

```
1    EMOTIONS EXPRESSED IN GOSSIP
     1    Concern
          1              Feeling concern about others
          2              Caring about others
                         1         Patients
                         2         Colleagues
     2    Anxiety
          1              Concern for self
     3    Frustration
          1              Anger towards others
          2              Irritation
     4    Annoyance
          1              With self
          2              With others
                         1         Unprofessional behaviour

2    EMOTIONAL OUTCOMES OF GOSSIPING
     1    Concern
          1              Feeling concerned for others
                         1         Patients
                         2         Colleagues
     2    Stress relief
          1              Support
          2              Reassurance
          3              Relaxed
     3    Discomfort
          1              Guilty
          2              Embarrassed
          3              With own unprofessional behaviour
          4              Hurt
```

Figure 10.3 Extract from diary study coding template

Integrating quantitative and qualitative data analysis: This is represented in the second-level analysis and immersion/crystallization style in Figure 10.2, and was achieved by using 'vertical passes through the data' (Borkan, 1999, p. 186) to further develop and refine the coding template. For example, with regard to anxiety, the underlying issues from an incident/individual level of analysis relating to uncertainty and anxiety about the future was intertwined with qualitative telephone interview data to reveal organizational issues relating to power, role, and job security:

> A tremendous effect [organizational uncertainty and change] – in nursing and in the public sector the pay is not good, but you do have some job security. When that gets threatened people tend to talk about the uncertainty and their anxieties about the future. There's a lot of inaccurate information about redundancies, particularly among the ancillary staff – doctors and nurses have

their professional status to protect them, so I think they feel a bit more secure, ancillary staff don't have this, they get sucked into the rumours.

(Extract from telephone interview)

The data analysis task in the diary study was complex and time consuming, partly because of the volume of data generated, and partly because of the iterative nature of template analysis in qualitative research. Quantitative data was a useful adjunct in this regard and provided orienting points for refining and developing the template. The lightly structured diary records also helped to orient respondents towards incidents of gossip in the workplace and the emotions invoked, which were the basis for qualitative diary data and interviews regarding critical incidents.

Implications for future research: Gossip is emerging as a topic of interdisciplinary interest in the social and organizational sciences, yet to date there are still relatively few empirical studies. The value of diaries in future research into organizational gossip is evident, providing a means of capturing gossip *in situ*. As we note in van Iterson, Waddington, and Michelson (2011), diaries provide an excellent opportunity for longitudinal organizational culture research, while another methodological possibility includes secondary analysis of data published in political diaries.

Researching Emotion at Work

Having looked at the role of diaries in a broad social research context, as well as their use in researching work-related gossip, the focus now shifts more specifically to their role in researching emotion at work. Emotion is a dynamic and multi-faceted concept, involving transient feelings in response to a particular cause or target, cognitions, expressive behaviour, and neurological and physiological changes (Grandey, 2008). There is however huge variety in the ways in which researchers have approached the definition of emotion, the most widely held and concise being 'emotions are adaptive responses to the demands of the environment' (Elfenbein, 2007, p. 316). Happiness can be understood in terms of positive emotional states, such as contentment, joy, and pleasure, in broader conceptual terms, such as affect and well-being, and in relation to more negative perspectives, such as anxiety, stress, or dissatisfaction (Warr, 2007).

As Elfenbein (2007) notes, from a psychological perspective the field of emotion at work and in organizations has grown rapidly, and messily, over the last 20 years or so, into a popular and popularized area of inquiry and in some respects this has been problematic. For example, Briner and Kiefer's (2005, 2009) reviews of research in the field found a relatively uncritical approach to empirical studies, a lack of attention to event-based data collection methods, and other serious limitations, including poor quantification and methods that are incongruent with psychological theory of emotion. Of particular relevance to qualitative diary research is the lack of event-based methods because: 'Without some understanding of the specific emotion-provoking event and context, and meaning of that event, we are only assessing emotion in a very partial way' (Briner and Kiefer, 2005,

p. 308). The incongruence between theory and methods is also pertinent to the focus of this chapter, not least because of the extensive body of knowledge and literature which forms the interdisciplinary foundations of our understanding of emotion at work (Elfenbein, 2007; Grandey, 2008; Lewis *et al.*, 2008). Interdisciplinary research seeks to integrate information, data, techniques, tools, perspectives, concepts, and theories to advance understanding and solve problems for which the solutions lie beyond the scope of a single discipline or field of research practice (Calhoun & Rhoten, 2010). Interdisciplinary approaches are important, therefore, in promoting coherence between theories and methods, and developing new and more comprehensive ways of assessing emotion.

Lucas and Diener (2008) point out, with regard to the study of subjective well-being (SWB), that some of the most exciting developments are taking place outside the traditional boundaries of psychology: 'Thus, although SWB research was initially developed within the context of existing psychology theory, it has important implications for research, theory, and application in a wide variety of domains' (p. 481). What is known about emotion is drawn from diverse disciplines, including biology, genetics, health, neuroscience, anthropology, sociology, psychology, and more recently economics (Lewis *et al.*, 2008). Development of an integrated interdisciplinary approach to research in the complex and messy field of emotion at work is pertinent, but also not unproblematic in terms of establishing linkages across disciplinary boundaries. However as Alaszewski (2006) points out, qualitative (and quantitative) diary studies have been used in a wide range of research domains and disciplines, and are one way of establishing such linkages.

Uncritical adoption of an interdisciplinary approach is as problematic as an uncritical approach to empirical studies in psychological research into emotion at work. Interdisciplinarity brings with it the risk of epistemological chaos as disciplinary ideas are disassembled and reassembled, and care is needed when working across paradigms and perspectives (Waddington, 2011). Nevertheless, as von Scheve and von Luede have pointed out:

> Although the disciplines involved in emotion research scarcely present a coherent picture or unified interpretation of their data, there are certain paradigms aiming at the advancement of consistent frameworks that are capable of dealing with other disciplines' findings and also with some of the infamous pitfalls of interdisciplinary work.
> (von Scheve and von Luede, 2005, p. 305)

Von Scheve and von Luede go on to advocate interfacing sociological models and theories with appraisal theories of emotion, and the incorporation of neuroscientific data into this framework, in order to produce a more detailed picture of emotions as the glue holding society together. Adoption of an interdisciplinary approach brings with it opportunities to develop methodologies to address the incongruence of theory and methods and poor quantification identified by Briner and Kiefer (2009).

Interdisciplinary methodologies will, of necessity, need to transcend the boundaries of work and organizational psychology and its *traditional* reliance upon psychometric testing and quantitative methods. This is of course not the case across the discipline today, and qualitative methods now have a strong profile and visibility (e.g. Cassell & Symon, 2006; Lee *et al.*, 2011). Warr (2007) suggests that researchers and practitioners in organizations and elsewhere need to develop their thinking about happiness in the following ways: (i) consider multiple aspects; (ii) examine a wide range of environmental sources; (iii) look for non-linear patterns; (iv) explore mental processes as well as environmental features; (v) recognize the importance of personal baselines; and (vi) acknowledge that unhappiness is essential to happiness. Qualitative diary research methods which draw upon interdisciplinary perspectives provide a means with which to consider multiple aspects of happiness, and link workplace emotion with organizational processes and outcomes.

Research Diaries and Reflexive Practice

Planned data collection in the diary study reported in this chapter was interrupted for over a year by unexpected health problems; I developed a post-viral arthritis, resulting in extremely swollen and painful joints. An unanticipated outcome (at that time) was a shift in the focus and content of my reflective research diary entries, from frustrations with the enforced interruption to a 'patient's' diary, recording my emotions and reactions to pain, immobility, and chronic illness. After I recovered and re-commenced Ph.D. studies, I found my reflective research writing had changed and my reflexive engagement with the data had also changed; I was more mindful and reflexively aware of my cognitive and emotional responses and processes. Clearly I am not advocating that the only way to develop researcher reflexivity is to experience ill health or pain. Rather, the lesson is that researchers need to make time to be present and engaged with their data and *notice* the feelings which emerge.

For example, a little later, when taking vertical passes through multiple data sources from all three phases of the research and 'immersed' in participants' experiences of gossip and emotion in their clinical work, I experienced a strong sense of 'academic voyeurism'. I questioned whether for me, as a nurse, doing a Ph.D. was nothing more than the individual defence mechanism of intellectualization. I felt uncomfortable, but staying with the feeling and thinking around it helped me appreciate the value of research diaries and reflective writing as a means of reflexively understanding my emotions in a research context.

Research diaries, therefore, are an important tool for reflexive practice, affording a deeper understanding of the role and impact of the researcher in their research encounters and endeavours, giving increased 'trustworthiness' of the data and 'integrity' in the research process (Nadin & Cassell, 2006, p. 209). They create a record of reactions, thoughts, feelings, insights, and intuitions in relation to the research process, and can form the basis for an ongoing iterative and reflexive dialogue with self (see Waddington, 2010).

Researcher Emotion

Researchers are not immune to emotion, and diaries are a means of managing emotions associated with the research process, such as 'worrying about sample size' (Silverman, 2010, p. 36). Nicholson's (2009) psychoanalytically informed account of the importance of the researcher's emotional experience in 'practice-near' (p. 451) research with frail older people has particular resonance for qualitative researchers working with emotion in health and social care settings. The wider principles are also relevant for researchers working with emotion in other sectors and settings. Nicholson argues that the emotional experiences of the researcher as well as the participants are important data, but there is a need for an overarching theoretical framework – in her case, psychoanalytic approaches – to give validity to these emotional processes. As we have seen, emotion is a complex, messy, interdisciplinary field of inquiry and other theoretical frameworks and epistemological positions can be used to help researchers make sense of the emotions experienced in research work.

For example, Hanna Weir and I drew upon theoretical perspectives from sociology, organizational psychology, and nursing in our research into recruitment and retention in health service call centres (Weir & Waddington, 2008). In this study we were able to link and then integrate theoretical perspectives around caring, emotion work, surveillance, and control to better understand participants' emotional dissonance and feelings of disappointment and professional dissatisfaction. We have returned to our data, field notes, and reflective writing to illustrate, below, how we engaged reflexively with our emotions as researchers during the data collection, analysis, and reporting of the findings. This is then followed by an extract from Angie Bistaraki's reflective diary as an example of a new researcher's reflections upon the emotions experienced at the beginning of her Ph.D. studies.

Hanna and Kathryn's Reflections

The call centre was one of a number that had been established nationally as part of a wider programme of health service reforms and hailed as an innovative 'nurse-led service'. What we found was a service that was over-managed and under-led. Communication and information giving took place through e-mails, or not at all, which seemed incomprehensible to staff who expected more 'visible leadership'. This was in stark contrast to the tangible management practices, which many felt were oppressive. Participants were very direct in their approach to 'telling it as it is':

> Meeting with Joe and Fran (not their real names). For this meeting we had to go to the corridor venue again. I sensed caution in their approach and told them a bit more about my being there, and said that I wanted to get to know what people do and get the picture of the call centre, and my notes were to remind me of conversations, confidentially – so what was their job? 'It is the shittiest job here' said one looking straight at me. I was a bit surprised at such straightforward opening.
>
> (Extract from Hanna's field notes)

As we collected, analysed, and interpreted data about participants' emotion work, we also reflected upon our own emotions as researchers. It became clear that for some participants being interviewed had made them reconsider their motivation for call centre work, and had precipitated a decision to leave the service. The research was having a negative impact upon staff retention – the very topic we were researching – and we felt uncomfortable about this. We also felt uncomfortable about our role as 'truth tellers', feeding back findings that were discordant with government policy, whilst retaining our integrity and authenticity as researchers. Our reflexive research conversations also revealed how some of the patterns and themes in the data interconnected with our emotional experiences of work in universities.

Angie's Reflections

> There are so many things to think and do and so little time. I wish I didn't have to work so much so as to have more time for my Ph.D. Although I am tired and have so many things in my mind, I feel optimistic today... It's very easy now to abandon the whole Ph.D. Nothing goes well. I am waiting to see what will happen in London. I wanted it so much but now I am very disappointed . . . Now, after a few days and having the retreat experiences [a two-day event for Ph.D. students and their supervisors] and some supportive meetings, I feel very good with myself and with the decisions I have made. I am very happy with the work that I am doing with my supervisors and with their support I feel that I will be able to enjoy this journey.
>
> (Extract from Angie's reflective diary)

Angie's Ph.D. journey is beginning, as it does for many students, as something of an emotional roller-coaster. Writing a reflective research diary helps us to notice and record observations about ourselves, such as our feelings, and is a valuable way of understanding our emotional engagement with research processes and transitions.

Conclusion

This chapter has reflected upon the use and value of qualitative diary research in understanding the phenomenon of work-related gossip, emotion at work, and emotional aspects of researchers' work and reflexive practice. Despite acknowledgement of the emotional nature of qualitative research, there is little empirical evidence about researchers' experiences of undertaking qualitative research. I would argue that diary studies in work and organizational psychology, particularly when positioned within an interdisciplinary approach to researching emotion, have an important role for future research agendas.

Acknowledgements

I would like to thank Angie Bistaraki and Hanna Weir for conversations which have contributed to this chapter and for permission to use extracts from their reflective diaries and field notes.

References

Alaszewski, A. (2006). *Using diaries for social research*. London: Sage.
Bolger, N., Davis, A., & Rafaeli, E. (2003). Diary methods: Capturing life as it is lived. *Annual Review of Psychology, 54*, 579–616.
Borkan, J. (1999). Immersion/crystallization. In B.F. Crabtree & W.L. Miller (Eds), *Doing qualitative research* (2nd ed., pp. 279–294). Thousand Oaks, CA: Sage.
Briner, R.B. & Kiefer, T. (2005). Psychological research into the experience of emotion at work: Definitely older, but are we any wiser? In N.M. Ashkanasy, C.E.J. Härtel & W.J. Zerbe (Eds), *Research on emotion in organizations: The effects of affect in organizational settings* (Vol. 1, pp. 289–315). Oxford: Elsevier.
Briner, R.B. & Kiefer, T. (2009). Whither psychological research into emotion at work? Feeling for the future. *International Journal of Work, Organisation and Emotion, 3*, 161–173.
Calhoun, C. & Rhoten, D. (2010). Integrating the social sciences: Theoretical knowledge, methodological tools and practical applications. In J. Thompson Klein & C. Mitcham (Eds), *The Oxford handbook of interdisciplinarity* (pp. 103–118). Oxford: Oxford University Press.
Cassell, C. & G. Symon (2006). Qualitative methods in industrial and organizational psychology. *International Review of Industrial and Organizational Psychology, 21*, 339–380.
Chell, E. (2004). Critical incident technique. In C. Cassell & G. Symon (Eds), *Essential guide to qualitative methods in organizational research* (pp. 45–60). London: Sage.
Clarkson, G.P. & Hodgkinson, G.P. (2007). What can occupational stress diaries achieve that questionnaires can't? *Personnel Review, 36*, 684–700.
Duncan, M. (2004). Autoethnography: Critical appreciation of an emerging art. *International Journal of Qualitative Methods, 3*, Article 3. Retrieved from: www.ualberta.ca/~iiqm/backissues/3_4/pdf/duncan.pdf (accessed 30th November 2010).
Elfenbein, H.A. (2007). Emotion in organizations: A review and theoretical integration. *Academy of Management Annals, 1*, 371–457.
Grandey, A.A. (2008). Emotions at work: A review and research agenda. In J. Barling & C.L. Cooper (Eds), *Handbook of organizational behavior* (pp. 235–261). London: Sage.
Guillemin, M. & Gillam, L. (2004). Ethics, reflexivity, and 'ethically important moments' in research. *Qualitative Inquiry, 10*, 261–280.
Heavey, C.L., Hurlburt, R.T., & Lefforge, N.L. (2010). Descriptive experience sampling: A method for exploring momentary inner experience. *Qualitative Research in Psychology, 7*, 345–368.
Lee, T.W., Mitchell, T.R., & Harman, W.S. (2011). Qualitative research strategies in industrial and organizational psychology. In S. Zedeck (Ed.), *APA handbook of industrial and organizational psychology, volume 1: Building and developing the organization* (pp. 73–83). Washington DC: APA Association.
Lewis, M., Haviland-Jones, J.M., & Barrett, J.F. (Eds) (2008). *Handbook of emotions* (3rd ed.). New York: The Guildford Press.

Lucas, R.E. & Diener, E. (2008). Subjective well-being. In M. Lewis, J.M. Haviland-Jones, & J.F. Barrett (Eds), *Handbook of emotions* (3rd ed., pp. 471–484). New York: The Guildford Press.

Michelson, G., van Iterson, A., & Waddington, K. (2010). Gossip in organizations: Contexts, consequences and controversies. *Group and Organization Management, 35*, 371–390.

Milligan, C., Bingley, A., & Gatrell, A. (2005). Digging deep: Using diary techniques to explore the place of health and well-being amongst older people. *Social Science and Medicine, 61*, 1882–1892.

Mullin, C. (2010). *Decline and fall.* London: Profile Books Ltd.

Nadin, S. & Cassell, C. (2006). The use of a research diary as a tool for reflexive practice: Some reflections from management research. *Qualitative Research in Accounting and Management, 3*, 208–217.

Nicholson, C. (2009). Researcher emotions: A way into the experiences of frail older people. *Journal of Social Work Practice, 23*, 451–459.

Patterson, A. (2005). Processes, relationships, settings, products and consumers: The case for qualitative diary research. *Qualitative Market Research: An International Journal, 8*, 142–156.

Pepys, S. (1985/2003). *The diaries of Samuel Pepys: A selection.* London: Penguin Books.

Plowman, P.J. (2010). The diary project: Revealing the gendered organisation. *Qualitative Research in Organizations and Management: An International Journal, 5*, 28–46.

Silverman, D. (2009). *Doing qualitative research* (3rd ed.). London: Sage.

Srivastava, P. & Hopwood, N. (2009). A practical iterative framework for qualitative data analysis. *International Journal of Qualitative Methods, 8*, 76–84.

Symon, G. (2004). Qualitative research diaries. In C. Cassell & G. Symon (Eds) *Essential guide to qualitative methods in organizational research* (pp. 98–113). London: Sage.

Teddlie, C. & Tashakkorie, A. (2009). *Foundations of mixed methods research: Integrating quantitative and qualitative approaches in the social and behavioural sciences.* Los Angeles: Sage.

Theodosius, C. (2006). Recovering emotion from emotion management. *Sociology, 40*, 893–910.

van Iterson, A., Waddington, K., & Michelson G. (2011). Breaking the silence: The role of gossip in organizational culture. In N.M. Ashkanasy, C.P.M. Wilderom, & M.F. Petersen (Eds) *Handbook of organizational culture and climate* (2nd ed., pp. 375–392). Thousand Oaks CA: Sage.

von Scheve, C. & von Luede, R. (2005). Emotion and social structures: Towards an interdisciplinary approach. *Journal for the Theory of Social Behaviour, 35*, 303–328.

Waddington, K. (2005). Using diaries to explore the characteristics of work-related gossip: Methodological considerations from exploratory, multimethod research. *Journal of Occupational and Organizational Psychology, 78*, 221–236.

Waddington, K. (2010). Organizational gossip, sense-making and the spookfish: A reflexive account. *International Journal of Management Concepts and Philosophy, 4*, 311–325.

Waddington, K. (2011). Watch this space: Working between disciplines and paradigms in the scholarship of organizational gossip, *The International Journal of Interdisciplinary Social Sciences, 5*, 323–330.

Waddington, K. (2012). *Gossip and organizations.* London: Routledge.

Waddington, K. & Fletcher C. (2005). Gossip and emotion in nursing and health-care organisations. *Journal of Health, Organisation and Management, 19*, 378–394.

Warr, P. (2007). *Work, happiness, and unhappiness.* Mahwah NJ: Erlbaum.

Weir, H. & Waddington, K. (2008). Continuities in caring? Emotion work in a NHS Direct call centre. *Nursing Inquiry, 15*, 67–77.

Willig, C. (2009). 'Unlike a rock, a tree, a horse or an angel...' Reflections on the struggle for meaning through writing during the process of cancer diagnosis. *Journal of Health Psychology, 14(2)*, 181–189.

Willig, C. & Stainton-Rogers, W. (Eds) (2008). *The SAGE handbook of qualitative methods in psychology*. London: Sage.

11 Research Agenda

Peter Totterdell, David Holman, and Karen Niven

What more do we need to know about a day in the life of a happy worker? The previous chapters have described some exciting current avenues of research in this area and have outlined some state-of-the-art research methods for their investigation. This final chapter aims to integrate these different perspectives on daily happiness at work and the different research methodologies that are being used. Drawing on this integration and on related developments, we offer a possible agenda for future research. This agenda will consider what we do not know about a day in the life of happy worker and how we might study it. To identify some central themes that can guide this endeavor, we begin this chapter by reflecting on what it is that makes the topic important.

Why a Day in the Life of a Happy Worker Matters

There are a number of implicit assumptions embedded in the contents of this volume that reveal its theoretical and practical importance as a topic for research. We have identified nine such assumptions in Table 11.1. The assumptions revolve around three main themes: the nature of work happiness (assumptions 1–3), the temporal structure of work happiness (assumptions 4–6), and enabling work happiness (assumptions 7–9). The first of these three themes – the nature of work happiness – is probably the least explored as a research issue in the current volume. We will therefore comment only briefly on the assumptions associated with the nature of work happiness, and then focus on the other two themes in greater depth.

Nature of Work Happiness

Being happy is a highly valued goal in most societies (Diener, 2000). Ideas concerning the meaning and place of happiness in society have a long history. Yet the nature and causes of happiness have only gained prominence in psychology in recent years, partly through the advent of "positive psychology," which focuses on positive mental states and how they arise, in contrast to the more dominant disease approach, which focuses on ameliorating problematic negative mental states (Seligman & Csikszentmihalyi, 2000). This new approach has been adopted in studies of positive organizational behavior (Luthans & Avolio, 2009).

Table 11.1 Implicit assumptions guiding research in previous chapters

	ASSUMPTIONS	RELEVANT TO:
	NATURE OF WORK HAPPINESS	
1.	Attaining happiness is important to people and has intrinsic value.	Value of happiness.
2.	Happiness at work can be defined, measured, and studied.	Conceptual basis of happiness.
3.	A person who is happy is better able to accomplish his or her job.	Consequences of happiness.
	TEMPORAL STRUCTURE OF WORK HAPPINESS	
4.	Daily happiness relates to general happiness but is also distinct from it.	Temporal experience of happiness.
5.	What people feel at work varies from day to day.	Temporal variation in happiness.
6.	Variations in work happiness depend on people's experience of daily events.	Temporal influences on happiness.
	ENABLING WORK HAPPINESS	
7.	Enabling daily happiness at work is not the same as preventing daily unhappiness at work.	Specificity of enabling happiness.
8.	The personal and situational conditions that enable daily happiness at work can be determined by characterizing those occasions when people are happy at work.	Conditions that enable daily happiness.
9.	Daily happiness at work can be enhanced by determining the enabling conditions of daily happiness.	Means of enabling daily happiness.

Definitions of happiness can be divided into those that emphasize a life of virtue, meaning, and personal growth (eudaimonic well-being), involve a positive cognitive evaluation or judgment of one's life (life satisfaction), or involve pleasant affective experiences (positive emotional or mood states) (e.g. Diener, 1984). Research on the structure of affective experience can also be divided into those models which place emotions into discrete categories and those models which characterize emotions and moods in terms of underlying dimensions, such as pleasantness and activation (Cropanzano *et al.*, 2003). In categorical models, happiness is always seen as one of the fundamental discrete emotions, and in dimensional models happy mood (or its equivalent, such as cheerfulness) always anchors the positive end of the hedonic unpleasant–pleasant dimension. Those scholars who adopt a wider lens on happiness include other positive affective states within the construct, such as states involving high levels of activation as well as pleasantness (e.g. enthusiasm).

In relation to happiness in the workplace, research has mostly focused on happiness in the form of positive judgments (e.g. job satisfaction) or pleasant experiences (e.g. moods and emotions), but a wide array of happiness-related concepts have been studied. These constructs include job satisfaction, affective commitment, job involvement, engagement, thriving, vigor, flow, intrinsic motivation, and affect (Fisher, 2010); some of which have been represented in the current volume. For example, Xanthopoulou and Bakker (this volume) focused on state work engagement, which they conceptualized as a state of pleasurable activation involving vigor, dedication, and absorption, while Fullagar and Kelloway (this volume) focused on work-related flow, which they conceptualized as the holistic pleasure of acting with total involvement comprising a number of elements, including absorption and intrinsic motivation.

As well as having intrinsic value, happiness also generates individual and social value because of its mostly positive consequences. A meta-analysis by Lyubomirsky, King, and Diener (2005) revealed that individual happiness relates positively to career success, satisfying relationships, health, and life expectancy. Their analysis indicated that these associations arise because happiness leads to success, and not just because success leads to happiness. Happiness at work, more specifically, has been associated with positive outcomes both for individuals and for organizations. These outcomes include job performance, staff retention, and customer satisfaction (see Fisher, 2010).

However, the focus in this volume has been on happiness at work at a state level (i.e. momentary happiness that varies across time), rather than on general individual happiness. There is evidence that momentary happiness can also have positive consequences, particularly in relation to worker well-being, creativity, proactivity, task performance, and goal attainment (see Fisher, 2010). According to Fredrickson's (2001) broaden and build theory, momentary positive affect engenders success by broadening people's thought-action repertoires and building their social and psychological resources. Positive affect may also undo the deleterious effects of negative events (Fredrickson *et al.*, 2000).

While there is good evidence that happiness is valued by people, that it has a strong conceptual basis, and that it has positive short- and long-term consequences for workers and organizations, we should also point out that these benefits are not immutable. We highlight three areas of emotion research which illustrate this point: culture, history, and function. First, with respect to culture, it is apparent that some cultural groups place a higher premium on the value of happiness than others. For example, North America has an independent culture that sees the pursuit of happiness as so important that it is a right in its national constitution, whereas interdependent cultures place greater value on collective harmony (Suh *et al.*, 1998). Second, with respect to history, it is apparent that the social value placed on particular emotions changes over time. For example, cheerfulness is highly valued in Western society at this point in history, but at other times more intense emotions and different emotions such as melancholy have been cherished (Kotchemidova, 2005). Third, with respect to function, happiness can sometimes be at odds with the cognitive demands of the task at hand. For example, for some tasks, happy moods have been associated with information-processing deficits (e.g. Mackie & Worth, 1989). Happiness at work should therefore be understood through its

Integrating Research Perspectives

Temporal Structure: Research Approaches

Research on happiness at work has mostly focused on the happiness of individual workers over relatively long periods of time (> 1 day) and happiness has usually been measured indirectly through other constructs, such as job satisfaction. However, it is apparent that happiness varies not only between people (and groups) but also across time. When different time-frames for affect are compared, it is clear that, while averaged momentary experiences of affect correspond to affect reported for the time period that incorporates those experiences, there also differences; for example, longer time-frames are more sensitive to concurrent mood and a positivity bias (e.g. Parkinson et al., 1995).

Aside from possible differences in what is measured when temporal focus changes, examining shorter time-frames for happiness appears to have had a major impact on the constructs that are studied. For example, researchers have begun to study momentary affect, state engagement, flow, and vigor, rather than constructs such as job satisfaction, organizational commitment, affective well-being, and positive affectivity (Fisher, 2010). The current volume has reflected this trend. Specifically, it has reported studies of state work engagement (Xanthopoulou & Bakker, this volume), flow (Fullagar & Kelloway, this volume), and vigor (Gross, Meier, & Semmer, this volume). This has led to novel findings, such as the fact that day-to-day work engagement can cross over from one worker to another (Xanthopoulou & Bakker, this volume), and the observation that frequent positive feedback may prevent some workers from experiencing midweek energetic lows (Gross et al., this volume).

The strength of relationships between happiness at work and other work-related variables can also change, sometimes substantially, when researchers compare time-points rather than individuals (Daniels, this volume). A good example of this is the correlation between satisfaction and performance, which is usually weak when looking at whether workers who are more satisfied with their jobs perform better (Judge & Bono, 2001), but seems to be much stronger when looking at whether workers perform better at times when they feel more satisfied with their work tasks (Fisher, 2003).

There would of course be little point in studying workplace happiness over short timescales if happiness did not fluctuate over short periods of time, such as within a workday or between workdays. In this respect, the research reported in this volume has a common ancestry in that it has emerged from studies demonstrating considerable within-person variation in affect within-day (e.g. Miner et al., 2005), between-days (e.g. Williams & Alliger, 1994), and between-weeks (e.g. Totterdell et al., 2006). Likewise, the research reported in this volume has reported substantial (25–75 percent) within-person daily variance in state work engagement

(Xanthopoulou & Bakker, this volume), flow (Fullagar & Kelloway, this volume), momentary affect (Hertel & Stamov-Roßnagel, this volume), and vigor (Gross *et al.*, this volume).

Another reason why research has turned its attention to temporal structure in trying to understand happiness is that stable characteristics of people and their environment only appear to account for about 60 percent of the variance in happiness; the remainder must therefore come from what people do during their days (Sheldon & Lyubomirsky, 2007). In this vein, studies have shown that the daily hassles and uplifts that people experience have an impact on what they feel (Kanner *et al.*, 1982) and have contributed to a "bottom-up" view of happiness in which happiness arises from momentary everyday experiences. However, "top-down" personal dispositions can affect the challenges that people seek out, and people's appraisals of whether they have the skills to match those challenges can affect their happiness (Fullagar & Kelloway, this volume).

Likewise, job characteristics have an influence on worker's happiness over time because they are enacted rather than stable, which means that they are dynamic, emergent, and shaped by workers (Daniels, this volume). According to Daniels, the precise benefits to happiness of an enacted job characteristic (e.g. getting support to solve a work problem associated with well-being) is likely to depend on its purpose (instrumental or motivational) and the timescale considered (e.g. short- or long-term). Relatedly, Beal and Weiss (this volume) propose that goal-based episodes (rather than momentary experiences) are the appropriate framework for understanding how the various elements of daily experience interconnect. In their view, people partition their everyday experiences into episodic segments that are organized around personal goals. They refer to the segment as a performance episode when those goals are organizationally relevant. In contrast, discrete emotion episodes are seen as being organized around instigating events and provide the experiential aspect of experience, but not its temporal structure.

Temporal Structure: Research Methods

Investigating how feelings unfold over time has required the development of appropriate methods for conducting those investigations. These methods are progressing hand-in-hand with empirical advances, and for that reason methods have been prominent in the current volume (mostly Chapters 6–10). Traditional methods, such as workplace surveys, although informative, are not suitable for investigating workday processes because they are unable to capture events as they occur. Surveys rely heavily on people's memories of past events and the time-course of those events – such memories may be unreliable and distorted by normative beliefs. Work surveys also typically contain long questionnaire scales; completing these scales would place an undue burden on participants if they had to complete them on many occasions. Hence, a number of methods have been developed that enable researchers to collect data from each participant on numerous occasions over a period of time.

These time-sampling methods go by various names, such as diary methods (e.g. Binnewies & Sonnentag, this volume), experience-sampling (e.g. Dimotakis & Ilies, this volume), and ecological momentary assessment (e.g. Beal & Weiss, 2003). They enable an in-depth study of everyday experiences and ongoing behavior in its natural environment (Csikszentmihalyi & Larson, 1987). Not only do these methods provide high ecological validity, but they also enable a better understanding of the temporal nature of work experience (such as how long effects last).

Study designs using these methods can be categorized into signal-, interval-, or event-contingent (Wheeler & Reis, 1991). Signal-contingent designs require participants to report on their current experience when prompted by a signal, sent on a fixed or quasi-random schedule. Interval-contingent designs also signal participants but require them to report on their experiences since the last signal (usually sent at equal intervals). Finally, event-contingent designs require participants to report on their experiences whenever a pre-specified event occurs (e.g. a work meeting). Dimotakis and Ilies (this volume) explain how it is possible and sometimes useful to: a) combine event-contingent and signal-contingent designs; and b) combine fixed and random interval signals.

Study designs vary in their rate of time-sampling. For example, they may sample experiences several times a day (Gross *et al.*, this volume), daily (Xanthopoulou & Bakker, this volume), or even weekly (Totterdell *et al.*, 2006). There are also various options available to the researcher for signaling participants and recording data. These options have expanded as technology has advanced. For example, whereas early studies were restricted to using pagers and watch alarms for signaling and paper booklets for recording, researchers can now use personal digital assistants (PDAs, also known as palmtop computers) and cell phones for both signaling and recording (see Dimotakis & Ilies, this volume).

Some of these methods have been described in greater depth in this volume. Additional methodological temporal problems have been addressed too. For example, in relation to collecting data, Hertel and Stamov-Roßnagel (this volume) describe how people tend to act as "cognitive misers" when asked to recall specific experiences because they usually resort to earlier global judgments rather than make new ones about their recent experiences. The reconstruction methods – for days or for events – described by Hertel and Stamov-Roßnagel overcome this problem by prompting people to re-experience an episode and thereby make use of episodic memory traces to access the momentary experience. This can be particularly useful when experience-sampling is either impractical or problematic. Likewise, Beal and Weiss (this volume) point out that, by measuring episodes rather than momentary experiences, it may be possible to capture all the critical elements of a workday rather than a sample of them.

In relation to analysis, Gross *et al.* (this volume) provide an accessible introduction to latent growth modeling as a method that enables researchers to account for individual differences in the structure and rate of change in variables over time. They also point to cutting-edge techniques, such as growth mixture modeling for identifying subpopulations of workers that show similar patterns of

Enabling Happiness: Research Approaches

When it comes to identifying the events that lead to happiness at work, it has been known for a long time that they are not necessarily the same as the events that lead to unhappiness (Herzberg et al., 1959). In particular, events that are associated with interesting work, goal achievement, and rewarding interactions are likely to cause positive feelings, in contrast to daily stressors that lead to negative feelings (Basch & Fischer, 2000; Totterdell & Holman, 2003).

Affective events theory (Weiss & Cropanzano, 1996) has been influential in explaining how stable characteristics of the work environment can make some daily events at work more likely than others and thereby influence how people feel at work. For example, transformational leaders may provide workers with challenging task opportunities and positive feedback during their working week, and such events may cause those workers who have transformational leaders to feel happier (Bono et al., 2007) and more engaged (Tims et al., 2011).

Although research has identified a variety of conditions that appear to enable happiness in organizations, few studies have used interventions to determine whether changing those conditions does enhance happiness at work. In relation to changing workers' personal resources, teachers trained to use engagement as an effective affect regulation strategy were found to experience greater cheerfulness (Totterdell & Parkinson, 1999). Likewise, Luthans, Avey, Avolio, Norman, and Combs (2006) successfully used a micro-intervention to enhance the psychological capital (e.g. efficacy, optimism) of managers, and psychological capital has been shown to predict subsequent happiness (Culbertson et al., 2010). Stress management interventions, of which there have been many, have focused on reducing workers' feelings of unhappiness, such as depression and anxiety, usually by changing stable features of their work environment (Hurrell Jr., 2005) or by changing how individuals respond to their work demands (Cartwright & Cooper, 2005).

Enabling Happiness: Research Methods

Waddington (this volume) points out that the methods frequently used in researching daily happiness at work, such as diary methods (Binnewies & Sonnentag, this volume) and experience-sampling (e.g. Dimotakis & Ilies, this volume), may in themselves act as an intervention because their intensity causes participants to self-reflect on their experiences and potentially change their behaviors. This may be a blessing if it produces a desired effect but a curse if it alters the phenomenon being studied. Diaries that involve self-reflection (such as those likely to be used in a qualitative method) can have therapeutic outcomes, but this has yet to be demonstrated for diaries that involve quantitative ratings (Bolger et al., 2003).

On a positive note, Waddington (this volume) observes that the use of diary methods is able to address Briner and Kiefer's (2009) concern that research on organizational emotion has largely neglected event-based methods in favor of methods that are incongruent with theory concerning the time-course of emotions. The methods described in Chapters 6–10 are also ideally suited to identifying the situational and personal conditions that give rise to daily variations in happiness at work. Use of such methods in the earlier chapters showed how this can be achieved. For example, Xanthopoulou and Bakker (this volume) described how diary studies have identified job resources (e.g. autonomy, supportive colleagues) and personal resources (e.g. self-efficacy, optimism) as precursors of state work engagement. Relatedly, Fullagar and Kelloway (this volume) observed that job and personal resources also contribute to preconditions of work-related flow, such as challenge–skill balance, goal clarity, and feedback on progress.

The methods that have been described in this volume do not confine researchers to examining workers' perceptions and subjective experiences. For example, Dimotakis and Ilies (this volume) described how physiological measures, such as heart rate and blood pressure, can be incorporated into experience-sampling methods, and in our own research we have used cognitive performance measures (e.g. Totterdell *et al.*, 1995). Options like these expand the potential bandwidth of research for understanding when and how enabling conditions translate into worker happiness.

We finish this section by drawing readers' attention to the potential use of qualitative diary methods (Waddington, this volume). Very few studies have made use of qualitative diaries and yet they seem ideal for obtaining rich data on how happiness-relevant processes arise and unfold at work for different workers. Even for researchers who prefer more orthodox qualitative methods, such as interviewing, qualitative diaries provide an excellent basis for discussion because they enable participants to record and reflect on their experiences as they happen, and these experiences can then be explored in greater depth during subsequent interviews. Qualitative diaries could also be fruitfully used in conjunction with the experience reconstruction methods described by Hertel and Stamov-Roßnagel (this volume). We anticipate that qualitative diary methods will be used more and developed further by researchers in years to come. Next, we specify some of the other directions that we think future research should take.

Agenda for Future Research

Temporal Structure: Research Approaches

A strength of the research reported in this volume is that it has adopted an approach in which changes in responses within a worker over short periods of time are seen as central to an understanding of the psychological processes that underlie happiness at work. McGrath and Kelly (1986) observed that time is part of the fabric of our lives and yet many of our research methods try to remove or change time in order to reduce complexity. For example, survey measures often require respondents to sum up how they felt over quite long periods of time.

Researchers also tend to give insufficient consideration to the likely duration of effects when designing studies. Following a study of the relationship between perceptions of work and the bottom line performance of organizations, Harter, Schmidt, Asplund, Killham, and Agrawal (2010) commented that:

> A universal limitation of studies of this sort is the fact that it is not known whether the time intervals used are those that are theoretically appropriate – because virtually no social science theories are precise enough to specify how much time is required for the postulated causes to have their effects.
>
> (p. 387)

This can lead researchers into choosing designs with sampling frequencies that are simply based on convenience for conducting the research. It can also lead researchers to expect the impossible from their own or from their colleagues' data. For example, they may hope for lagged associations between variables in order to establish causality (e.g. trying to identify an event that influences feelings at a later time point after controlling for current feelings), even though the concurrent association is likely to be much greater because the two variables are temporally closer. Recent evidence from experience-sampling studies suggests that many emotions have a short life span (< 2 hr) unless reinstated (Verduyn et al., 2009).

Researchers may also miss effects if they do not sample for long enough. We earlier mentioned how broaden and build theory (Fredrickson, 2001) specifies that positive affect enables individuals to build resources, but it is not clear how long the affect must persist or how long the build takes; this may explain the lack of empirical evidence to date. Clearly a more careful consideration of time is needed in the design of future research. Dimotakis and Ilies (this volume) describe how experience-sampling studies can be used to measure how relationships change with greater temporal distance from an initial event, and yet few studies have done this.

Empirical research would also be helped by better theories of psychological time. Such theories might, for example, explain how work events can have different effects at different times of day. For instance, the timing of work shifts is known to have a major impact on workers' affect and well-being (see Totterdell, 2005). It is also apparent that the psychological experience of time varies and that time influences psychological experience. For example, time perception is distorted during flow experiences (Fullagar & Kelloway, this volume) and age appears to affect the specificity and accuracy with which momentary affect is recalled (Hertel & Stamov-Roßnagel, this volume). Research should also devote more attention to understanding the basis on which people chunk their continuous temporal experience of work into meaningful episodes (Beal & Weiss, this volume).

Temporal matters are relevant for new lines of research too, and we identify four lines of research here: happiness stability, happiness shifts, anticipated happiness at work, and the stability, shifts, and anticipation of happiness in groups. Happiness stability refers to the time-course by which happiness moves away from and returns to its baseline once it has been disturbed. Research has established that individuals have a set-point or equilibrium level for happiness that is usually mildly positive but varies between individuals (see Parkinson *et al.*, 1996). Events at work can deflect individuals from this baseline, but individuals can differ in their sensitivity to events and may return to the baseline at different rates (Bowling *et al.*, 2005). Research has yet to identify the characteristics of individuals that determine their recovery rate. Individual differences in self-regulatory capacity may account for some of the variation, together with the ability of individuals to deploy effective emotion regulation strategies to deal with their work circumstances (e.g. Totterdell & Parkinson, 1999). In light of the fact that individuals seem to return to their baseline even after very positive or negative events (e.g. Brickman *et al.*, 1978), it raises the question of whether interventions at work will be able to successfully raise happiness levels in the long-term.

Although happiness may have a set level around which it varies, the experience of this variation may differ from individual to individual. Some might be more likely to experience abrupt changes in happiness, while others might experience more gradual changes in happiness; such differences might also occur with regard to changes from happiness to other affective states and vice versa. Such differences might be related to the ability of individuals to differentiate between affective states (Barrett, 1998, 2004). Thus, some people are able to describe and clearly differentiate between the different discrete types of affect and emotion they are experiencing. In contrast, others tend to describe their affective experiences in a relatively undifferentiated manner and use similarly valenced terms interchangeably. Emotion differentiation has been proposed to be functional with regard to decision-making. Those with higher emotion differentiation are thought to be better at identifying and correcting sources of affective bias that might impair decision-making (Barrett *et al.*, 2001; Seo & Barrett, 2007) and have a wider variety of affective knowledge on which to draw when making decisions. It is interesting to therefore speculate whether emotion differentiation is linked to the experience of affective change. Those with high emotion differentiation might be more likely to experience affective change as an abrupt movement between discrete states, whereas those with low emotion differentiation might be more likely to experience affective change as a smooth transition. A question for future research might be to establish when smooth affective transitions into or out of happiness are advantageous for task performance (e.g. tasks requiring extended periods of concentration or attention to detail) and when abrupt affective transitions might be more effective for task performance.

Anticipated happiness brings in a new temporal dimension because it refers to individuals' use of mental time travel to anticipate how they will feel in the future based on their current circumstances and their past experiences. Most research on this topic has occurred outside of organizational psychology, but it offers potentially fertile ground for understanding work behavior. It has been proposed, for example, that while feelings sometimes directly drive behavior, it is more common for behaviors to pursue anticipated emotions (Baumeister *et al.*, 2007). In this conception, individuals anticipate how they will feel were they to follow particular courses of action and then choose behaviors that they believe will attain the feelings they desire. Thus, in a work context, workers will make daily decisions about their work behavior based on how they anticipate they will feel if they act that way, using feedback from past experiences. If this is correct, then it would be important to ensure that workers have pleasurable experiences in relation to positive work behaviors because they are then more likely to repeat them. In other words, happiness becomes the driver of future work events and not just a passive outcome of events as they occur. We therefore envisage researchers adopting a more active conception of workers with respect to their happiness at work. Such a conception would recognize that workers do not just respond to events at work (see Daniels, this volume), they also shape how they feel through continual processes involving imagination, regulation, feedback, and learning.

It is also worth speculating on how happiness stability, happiness shifts, and anticipated happiness relate to group-level affective processes (Niedenthal & Brauer, 2012), such as whether these constructs exist at the group level of analysis and whether they have any functionality at the group level. For example, with regard to happiness stability, is it the case that groups establish a set point for group happiness, and, if they do, to what extent might a set point impact on group effectiveness? Indeed, a group happiness set point might be more malleable than an individual's set point, and this could be a target for intervention-based research. It might also be interesting to establish whether group behavior is shaped by anticipated group affect – for example, group members collaborating because they anticipate that it will improve group happiness.

Temporal Structure: Research Methods

Research on daily happiness at work faces a number of methodological challenges, some of which arise from temporal structure. Gross (2010) observed that "catching emotions as they unfold is a bit like catching butterflies, only harder" (p. 213). The problem arises because emotions develop over time so there is not always an obvious transition from a non-emotional state to an emotional state; indeed, it is not clear that a non-emotional state exists per se. This problem is compounded by the fact that, although emotion can be measured using different types of response (e.g. physiological, behavioral, self-report), these responses often show low coherence (Mauss & Robinson, 2009). Greater understanding of how to reconcile data from different measures is therefore needed.

This need is particularly pertinent because new opportunities are arising for collecting and integrating different sources of data from workers during work time. Wilhelm and Grossman (2010) describe how many of the methods for assessing emotions that could formerly only be used in the laboratory can now be employed in field studies using ambulatory assessment. Portable recordings of physiological parameters (e.g. heart rate, blood pressure), movement, speech, geographic location, and visual environment are now feasible. The measurement instrument of choice in the last decade of time-sampling studies has been the palmtop computer (or PDA). We anticipate that smartphones and tablet computers will mark the next generation of studies. Indeed, such studies are already emerging (Killingsworth & Gilbert, 2010; Raento *et al.*, 2009). The ability of these devices to remotely connect to the internet opens up a host of new possibilities to the researcher, including the potential for context-sensitive interventions (Ebner-Priemer & Trull, 2009). For example, geographic location could be used as a trigger event (Dimotakis & Ilies, this volume) such that participants are prompted with specific questions when they enter a particular location. Proximity to other people or contact with them could also be used as trigger events. This opens up the possibility of studying intra-individual changes in affect as a person moves though a physical or social space to gain more insight into the effect of contextual moderators. A further implication is that interventions could be triggered depending on the type of physical or social space entered or at random when a certain type of space is entered. This would help to establish whether the effect of the intervention is dependent upon context. The latest devices are also likely to become commonplace consumer accessories, which would potentially reduce the financial investment required to conduct such studies. This additionally expands the potential reach of samples and contexts and opens up the possibility for people and organizations to participate more fully in the research and obtain more benefit (Picard, 2010).

As well as advances in the means of collecting data from workers in real time, there needs to be advances in capabilities for analyzing the temporal dynamics of the resulting data. This will include developments in traditional statistical techniques, such as the recent emergence of dynamic mediated longitudinal analysis (Pitariu & Ployhart, 2010) and latent growth modeling techniques (Gross *et al.*, this volume). We suggest that organizational research would also benefit from greater use of computer simulation models. Such models would enable researchers to encapsulate and test their assumptions about how affective processes at work arise and develop over time (Farrell & Lewandowsky, 2010). They are particularly suited to the study of temporal structure, such as duration and rate of change, and allow for assessment of complex temporal dynamics in affect (Bosse *et al.*, 2010). Fullagar and Kelloway (this volume) identify computer microworlds as potential controlled testing environments capable of recreating complex dynamics in affect. Computer simulations of affect might therefore be tested by examining whether they can reliably predict the human affect dynamics that arise in these microworlds. In other words, the researcher would examine whether the simulation model provides accurate estimates of what agents in the microworld feel over time when the model is given the starting conditions and the events that the agents encounter.

Enabling Happiness: Research Approaches

What does the future hold for determining how to bring about happiness at work on a day-to-day basis? In a recent article concerning future challenges for emotions research in organizational behavior, Gooty, Gavin, and Ashkanasy (2009) argued that research needed to: define emotion consistently, deal with discrete rather than aggregated emotions, treat emotions as dynamic phenomena, and examine discrete emotions in context. This last point concerning context was motivated by their analysis that less than ten percent of research on emotion published in leading management journals has been based on field tests of discrete emotions. The context in which emotions occur can greatly affect outcomes, and hence an approach that entails conducting field studies in organizations (complemented by other types of study) should be an integral part of the research agenda.

Research has converged on a number of related work conditions that appear to be crucial in generating not only happiness at work but also business competitiveness (Harter *et al.*, 2010). These include role clarity, feeling appreciated, good coworker relationships, supervisor support, and learning opportunities, and they are hallmarks of engaging workplaces. It has been suggested that engagement is a general work attitude construct, and may be part of the higher-order construct of happiness (see Harter *et al.*, 2010; Fisher, 2010). Xanthopoulou and Bakker (this volume) and Fullagar and Kelloway (this volume) discuss the distinction between state work engagement and flow, but clearly more work is required to map out and distinguish these and their conceptual cousins. There also needs to be a clear difference drawn between such concepts and the conditions that give rise to them. This is a problem that has hampered research on stress, wherein the term stress has been used interchangeably to refer to both the conditions (stressors) and the outcomes that arise from them (strain).

The interpersonal or relational nature of many of the enabling conditions is apparent (e.g. good relationships, recognition), so greater consideration ought to be given to the way in which workers' feelings are regulated both unconsciously and consciously by the actions and feelings of their colleagues (e.g. Kelly & Barsade, 2001; Niven *et al.*, 2009; Rimé, 2009; van Kleef, 2009). Some of these effects appear to occur at a group (or team) as well as an individual level, so the unit of investigation will also need to be considered in future studies. Another apparent feature of some of the identified enabling conditions for happiness is that they connect workers with the social meaningfulness of their work (e.g. Grant & Campbell, 2007); this deserves more research exploration.

Organizational researchers can also look to non-organizational research for inspiration. Sheldon and Lyubomirsky's (2007) sustainable happiness model proposes that changing goals and activities is the best route to sustainable happiness, but the goals and activities "must be of certain positive types, must fit one's personality and needs, must be practiced diligently and successfully, must be varied in their timing and enactment, and must provide a continued stream of fresh positive experience" (p. 129). Their review highlights a number of interventions that have had some success in enhancing happiness, including expressing gratitude, acts of kindness, savoring daily experiences (see also Frijda & Sundararajan, 2007), employing personal strengths, and reflecting on best possible selves. It may be possible to automate some of these behaviors using implementation intentions, which specify in advance how a person should act when he/she encounters a particular situation. This method has been used to overcome undesirable effects of negative feelings (e.g. Varley *et al.*, 2011), but has not yet been directed at enhancing daily happiness. Methods, such as this, that rely less on effortful cognition may help overcome some of the information processing and motivational constraints that can reduce regulatory effectiveness (see Beal & Weiss, this volume). It may be possible to use response latencies to test whether behaviors are under the guidance of automatic or controlled processes. Specifically, people should respond faster to questions that pertain to things that rely on automatic processes.

Enabling Happiness: Research Methods

Research is needed to identify the situational and personal factors that help convert enabling conditions into happiness, and happiness into other positive consequences (Fisher, 2010). A method that could elicit such information would be of great use in the design of effective interventions. Previously we identified qualitative diary methods as having an important future role in understanding happiness at work and it may be the case that they can contribute to this issue.

We also identified relationships as an important source of happiness at work and in need of further research. There are a range of methods suitable for studying relationships. One method that is particularly useful is social network analysis, which has been used effectively in other areas of organizational research (Borgatti & Foster, 2003). An advantage of social network analysis is that it can be used to examine how people are influenced by all those with whom they have a social tie. Social network studies in communities (Fowler & Christakis, 2008) and organizations (Totterdell et al., 2004) have established that people's happiness depends on the happiness of the people with whom they are connected. What are needed, however, are methods that can track and analyze the ebb and flow of happiness in organizational networks over time. Exponential random graph modeling is one method that offers promise in this direction (Robins et al., 2007). This method allows researchers to assess the probability that an observed social network structure has arisen from specified dependencies in the ties that connect the members of that network.

Earlier we pointed out that very few research studies have tested interventions that alter work conditions or worker behavior to enhance happiness at work. Intervention studies are needed for three reasons. First, they will help to establish that the associations between conditions and happiness are causal rather than spurious. Second, they will confirm whether associations that hold between people also hold within people over time (e.g. people with challenging work may report feeling happier, but it does not necessarily follow that making a person's work tasks more challenging will increase his or her happiness). Third, they have the potential to contribute positively to workers' work life and organizational performance. However, only a few studies have utilized diary or experience-sampling methods to evaluate interventions (e.g. Nielsen & Daniels, 2012; Totterdell & Parkinson, 1999), which is somewhat surprising given that these methods are particularly appropriate when evaluating interventions aimed at changing daily experiences. As we have noted, the diary method can also be used as a form of intervention. Research on "disclosure" has shown that getting people to record and reflect on their affective experiences can improve a person's psychological well-being (Frattaroli, 2006; Pennebaker, 1993). The meta-analysis of Frattaroli (2006) also provides a useful overview of some of the factors that could be used in daily diary

Table 11.2 Future research agenda

Themes	Research Needs	Examples of Use
Temporal Structure *Research Approaches*	Consideration of time in research designs.	Addressing temporality of cause and effect.
	Understanding stability of happiness.	Investigating individual differences in temporal responses to work events.
	Investigating anticipated happiness.	Workers understood as active agents in shaping their happiness.
Temporal Structure *Research Methods*	Integrating different types of emotion response.	Combining self-report, physiological and behavioral data.
	Multi-channel internet-enabled ambulatory measurement and intervention.	Using smartphones to collect data and administer interventions.
	Computer simulation models.	Simulating temporal dynamics of happiness.
Enabling Happiness *Research Approaches*	Context-sensitive studies.	Conducting field studies in different organizational contexts.
	Identifying key happiness enablers.	Studying work engagement, interpersonal and group influences, and social meaning of work.
	Interventions to enhance happiness.	Savoring experiences; personal strengths; implementation intentions.
Enabling Happiness *Research Methods*	Understanding how enablers are translated into outcomes.	Designing effective interventions.
	Longitudinal social network analysis.	Analyzing changes in happiness in organizational networks.
	Evaluation of interventions.	Use of diary methods and experience-sampling.

interventions to improve their effectiveness – for example, number, length, and scheduling of diary sessions and the type of questions that prove most effective.

Conclusion

In this chapter we have identified and integrated some of the research themes and contributions from this volume on daily happiness at work. We have particularly focused on the temporal aspects of happiness (*temporal structure*) and the conditions that give rise to happiness (*enabling happiness*). Using these issues as an organizing framework, we have set out a proposed agenda for future research that addresses research approaches and research methods. Table 11.2 summarizes the research needs embodied in this agenda and provides examples of research that would address those needs. Our agenda draws on ideas, developments, and trends from emotion research in general. Research on happiness at work can benefit by looking beyond organizational research to related fields. Yet it is also true that other fields can benefit from the theoretical, empirical, and methodological developments of the kind reported in this volume. Emotion researchers have called for research that moves out of the laboratory into the field to address the practical problems that people face (Gross, 2010; Picard 2010). Organizational research on daily happiness has already begun to answer that call and is well-placed to make a significant contribution to scientific understanding and to people's lives.

Acknowledgements

This research was part funded by ESRC UK grant RES-060-25-0044: "Emotion regulation of others and self (EROS)."

References

Barrett, L.F. (1998). Discrete emotions or dimensions? The role of valence focus and arousal focus. *Cognition and Emotion, 12*, 579–599.
Barrett, L.F. (2004). Feelings or words? Understanding the content in self-report ratings of experienced emotion. *Journal of Personality and Social Psychology, 87*, 266–281.
Barrett, L.F., Gross, J.J., Christensen, T.C., & Benvenuto, M. (2001). Knowing what you're feeling and knowing what to do about it: Mapping the relation between emotion differentiation and emotion regulation. *Cognition and Emotion, 16*, 713–724.
Basch, J. & Fisher, C.D. (2000). Affective job events–emotions matrix: A classification of job related events and emotions experienced in the workplace. In N. Ashkanasy, W. Zerbe, & C. Hartel (Eds), *Emotions in the workplace: Research, theory, and practice* (pp. 36–48). Westport, CT: Quorum Books.
Baumeister, R.F., Vohs, K., DeWall, C.N., & Zhang, L. (2007). How emotion shapes behavior: Feedback, anticipation and reflection, rather than direct causation. *Personality and Social Psychology Review, 11*, 167–203.
Beal, D.J. & Weiss, H.M. (2003). Methods of ecological momentary assessment in organizational research. *Organizational Research Methods, 6*, 440–464.
Bolger, N., Davis, A., & Rafaeli, E. (2003). Diary methods: Capturing life as it is lived. *Annual Review of Psychology, 54*, 579–616.

Bono, J.E., Jackson Foldes, H., Vinson, G., & Muros, J.P. (2007). Workplace emotions: The role of supervision and leadership. *Journal of Applied Psychology, 92*, 1357–1367.

Borgatti, S.P. & Foster, P.C. (2003). The network paradigm in organizational research: A review and typology. *Journal of Management, 29*, 991–1013.

Bosse, T., Pontier, M., & Treur, J. (2010). A computational model based on Gross' emotion regulation theory. *Cognitive Systems Research, 11*, 211–230.

Bowling, N.A., Beehr, T.A., Wagner, S.H., & Libkuman, T.M. (2005). Adaptation-level theory, opponent process theory, and dispositions: An integrated approach to the stability of job satisfaction. *Journal of Applied Psychology, 90*, 1044–1053.

Brickman, P., Coates, D., & Janoff-Bulman, R. (1978). Lottery winners and accident victims: Is happiness relative? *Journal of Personality and Social Psychology, 36*, 917–927.

Briner, R.B., & Kiefer, T. (2009). Whither psychological research into emotion at work? Feeling for the future. *International Journal of Work Organisation and Emotion, 3*, 161–173.

Cartwright, S. & Cooper, C. C. (2005). Individually targeted interventions. In J. Barling, E.K. Kelloway, & M.R. Frone (Eds), *Handbook of Work Stress* (pp. 607–622). London: Sage Publications.

Cropanzano, R., Weiss, H., Hale, J., & Reb, J. (2003). The structure of affect: Reconsidering the relationship between negative and positive affectivity. *Journal of Management, 29*, 831–857.

Csikszentmihalyi, M. & Larson, R. (1987). Validity and reliability of the experience-sampling method. *The Journal of Nervous and Mental Disease, 175*, 526–536.

Culbertson, S.S., Fullagar, C.J., & Mills, M.J. (2010). Feeling good and doing great: The relationship between psychological capital and well-being. *Journal of Occupational Health Psychology, 15*, 421–433.

Diener, E. (1984). Subjective well-being. *Psychological Bulletin, 95*, 542–575.

Diener, E. (2000). Subjective well-being: The science of happiness and a proposal for a national index. *American Psychologist, 55*, 34–43.

Ebner-Priemer, U.W. & Trull, T.J. (2009). Ecological momentary assessment of mood disorders and mood dysregulation. *Psychological Assessment, 21*, 463–475.

Farrell, S. & Lewandowsky, S. (2010). Computational models as aids to better reasoning in psychology. *Current Directions in Psychological Science, 19*, 329–335.

Fisher, C.D. (2003). Why do lay people believe that satisfaction and performance are correlated? Possible sources of a commonsense theory. *Journal of Organizational Behavior, 24*, 1–25.

Fisher, C.D. (2010). Happiness at work. *International Journal of Management Reviews, 12*, 384–412.

Fowler, J. & Christakis, N. A. (2008). The dynamic spread of happiness in a large social network: Longitudinal analysis over 20 years in the Framingham heart study. *British Medical Journal, 337*, a2338.

Frattaroli, J. (2006). Experimental disclosure and its moderators: A meta-analysis. *Psychological Bulletin, 132*, 823–865.

Fredrickson, B.L. (2001). The role of positive emotions in positive psychology: The broaden-and-build theory of positive emotions. *American Psychologist, 56*, 218–226.

Fredrickson, B.L., Mancuso, R.A., Branigan, C., & Tugade, M.M. (2000). The undoing effect of positive emotions. *Motivation and Emotion, 24*, 237–258.

Frijda, N.H. & Sundararajan, L. (2007). Emotion Refinement: A theory inspired by Chinese Poetics. *Perspectives on Psychological Science, 2*, 227–241.

Gooty, J., Gavin, M., & Ashkanasy, N.M. (2009). Emotions research in OB: The challenges that lie ahead. *Journal of Organizational Behavior, 30*, 833–838.

Grant, A. & Campbell, E.M. (2007). Doing good, doing harm, being well and burning out: The interactions of perceived prosocial and antisocial impact in service work. *Journal of Occupational and Organizational Psychology, 80*, 665–691.
Gross, J. (2010). The future's so bright, I gotta wear shades. *Emotion Review, 2*, 212–216.
Harter, J.K., Schmidt, F.L., Asplund, J.W., Killham, E.A., & Agrawal, S. (2010). Causal impact of employee work perceptions on the bottom line of organizations. *Perspectives on Psychological Science, 5*, 378–389.
Herzberg, F., Mausner, B., & Snyderman, B. (1959). *The motivation to work*. New York: Wiley.
Hurrell, Jr., J.J. (2005). Organizational stress interventions. In J. Barling, E.K. Kelloway, & M.R. Frone (Eds), *Handbook of work stress* (pp. 623–646). London: Sage Publications.
Judge, T.A., & Bono, J.E. (2001). Relationship of core self-evaluations traits – self-esteem, generalized self-efficacy, locus of control, and emotional stability – with job satisfaction and job performance: A meta-analysis. *Journal of Applied Psychology, 86*, 80–92.
Kanner, A.D., Coyne, J.C., Schaeter, C., & Lazarus, R.S. (1982). Comparison of two modes of stress measurement: Daily hassles and uplift versus major life events. *Journal of Behavioral Medicine, 4*, 1–39.
Kelly, J.R. & Barsade, S.G. (2001). Moods and emotions in small groups and work teams. *Organizational Behavior and Human Decision Processes, 86*, 99–130.
Killingsworth, M.A. & Gilbert, D. (2010). A wandering mind is an unhappy mind. *Science, 330*, 932.
Kotchemidova, C. (2005). From good cheer to "drive-by-smiling": A social history of cheerfulness. *Journal of Social History, 39*, 6–37.
Luthans, F. & Avolio, B.J. (2009). The point of positive organizational behavior. *Journal of Organizational Behavior, 30*, 291–307.
Luthans, F., Avey, J.B., Avolio, B.J., Norman, S.M., & Combs, G.M. (2006). Psychological capital development: Toward a micro-intervention. *Journal of Organizational Behavior, 27*, 387–393.
Lyubomirsky, S., King, L.A., & Diener, E. (2005). The benefits of frequent positive affect: Does happiness lead to success? *Psychological Bulletin, 131*, 803–855.
McGrath, J.E. & Kelly, J.R. (1986). *Time and human interaction: Toward a social psychology of time*. New York: Guilford.
Mackie, D.M. & Worth, L.T. (1989). Processing deficits and the mediation of positive affect in persuasion. *Journal of Personality and Social Psychology, 57*, 27–40.
Mauss, I. & Robinson, M.D. (2009). Measures of emotion: A review. *Cognition and Emotion, 23*, 209–237.
Miner, A.G., Glomb, T.M., & Hulin, C. (2005). Experience sampling mood and its correlates at work. *Journal of Occupational and Organizational Psychology, 78*, 171–193.
Niedenthal, P.M. & Brauer, M. (2012). Social functionality of human emotion. *Annual Review of Psychology, 63*, 259–285.
Nielsen, K. & Daniels, K. (2012). Enhancing team leaders' well-being states and challenge experiences during organizational change: A randomized, controlled study. *Human Relations, 65*, 1203–1227.
Niven, K., Totterdell, P., & Holman, D. (2009). A classification of controlled interpersonal affect regulation strategies. *Emotion, 9*, 498–509.
Parkinson, B., Briner, R.B., Reynolds, S., & Totterdell, P. (1995). Time frames for mood: Relations between momentary and generalized ratings of affect. *Personality and Social Psychology Bulletin, 21*, 331–339.

Parkinson, B., Totterdell, P., Briner, R.B., & Reynolds, S. (1996). *Changing moods: The psychology of mood and mood regulation*. Harlow: Longman.

Pennebaker, J.W. (1993). Putting stress into words: Health, linguistic & therapeutic implications. *Behavior Research and Therapy, 31*, 539–548.

Picard, R.W. (2010). Emotion research by the people, for the people. *Emotion Review, 2*, 250–254.

Pitariu, A.H. & Ployhart, R.E. (2010). Explaining change: Theorizing and testing dynamic mediated longitudinal relationships. *Journal of Management, 36*, 405–429.

Raento, M., Oulasvirta, A., & Eagle, N. (2009). Smartphones: An emerging tool for social scientists. *Sociological Methods & Research, 37*, 426–454.

Rimé, B. (2009). Emotion elicits the social sharing of emotion: Theory and empirical review. *Emotion Review, 1*, 60–85.

Robins, G., Pattison, P., Kalish, Y., & Lusher, D. (2007). An introduction to exponential random graph (p^*) models for social networks. *Social Networks, 29*, 173–191.

Seligman, M.E.P. & Csikszentmihalyi, M. (2000). Positive psychology: An introduction. *American Psychologist, 55*, 5–14.

Seo, M.G. & Barrett, L.F. (2007). Being emotional during decision making – Good or bad? An empirical investigation. *Academy of Management Journal, 50*, 923–940.

Sheldon, K.M. & Lyubomirsky, S. (2007). Is it possible to become happier? (And if so, how?). *Social and Personality Psychology Compass, 1*, 129–145.

Suh, E., Diener, E. Oishi, S., & Triandis, H.C. (1998). The shifting basis of life satisfaction judgments across cultures: Emotions versus norms. *Journal of Personality and Social Psychology, 74*, 482–493.

Tims, M., Bakker, A.B., & Xanthopoulou, D. (2011). Do transformational leaders enhance their followers' daily work engagement? *Leadership Quarterly, 22*, 121–131.

Totterdell, P. (2005). Work schedules. In J. Barling, E.K. Kelloway, & M.R. Frone (Eds), *Handbook of work stress* (pp. 35–62). London: Sage Publications.

Totterdell, P. & Holman, D. (2003). Emotion regulation in customer service roles: Testing a model of emotional labor. *Journal of Occupational Health Psychology, 8*, 55–73.

Totterdell, P. & Parkinson, B. (1999). Use and effectiveness of self-regulation strategies for improving mood in a group of trainee teachers. *Journal of Occupational Health Psychology, 4*, 219–232.

Totterdell, P., Spelten, E.R., Smith, L.R., Barton, J., & Folkard, S. (1995). On-shift and daily variations in self report and performance measures in rotating-shift and permanent night nurses. *Work & Stress, 9*, 187–197.

Totterdell, P., Wall, T., Holman, D., Diamond, H., & Epitropaki, O. (2004). Affect networks: A structural analysis of the relationship between work ties and job-related affect. *Journal of Applied Psychology, 89*, 854–867.

Totterdell, P., Wood, S., & Wall, T. (2006). An intraindividual test of the demands- control model: A weekly diary study of job strain in portfolio workers. *Journal of Occupational and Organizational Psychology, 79*, 63–84.

Van Kleef, G.A. (2009). How emotions regulate social life: The emotions as social information (EASI) model. *Current Directions in Psychological Science, 18*, 184–188.

Varley, R., Webb, T.L., & Sheeran, P. (2011). Making self-help more helpful: A randomized controlled trial of the impact of augmenting self-help materials with implementation intentions on promoting the effective self-management of anxiety symptoms. *Journal of Consulting and Clinical Psychology, 79*, 123–128.

Verduyn, P., Delvaux, E., van Coillie, H., Tuerlinckx, F., & van Mechelen, I. (2009). Predicting the duration of emotional experience: Two experience sampling studies. *Emotion, 9*, 83–91.

Weiss, H.M. & Cropanzano, R. (1996). Affective events theory: A theoretical discussion of the structure, causes and consequences of affective experiences at work. *Research in Organizational Behavior, 18*, 1–74.

Wheeler, L. & Reis, H.T. (1991). Self-recording of everyday life events: Origins, types, and uses. *Journal of Personality, 59*, 339–354.

Wilhelm, F.H. & Grossman, P. (2010). Emotions beyond the laboratory: Theoretical fundaments, study design, and advanced analytic strategies for advanced ambulatory assessment. *Biological Psychology, 84*, 552–569.

Williams, K.J. & Alliger, G.M. (1994). Role stressors, mood spillover, and perceptions of work–family conflict in employed parents. *Academy of Management Journal, 37*, 837–868.

Index

ability 12–13
absorption: flow 44, 45; positive affect 81; work engagement 25, 26–7, 28, 33, 35
Actor-Partner Independence Model (APIM) 33–4
Adlai-Gail, W.S. 49
affective events theory 78, 156
affective states 1, 151; ability to differentiate between 159; multiple rating sources 95; organizational citizenship behavior 87; performance episodes 16, 17–18; reconstruction methods 106–7; recovery 75, 77, 78; signal-contingent delivery schedules 90; spillover from work into private life 75, 78; *see also* emotions
age 105, 106, 108–9, 158
Agrawal, S. 158
agreeableness 75
Aiken, L.S. 126
Alaszewski, A. 133, 143
Allen, B.P. 26
Allport, Gordon 6, 133
anxiety 1, 42, 142; flow incompatibility with 48; gossip 140, 141; stress management interventions 156
Appelbaum, E. 61
Ashkanasy, N.M. 161
Asplund, J.W. 158
assembly line workers 31, 32
attention: allocation of 11–12, 14; attentional pull 13; cognitions 18; flow 44, 47, 48; regulation of 12–14
attitudinal measures 100, 102, 104, 105, 108, 109–10
automaticity 47, 48, 162–3
autonomy 30, 36, 51, 61
autotelic personality 48, 49
Avey, J.B. 156
Avolio, B.J. 156

Bakker, Arnold B. 1–7, 25–40, 45, 51, 152, 157, 162
Bal, P.M. 28, 30, 32
Barker, R.G. 21
Baron, R.A. 87
Barros, E. 32
Baumeister, R.F. 13
Bayer, U.-V. 78, 79, 90
Beal, Daniel J. 2, 4, 8–24, 32, 35, 74, 76, 154, 155
Beckers, D.G.J. 78
behaviors 16, 18–19
Berkhof, J. 87
Binnewies, Carmen 5, 72–84, 93
Bistaraki, Angie 145, 146
Bless, H. 49
Bodner, T. 128
Bolger, N. 73, 132, 135–6
Bollen, K. 125
boredom 42, 51
brain processes 47
breaks 13, 76
Breevaart, K. 27
Briner, R.B. 142, 143, 156–7
broaden and build theory 52, 152, 158
burnout 13, 81

challenge/skill balance 42–3, 46, 49, 50, 51
change: latent growth modeling 122–4, 128; versus variability 117–18
Cifre, E. 35
circumplex model of affect 26
cognitions 16, 18, 19
Combs, G.M. 156
computer simulations 46, 161, 164
confidentiality 136, 138
conflict 61, 115
conscientiousness 75
control, sense of 44; *see also* job control

control theory 12, 14
Cook, W. 33
coping 62–3
co-worker support 30; *see also* social support
Cranford, J. 116, 117, 123
creativity 52, 59, 67, 68, 107, 152
Cropanzano, R. 17
Cropley, M. 79
Csikszentmihalyi, Mihaly 41, 42–5, 46–7, 48–50, 86
cultural context of happiness 152–3
Curran, P. 125

Daniels, Kevin 1–7, 29, 58–71, 154
data analysis 137, 140–2, 161
data collection 3, 160–1; diaries 72–3, 138, 144; experience-sampling method 86–9; flow 45–7; job characteristics 60
data protection 136
Daus, C.S. 74, 91–2
Day Reconstruction Method (DRM) 5, 103–5
De Manzano, O. 47–8
De Pater, I.E. 87, 91
dedication 25, 26–7, 28, 81
demands, control, support model (DCSM) 59, 63–4, 67
Demerouti, E. 27, 30, 31, 33, 51, 76
depression 77, 156
DeRue, D.S. 90
detachment 78, 79, 80–1
Dewey, J. 20
diaries 5, 6, 72–84, 132–49, 155, 163–5; data analysis 137, 140–2; development of diary research 133–4; emotion at work 142–4; enabling happiness 156–7; ethical issues 135–6; gossip 137–42; job characteristics 60, 64, 66; limitations of 101, 107–8; nature and core features of 72–3; practical considerations 136–7; reconstruction methods 103; record sheets 139; recovery from stress 75–81; reflexive practice 144–6; research questions 73–5; short-term growth processes 115; strengths and limitations of 134–5; theoretical and practical implications 81–2; vigor 117; work engagement 28, 30, 31, 32
Diener, E. 143, 152
Dietrich, A. 47
Dimotakis, Nikolaos 5, 85–99, 155, 157, 158
Dispositional Flow Scale 49

effectiveness 11, 12, 18
ego-depletion 13
Eisenberger, R. 52
electronic diaries 3, 73, 133, 135
Elfenbein, H.A. 142
emotions 17–18, 156–7; ability to differentiate between 159; anticipated 159–60; breaks 76; categorical and dimensional models 151; diary research 134, 142–4, 146; emotion episodes 15–16, 154; emotional contagion 128; flow 48; gossip 138, 140, 141; measuring 160; reconstruction methods 101, 102, 103, 104; research challenges 161–2; researcher's 132, 145; short life span of 158; *see also* affective states; negative affect; positive affect
enacted job characteristics 29, 61–2
enduring work engagement 25, 26, 27–9
Engquist, G. 21
enjoyment 34, 45
episodes *see* performance episodes
episodic memory 101–2, 103, 104, 108, 155
ethical issues 135–6, 138
Event Reconstruction Method (ERM) 5, 104–5, 106–7, 108, 110
event sampling 5, 60, 89–91
Event Segmentation Theory 21
event-contingent delivery schedules 89–91, 155
events 16, 17, 18–19
experience: episodic structure 8, 15–16, 19–20, 21; meaning of 20; stream of 16
experience-sampling method (ESM) 5, 86–97, 155, 156; diary comparison with 72; emotions 158; event- and signal-contingent delivery schedules 89–91; fixed and random delivery schedules 91–3; flow 44, 45–6; job characteristics 64; job satisfaction 100; limitations of 101, 102; multiple measurements 86–9, 96; multiple rating sources 94–5; performance episodes 10; physiological measures 157; reconstruction methods 103, 109–10; study length 93–4; technological survey delivery options 95–6
expertise 48

fatigue 77, 78
Fay, D. 35
feedback 43–4, 51, 126–7, 153
Ferrer, E. 120

172 Index

financial performance 32–3
Fisher, C.D. 100, 104
fixed delivery schedules 91–2
flight attendants 30, 32, 77
flow 4, 41–57, 152, 153–4, 157, 162;
  capturing 45–7; challenge/skill balance
  42–3, 46, 49, 50, 51; clear and specific
  goals 43; feedback 43–4; physiology of
  47–8; state or trait 48–9, 50; time
  perceptions 158; work engagement and
  34–5, 45; work-related 50–2
Flow State Scale 46, 49
Foo, M.D. 87, 93
Frattaroli, J. 163–5
Fredrickson, B.L. 52, 152
Frijda, N.H. 15
Fritz, C. 32, 74
Fullagar, Clive J. 4, 35, 41–57, 152, 157,
  161, 162
functional context of happiness 152–3

Gavin, M. 161
George, J.M. 29
Gerstorf, D. 117
Geurts, S.A.E. 30, 31, 78, 79
Ghandour, L. 17, 74
Gnys, M. 93
goals: clear and specific 43; control theory
  12, 14; emotion episodes 15; goals
  orientation 51; job crafting 61, 62, 63;
  motivation 106; performance episodes
  9–10, 16, 154; work engagement 36
Gonzàlez-Romà, V. 25
Goodie, J.L. 93
Gooty, J. 161
gossip 137–42
Grant, A.M. 60
Green, S.G. 76
Gross, Sven 6, 114–31, 155, 160
Grossman, P. 160
group-level affective processes 160, 162
growth mixture modeling (GMM) 127–8,
  155–6
Grube, A. 104, 105, 106

Hackman, J.R. 59
Hahn, V.C. 81
Hakel, M. 115
happiness 1, 2–3, 142; anticipated 159–60,
  164; assumptions about 150, 151;
  definitions of 151; diary designs 73–4,
  82; enabling 151, 156–7, 161–5; flow
  34, 51; group-level affective processes
  160; interdisciplinary research 144;
  nature of 150–3; recovery 78, 80;
  stability 158–9, 160, 164; stress impact
  on 75; temporal structure 151, 153–6,
  157–61, 164; work engagement 26
Harter, J.K. 158
Hay, J.F. 108
health 59, 115
Heller, D. 78
Hentzschel, C. 105
Hertel, Guido 5, 100–13, 155, 157
Hetland, J. 27
historical context of happiness 152–3
Hobfoll, S.E. 31
Holman, David 6, 150–69
home, recovery at 76–8
Hopwood, N. 137
Huth, M. 91

Ilgen, D.R. 90
Ilies, Remus 5, 74, 75, 78, 85–99, 100,
  155, 157, 158
Implicit Association Test (IAT) 96
industrial/organization (I/O) psychology
  115, 129
innovation 51, 67, 68, 107–8
interdisciplinary research 143–4
interruptions 3, 16–17
interval-contingent delivery schedules 155
intervention studies 163, 164
interviews 64, 66, 137, 138
intrusions 12

Jackson, S.A. 46
James, W. 20
"Jangle Fallacy" 45
Janicki, D.L. 93
Jelden, S. 79
job characteristics 4–5, 60–1; dynamic
  processes 29; enacted 29, 61–2; flow 51;
  impact on happiness 154;
  methodological issues 64–6; recent
  studies 66–8
job characteristics theory (JCT) 59, 63
job control 59, 60, 62, 64, 65, 66, 68, 74
job crafting 31, 36, 61–6, 68
job demands 31–2, 37; DCSM model 59,
  63–4, 67; spillover from work into
  private life 78; stress 50
job design 58–71; methodological issues
  64–6; new developments 61–4; recent
  studies 66–8; traditional research 58–61
job satisfaction 1, 2, 151–2; diaries 74;
  experience-based measures 100; job
  crafting 61; organizational citizenship

behavior 75; performance relationship 153; reconstruction methods 104, 105, 108
Johnson, M. 90
Jones, K.M. 109
Jong, Y.K. 93
joy 48, 51, 142
Judge, T.A. 74, 88, 91, 92, 100

Kahneman, D. 103, 104, 105
Kamarck, T.W. 93
Karasek, R.A. 59, 63–4, 67
Keller, J. 49
Kelley, E.L. 45
Kelloway, E. Kevin 4, 35, 41–57, 152, 157, 161, 162
Kelly, J.R. 157
Kenny, D.A. 33
Kiefer, T. 142, 143, 156–7
Killham, E.A. 158
King, L.A. 152
Klebe Trevino, L. 52
Kompier, M.A.J. 78, 79
Koopman, J. 87
Kuppens, P. 89

Larson, R. 45, 86
latent growth models (LGMs) 6, 114–31, 155, 161; basic 118–20; change versus variability 117–18; covariates 124–7; growth mixture modeling 127–8, 155–6; measurement invariance 118, 120–1; specification of the form of change 122–4
latent job characteristics 29
Leana, C. 61
learning 67
leisure activities 50, 77–8
LePine, J.A. 31–2
LePine, M.A. 31–2
Levene, H. 88
Levine, B. 108
Llorens, S. 51
Lucas, R.E. 143
Luthans, F. 1, 41, 45, 156
Lyubomirsky, S. 152, 162

MacDermid, S.M. 32
Mäkikangas, A. 51, 128
Marco, C.A. 89
Marsh, H.W. 46
Mayo, M. 76
McGrath, J.E. 157
Meier, Laurenz L. 6, 114–31

memory: episodic structure 8, 10; reconstruction methods 100–2, 103, 104, 108–9, 110, 155
mental processes 19
methodological issues 3, 4, 5; diary research 134; enabling happiness 156–7, 163–5; job characteristics 64–6; temporal structure of happiness 154–6, 160–1, 164; within-person designs 66–7, 85–6, 96–7, 100; *see also* data collection; experience-sampling method; qualitative methods; quantitative methods
Michelson, G. 142
Mojza, E.J. 78, 80, 81, 93
mood 18, 107; emotional contagion 128; flow 51–2; mood induction technique 101; Profile of Mood States 117; sport activities 78; stress impact on 75
Moreno-Jiménez, B. 76
Moscovitch, M. 108
motivation 13–15; coping literature 63; extrinsic 50; growth 115; intrinsic 13, 35, 41–5, 50, 59, 152; job characteristics 51, 61, 64; personal resources 30; positive feedback 126; reconstruction methods 106–7; work engagement 31
Motowidlo, S.J. 10
Muldoon, M.F. 93
Mullin, C. 133
multilevel modeling 3, 27
multiple daily measurements 86–9, 96
multiple rating sources 94–5

Namuth, Hans 41
negative affect 1; impact on creativity 107; problem solving 67; reconstruction methods 103; recovery 76, 78; weekly patterns 74; *see also* affective states
Nesselroade, J. 117
Newtson, D. 21
Nicholas, J.P. 74, 91–2
Nicholson, C. 145
Nicolson, N.A. 87
Niessen, C. 29–30, 31, 80
Niven, Karen 6, 150–69
Norman, S.M. 156
nursing 141–2, 145–6

Oerlemans, W.G.M. 26
Ohly, S. 32, 74
Oldham, G.R. 59
online assessments 21–2
optimism 30, 48

Oravecz, Z. 89
organizational citizenship behavior (OCB) 2, 74, 75, 87
organizational culture 142

Parker, S.K. 60
participant fatigue 88–9, 93
partner effect 33–4
Paty, J.A. 93
Pepys, Samuel 133
perceived job characteristics 29
performance 1–2, 10–11; flow 52; happiness impact on 152; job crafting 63; job satisfaction impact on 153; recovery impact on 80; vigor 116; work engagement 29, 32–3, 36
performance episodes 2–3, 4, 8–22, 32, 154; allocation of attention 11–12; elements of the stream of experience 16–19; emotion episodes 15–16; regulation of attention 12–14; structure of work life 19–21; work engagement 35
Personal Digital Assistants (PDAs) 133, 135, 155
personal initiative 67–8
personal resources 30–1, 36, 37, 51, 156, 157
personality: autotelic 48, 49; organizational citizenship behavior 75; *see also* traits
Petrou, P. 31, 36
physiological measures 47–8, 79, 96, 157, 160, 164
Pinder, C.C. 106
Pitariu, A.H. 35
Plowman, P.J. 134
Ployhart, R.E. 35, 115
Podsakoff, N.P. 31–2
police officers 79
Pollock, Jackson 41
positive affect 1, 2, 142; age-related differences in recall 109; broaden and build theory 52, 152, 158; broaden and build theory of 52; flow 48, 51; job demands 31–2; motivation 106; organizational citizenship behavior 74, 75; problem solving 67; reconstruction methods 103; recovery 75–6, 78, 80–1; weekly patterns 74; *see also* affective states; emotions
positive organizational behavior (POB) 1
positive psychology 1, 50, 150
Potkay, C.R. 26

'pragmatist paradigm' 137
pressure 36, 74, 79
proactive behavior 74, 80, 152
problem solving 59, 62, 63–4; methodological issues 64–6; recent studies 66–8
productivity 2, 33
Profile of Mood States 117
psychological capital 156
psychosomatic health 1, 81

qualitative methods: data analysis 137; flow 45–6; interdisciplinary research 144; job characteristics 66; research design 135; *see also* diaries
quantitative methods 5–6; diary collection of quantitative data 134, 137, 138, 140, 142; flow 46–7; interdisciplinary research 144; job characteristics 64, 66
questionnaires 3, 154; experience-sampling method 86, 89, 91, 92, 95–6; job characteristics 60, 64–5; motivation 106; reconstruction methods 103, 110

Ram, N. 117
random delivery schedules 91–3
Rau, R. 79
Rauschenbauch, C. 110
reactive effects 89
Ready, R.E. 109
reconstruction methods 5, 100–13, 155, 157; affective biases 109; application of 108; Day Reconstruction Method 103–5; Event Reconstruction Method 104–5, 106–7, 108, 110; innovative work behavior 107–8; motivation 106–7; rationale of 101–2
recovery 5, 29–30; breaks 76; diary studies 75–81; at home 76–8; training intervention 81–2
recruitment of research participants 95
reflexive practice 137, 144–6
reflexivity, ethical 136
regulatory compatibility 42
Reis, H.T. 93
relationships 163
relaxation 78
Remote Associates Test (RAT) 96
rescheduling activities 62, 63
resources: allocation of 2; coping 62; ego-depletion 13; flow 51, 157; self-regulatory 79, 80; vigor 116; work engagement 29, 30–1, 36, 37, 157
retrospection bias 72, 73–4, 103

Rodriguez-Sánchez, A.M. 35
role ambiguity 61, 79
rumination 12, 79
Rupp, D.E. 20, 21
Russell, J.A. 26
Ryan, R.M. 52, 91

Salanova, M. 25, 29, 35, 51
Sanz-Vergel, A.I. 76
Schaufeli, W.B. 25, 29, 35, 45
Schmidt, F.L. 158
Schroer, J. 105
Schwartz, J.E 93
Schwarz, N. 104
Schwind, K.M. 78, 90, 94
Scott, B.A. 74, 87
the self 21
self-consciousness 44, 135
self-control 13
Self-Determination Theory (SDT) 13–14
self-efficacy 30, 51
self-esteem 30
self-reflection 156
self-regulation 79, 80, 159
Semmer, Norbert K. 6, 114–31
Seo, M. 93
Sevchuk, I. 61
Sheldon, K.M. 162
Shiffman, S. 93
signal-contingent delivery schedules 89–91, 155
Silverman, D. 145
Simbula, S. 30
Singer, J. 125
skill variety 51, 59
skill/challenge balance 42–3, 46, 49, 50, 51
Smithline, L. 93
social activities 77–8
social network analysis 163, 164
social support 59, 62; flow 51; problem solving 64, 65, 66, 68
Socioemotional Selectivity Theory 105
Sonnenschein, M. 35
Sonnentag, Sabine 5, 25, 27, 29–32, 35, 72–84, 90, 93
sport activities 77, 78, 79
Srivastava, P. 137
Stamov-Roßnagel, Christian 5, 100–13, 155, 157
state work engagement (SWE) 25–40, 152, 153, 157, 162; crossover of 33–4; defining 25–6; enduring work engagement distinction 27–9; future research 34–6; measuring 26–7, 37; performance 32–3; practical implications 36; predictors of 29–32
states 48–9, 50, 116
state-trait model (STM) 122, 123–4
stress 48, 142, 162; job demands 50; reconstruction methods 105; recovery from 75–81; stress management interventions 156
stressors 62, 63, 75, 79, 115, 162
structural equation modeling (SEM) 116, 128
subjective well-being (SWB) 103, 143
Suls, J. 89
survey delivery options 95–6
sustainable happiness model 162
Sutton-Tyrell, – 93
Svoboda, E. 108
Symon, G. 136

Taris, T.W. 79
teachers 30, 32, 77, 79
team working 59–60
technology 95–6, 155, 160–1
Theorell, T. 59, 63–4, 67
time: diaries 74; flow 44; intra-individual variability 117–18; latent growth modeling 118–20, 121; measurement invariance 118; random delivery schedules 92; reconstruction methods 105; temporal structure of happiness 151, 153–8, 157–61, 164; work engagement 35–6
time-invariant covariates (TICs) 124, 125–7
time-variant covariates (TVCs) 125
Tims, M. 30
Totterdell, Peter 6, 150–69
training 108
traits 26, 48–9, 50; organizational citizenship behavior 75; vigor 122, 126
transformational leadership 156
Triemer, A. 79
Trougakos, J.P. 13, 76
Tuerlinckx, F. 89

Utrecht Work Engagement Scale (UWES) 26, 27, 37
Uy, M.A. 87

Van Eck, M. 87, 89
Van Emmerik, H. 30, 31

Van Hooff, M.L.M. 78, 79
Van Iterson, A. 142
variability, change versus 117–18
vigor 114, 152, 153–4; change versus variability 117–18; latent growth modeling 115, 116–28; off-work activities 77, 78; positive affect 81; positive feedback 126–7; recovery 76, 80; as a state concept 116; work engagement 25, 26–7, 28, 31, 33, 34
Von Luede, R. 143
Von Scheve, C. 143

Waddington, Kathryn 6, 132–49, 156
Wagner, D.T. 90, 94
Wang, M. 128
Watson, D. 96
Webster, J. 52
Weinberger, M.I. 109
Weir, Hanna 145
Weiss, Howard M. 4, 8–24, 32, 74, 76, 91–2, 154, 155
well-being 1, 4–6, 142, 152; crossover 33; diary designs 82; disclosure research 163; dynamic processes 29; flow 51; job crafting 68; job design 59; multiple daily measurements 88; off-work activities 77; problem solving 66; recovery 80; short-term fluctuations 2, 3; subjective 103, 143
West, S.G. 126
Wheeler, L. 93
Wilhelm, F.H. 160
Willett, J. 125
Willig, Carla 133–4
Winocur, G. 108
within-person designs 66–7, 85–6, 96–7, 100
WOLF 45, 51
work engagement 2, 4, 25–40, 152, 153, 157, 162; crossover of 33–4; defining 25–6; enduring 25, 26, 27–9; flow and 34–5, 45; future research 34–6; measuring 26–7, 37; performance 32–3; positive affect 81; practical implications 36; predictors of 29–32
workload 31, 79
Wrzesniewski, A. 61

Xanthopoulou, Despoina 4, 25–40, 152, 157, 162
Xu, J. 104

Zacks, J.M. 9, 21
Zijlstra, F.R.H. 77